How to Walk in High Heels

Camilla Morton

How to Walk in High Heels

The Girl's Guide to Everything

NEW YORK

Copyright © 2006 Camilla Morton

Illustrations by Natasha Law

All rights reserved. No part of this book may be used or reproduced in any manner whatsoever without the written permission of the Publisher. Printed in the United States of America. For information address Hyperion, 114 Fifth Avenue, New York, New York 10011-5604.

Library of Congress Cataloging-in-Publication Data

Morton, Camilla.
  How to walk in high heels : the girl's guide to everything / Camilla Morton.
    p. cm.
  ISBN 978-1-4013-0275-7
  1. Young women—Conduct of life.   2. Young women—Life skills guides.   I. Title.

HQ1229.M72 2006
646.70084'22—dc22   2006043534

Hyperion books are available for special promotions and premiums. For details contact the HarperCollins Special Markets Department in the New York office at 212-207-7528, fax 212-207-7222, or email spsales@harpercollins.com.

FIRST EDITION

10   9   8   7   6

For aspiring Cinderellas everywhere . . . and to John and Manolo,
who opened Pandora's Box for me

The Camilla I know is unique: charming and chatty, but this much you could have guessed; the tangents she goes off on, you could not. She lives in the fashion front line, in the line of fire, and is the first with the gossip and the last to give up; like me, fashion is her lifeblood. She is a true Galliano Girl.

Our English eccentric might not have known how to change her light-bulbs when she lived in Paris, but she brought her own light, and an intrepid determination to anything she tries. Living by the flicker of Diptyque candles might not be for everyone, but for her it was all part of the unfolding adventure. Don't be fooled by those blue eyes, behind them is an inspiring, intelligent friend, who is one of a kind. Now, as well as being entertaining, she will be really handy around the home and in the studio.

Enjoy . . .

Love,

John Galliano
Paris
March 2006

Contents

Being Socially Adept

Tackling Your Technophobia

Homes & Gardens

Greeting Your Public

Cinderella, you shall go to the ball.
—*The Fairy Godmother*

How to Be Stylish

Fashion fades, style is eternal.
—*Yves Saint Laurent*

How to create the right atmosphere to get ready in

Being stylish takes time, patience, but above all *practice*. Gore Vidal said, "Style is knowing who you are, what you want to say, and not giving a damn."

Some people need music, some people need lights, and some people need scent. But, above all, before you even open the wardrobe, with creativity must come organization and calm.

First a mood must be established. Do this with scented candles, the ultimate being Diptyque. Freesia for day; John Galliano (as the name implies) for fabulous occasions; Tuberose for candlelit dinners; Baises (berries) in black wax for seduction.

Music is a helpful tool but can, if you are in a hurry, also become a hindrance. Sometimes it is not good to be leaping 'round the room agreeing with Aretha Franklin that you need R-E-S-P-E-C-T. Some songs should have "handle with care" labels attached, as they can whip you up into an inappropriate frenzy. It is terribly difficult to apply lipstick, brush your hair, or roll on sheer stockings with any hope of accuracy while trying to dance to the beat. If music *is* required, opt for classical, jazz, or synthesized and soothing mood enhancers, rather than distracters, and therefore delayers.

How to get dressed in five minutes*

1. **Venue:** Always know *where* you are going, and what the dress code is before deciding *how* to interpret it.

You never know where you are going to meet your future boss/boyfriend/best friend (delete as required) so ALWAYS dress to impress.

Take out a subscription to *OK* magazine if in any doubt on this. Stars without their makeup/dressed down/taking out the garbage are images that should never be seen, and are NEVER to be re-created. Imagine you have the paparazzi following you, and never give anyone the satisfaction of seeing you on a bad hair day.

That said, the old cliché that "beauty is lit from within" is true; designer labels and diamonds are merely the frosting to set it off. Sometimes the most mesmerizing person in the room is the one with the warmest smile.

2. **Layout:** Ideally you should lay out the look the night before, so you have time to "live with it," and you're not rushed into a decision. But if you don't have time for this, plan the outfit in your mind while you shower, and hope that when you pull the pieces out they have all the buttons attached and are immaculately pressed.

If struggling, remember a good pair of shoes can make any outfit. Likewise, a bad pair can do irrevocable damage.

3. **Point of focus:** Less is often more. Choose a point of focus and accessorize around this. One day, it could be the waist, or the décolletage, next the derrière. Learn what to exaggerate and which parts of your body to conceal.

To show off the waist Wear low-slung jeans, cropped tops and, if you really want to push the boat out, a belly button piercing. The latter only if you are on holiday and have a washboard-flat stomach. If not, don't; it destroys the line and drape of garments.

To show off the bottom Heels throw the buttocks out and back, and tighten the thighs terrifically. Tight pencil skirts, and anything by Azzedine Alaïa, can also prove lethal when showcasing this area. Remember: big is beautiful, ignore the whippets, think Monroe.

To show off the chest All hail the magical powers of the V-neck sweater. Whether it's plunging or demure, a V-neck draws the eye down to the point and enhances all cleavage. Essential for meetings with accountants.

If in any doubt about what to wear, always have a little black dress, a clean, crisp white T-shirt (Petit Bateau is a good choice), and a sassy pair of jeans (Stella McCartney would be my personal choice du jour) on standby. When in doubt keep it simple and chic.

4. **Teeth:** Teeth must be flossed, brushed, scrubbed, and, if you will insist on eating garlic, mouth-washed. Do this early in the proceedings, as toothpaste stains can be VERY trying to get off clothes, and must be done well before lip-gloss application.

5. **Makeup:** This is one of the most crucial stages in the evening's preparation. If this bit goes wrong, there could even be cause, in extreme cases, to develop a sudden acute illness or migraine. Breakouts, blotches, and, worst of all, tidemarks (an obvious line where you can see where your foundation meets your chin) MUST be banished.

Aim to look like a girl on the pages of a magazine. But comfort yourself with the knowledge that even they have never seen themselves look that good. A professional makeup artist, hairstylist, fashion editor, and photographer will have spent several hours achieving this result and the rest will have been done with Photoshop. Which, when you think about it, makes it ludicrously unfair that the mere mortal is given a paltry five minutes to compete with a supermodel. Is it any wonder they are where they are and you are feeling insecure?

First, wash face with water. The colder it is, the more it wakes you up and tightens the face. Next, cleanse, tone, and moisturize.

Learn a routine so you don't really have to think, you just know what follows what. Foundation, concealer, and a little liquid radiance and lift under the eyes – courtesy of Touche Éclat by YSL or any leading-brand liquid light wand – then get out the mascara. Apply liberally. Remember there can never be too much mascara; eyes are the window to the soul so enhance and open them as much as possible.

Always pick a feature to exaggerate, either the eyes or the mouth, not both. Red lips need softer eyes, while sockets rimmed with kohl should be counterbalanced with pouting nude lips.

But, as with your outfit, this is all venue dependent. Good lighting is crucial for application, but knowing what lighting you will end up in is even more so.

Find out if you will be:

Up close and intimate? If that is the case, you'll want to fudge the "nope not wearing any makeup, this is fresh-faced flawless little ol' me . . ." Yeah right.

Look don't touch? For this you need the red lipstick. Red is for occasions when you want to be circled and admired. A note of caution, however: not only is red the trickiest to apply but it *really* is not ideal for dinners or drinks with excessive talking. Lipstick on teeth is a big no-no and, with the threat of this in mind, when lips are red they should be kept, ideally, shut – only opened after discreetly running your tongue over your teeth, when you have something really startling to purr.

To avoid lipstick stains on a champagne flute casually lick the glass as you put your lips to it. If this fails, hold glass near rim and wipe stain away with thumb after your sip.

False eyelashes and black kohl-rimmed eyes False eyelashes can be the most seductive of accessories; Julie Christie and Audrey Hepburn leap to mind here. Though you should think incredibly carefully before wearing them to go swimming or to a tear-jerking movie. False eyelashes that have come adrift are very difficult to explain with style as they look like spiders. Streaking mascara, however, along with lipstick stains on champagne flutes, collars, etc., can be marvelous mementos to leave when you make a stylish exit.

6. **Underwear:** The choice of styles can be overwhelming, which is why when "rushing" things all needs to be in apple-pie order. (See *How to wear the appropriate underwear*, page 42.) We're talking sets; the basic rule is bra and underwear must match.

Do you need to wear a bra? Yes or no? And can you in that dress? Do you need to maximize or minimize?

Remember: a black bra under a white T-shirt is a sin. You really should not have colors that show through: dark on top, bright below; light on top, pastel and pale. Fact: white bras are ultraviolet in certain lights and go gray after a few too many washes; "nude" colors never show through and are easier to maintain.

Do not let lingerie go past its "wear by" date. When it starts to look old, frayed, or faded, toss it and start again.

Be wary of a G-string poking out. If underpants *are* on show, make it deliberate and something worth seeing. If low-slung jeans are your poison, invest in hipster G-strings.

7. **Perfume, phase one:** Think of Patrick Suskind's novel *Perfume*, the narrator of which is on a "quest for the intangible scent of a woman." Okay, so in this case it leads to murder, a little extreme, and not the effect you are after, but perfume is one of the few remaining (legal) sorceries we have left, so use it. Layer a few squirts over the body before your clothes go on so that it can soak into your skin. It should be applied right after deodorant, masking any cheap synthetic scent that this may have left, and blending with soaps and scented body lotions to create your own unique odor.

Remember: Coco Chanel said perfume should be worn "wherever one wants to be kissed."

8. **Dress:** Things really start to feel as if you are finally getting somewhere when you get to this stage. You should have decided what look you are after in the layout phase, but now you apply the labels, be it Dior or Gap; that is up to you. Dress in a bottom-to-top, top-to-bottom yo-yo and you will ensure you forget nothing, and can tuck everything in. Always ensure clothes are well pressed and well maintained. (See *How to iron the blues away*, page 348.)

9. **Makeup:** Take a quick glance in the mirror and assess the situation. Is the eye makeup heavy enough? Too heavy? Has any coverage been dislodged or indeed have any blemishes appeared? Is this look enhancing the clothes? Is your lighting harsh and honest enough?

10. **Hair:** Tousled or ironed straight? Up or down? This should already have been decided. NOW is the time to comb, tease, or tweak it into position.

But go easy on the hairspray, you don't want a concrete Ivana-like helmet to asphyxiate your neighbor.

11. **Shoes:** The higher, the more expensive, the better.

"It is totally impossible to be well dressed in cheap shoes," according to Sir Hardy Amies.

The higher the heel, the tighter the calves, while the thinner the heel the greater the optical illusion. Therefore the overall ratio to apply is:

Heel height + width – thighs + calves x 2 = legs + bottom/wiggle

12. **Perfume, phase two:** To avoid the smell being too intense, spray a mist of scent into the air and walk into it. Dab a little behind the earlobes and wrists and at the ankles – well . . . you never know who might want to kiss your feet. Note: the top layer can be a different scent from the one you used as a base coat.

13. **Hair:** Toss.

14. **Makeup and mirror:** One last check – teeth, tucked in, pushed up, done up, and face flawless.

15. **Smile:** Here would be when you can call "Coming! Ready!" to any waiting suitors/attending groupies. This way they are all primed, and ready to compliment you as you glide down the stairs.

16. **Check you have your handbag, and contents.** (See *How to fit everything into your handbag*, page 13.)

17. **Outer layering—the coat:** Always opt to be assisted into your coat; it's the best way to ensure people see you and your outfit at close range. Not only can they see the great labels you have put together but, on a practical note, having someone slip the coat onto your shoulders ensures that it is hung at the best angle and the drape and cut is shown off and smoothed out to its full advantage.

18. **Lip gloss:** Absolutely no point doing it till now – too many obstacles, and it's a good crowd pleaser.

19. **Finale:** One final "Mirror, mirror, on the wall, who is the fairest of them all?" and you're off.

* So here is the confession. The heading was *slightly* misleading, a female prerogative. With no fewer than eighteen ESSENTIAL steps it is inconceivable that you could be ready, and up to standard, in much under twenty minutes.

The key is to be realistic, even if you only admit this time frame to yourself, far better than rushing to be *badly* ready in five minutes.

The only time it's possible to be ready in five minutes is when going to bed. Do like Marilyn Monroe and wear Chanel No. 5. Providing the perfume is where you left it, how long can it take?

How to avoid confrontation whilst getting ready

Don't give a woman advice; one should never give
a woman anything she can't wear in the evening.
—*Oscar Wilde*

Remember the ancient proverb, Hell hath no fury like a woman scorned? Well, double the terror and consequences for a woman rushed. It is hard to focus under pressure. Arrange to meet your date at a venue. Or, if they will insist on collecting you, have freshly brewed coffee or tea, current magazines, and TV remote all laid out for them. You can't hurry meringues, couture, or the Hermès Birkin bag waiting list, so why try to hurry a vision of loveliness?

If you are living together they can assist with odd jobs, ironing, zips, and hard-to-reach buttons. Getting them involved will make them appreciate that it is truly impossible for you to go any faster. But do be wary of employing them in the "second opinion" category unless you really, truly value their opinion, and are going to take what they say seriously (and not slam the door and refuse to go out). This is particularly crucial advice if the person involved is a man, and even more so if he is *your* man.

To avoid initial confrontation, always have at least two clocks

One should be set at least seven to twenty-one minutes fast. NEVER set it to an easily calculable time, as you will eventually make the correct arithmetic adjustments automatically. This "booby" clock should be displayed prominently in the room: above a mirror is a popular spot. The real time should stay hidden in a drawer and never be referred to.

How to get ready in five minutes – really

Okay, sometimes due to your own, or more likely someone else's, bad planning (and downright bad luck on your part), you *really* do only have five minutes to change.

The key to success here is perfume and imagination.

Pull top off, and knot hair (if long enough) on head, and while still undressed, think, wash face, clean teeth, generally "freshen up."

Spray on deodorant and perfume.

Throw on nearest, cleanest top.

Reapply makeup, mascara, and gloss. Ensure no makeup spills on top, as this will delay departure; a way to do this is to wrap towel or dressing gown over clothes to catch any errors.

Change into heels, or select pair to change into en route and slip on pair of flats so you can run.

Empty bag on bed; repack mobile phone, wallet, keys in evening bag. Perhaps a shawl/scarf/cardigan option could be slipped in here.

Seize first pair of dangling earrings or necklace (that you don't wear every day) and either put them on or have ready to apply at first traffic light in car, if driving. Remember a little bit of crystal will throw extra light on your face and make you look radiant, even if you feel truly exhausted and harassed.

Jacket. Door. Hair down.

GO.

No time to clean teeth? Eat an apple.

No time to dry hair? Comb and turn car air conditioner on full.

If you are really, really, really late – yikes – what can you do en route? Change in the car? Call to say you're on your way? Do something, but make sure you are worth the wait.

Fashion designers Dolce & Gabbana advise:

If you have no time, and are really late, do not panic! That is the first rule! Choose clothes and accessories that you know you will feel at ease wearing, and do not exceed. Go for basic and natural makeup, add a jewel and a precious accessory, a drop of a sensual fragrance, and you are ready.

What matters most is to be confident and never betray your personality and personal taste. Be yourself and *that* is stylish.

How to make stylish excuses

Beautiful people are sometimes more prone to keep you waiting than plain people are because there's a big time differential between the beautiful and the plain.

—*Andy Warhol*

Too true.

Even with the best will in the world sometimes you just won't make it. It is a myth that timekeeping is unstylish. But while being fashionably late is one thing, being supremely delayed is tardy, chaotic, ill mannered, and downright rude.

Only fashion shows, and marriage proposals, can be truly delayed, and even they must have a cut-off point. For fashion shows it's three or four hours max for a new designer, and that's only if it's a really, really hot ticket. Marriage proposals: if it's nine months and there's no action, surely it's time to move on.

This handy guide will help you gauge the appropriate level of apology:

0–20 minutes

No excuse necessary. You have arrived. What is the problem?

20–45 minutes

Disarm irritated faces with compliments and follow with a casual apology, blaming external factors. Your opening gambit could run along the following lines: "Oh, how lovely to see you all again. You look so well. Nightmare getting a cab/traffic/parking, isn't it?" (Delete as appropriate.)

45 minutes–one hour

Vaguely suggest a day of exciting trauma, but be careful not to elaborate, settle in quickly and become absorbed in the current conversation. "What a day! You just couldn't imagine. Oh well, at least I'm here, so what have I missed? Anyone else have trouble getting a sedan chair to carry them over *ce soir?*" . . . and so on.

One hour plus

This requires the showstopper entrance, but it is no bad thing as it will remind everybody that you are a special creature and can't be expected to keep to standard timekeeping. As Marilyn Monroe once said, "I have often been on calendars, but I have never been on time."

For inspiring entrances, or ways to get ready, do your homework. Watch *Grease* for Sandy's jaw-dropping transformation, or how Eliza Doolittle becomes a lady in *My Fair Lady*. Molly Ringwald getting ready for the prom in *Pretty in*

Pink, or Julia Roberts in *Pretty Woman* are always worth rewatching; it just all depends on the dress code you are prepping. Select appropriate DVD to help you on your way.

How to fit everything into your handbag

A girl's handbag is her own private sanctuary and only the very privileged, loved, or trusted are ever invited in.

It is preferable to have two bags – a Mary Poppins–style bag that can carry everything you will need in it, and within that, the decoy, a dainty frivolous number that you can carry into dinner. Only an elite few can cope with a no-bag entrance, and then either their companion's suit is crammed with lipsticks, they have a driver outside, or they are truly fabulous.

Until you reach this status, it's best to be prepared for anything.

Things you *absolutely* need in your handbag and/or day bag include:

Mobile phone
Wallet and money
> You will always need a few dollars for cloakrooms and dire emergencies. Don't worry about enough for a taxi; any damsel in distress knows that can be figured out once you are safely away from the scene of the crime.

Notebook
> Inspiration can strike anywhere.

Pens or pencils
> You never know whose number you might need to scribble down and lipstick has never been that reliable. But remember: pens MUST have lids, if not they are liable to ruin the lining of a bag; do you have a pencil case?

Lipstick

Lip gloss

Adds shine and shimmer to a sexy pout, and very user-friendly to apply sans mirror.

Perfume

The sample bottles from the makeup counters are the perfect travel size.

Keys

Door keys and car keys. Even if you lose everything else, you want to concentrate really hard on not misplacing these. Always consider where to hide a spare, or who to give a spare to, but they must be the kind of person who appreciates a call at three in the morning. (See *How to be stylish when locked out*, page 304.)

Safety pins/sewing kit

No need to cry over spilt milk – buttons do pop at the most inappropriate moments, so come prepared. The complimentary mini sewing kits you get in hotels are perfect for this kind of emergency.

Compact

If you leave the house without your powder and mirror, go back. There's nothing worse than a shiny face, or having no mirror in which to check discreetly all is where it should be. Also, "I'm just going to powder my nose" is an excellent code for "I need to escape," so you need to have your alibi with you.

Road map/A–Z

Optional if getting cabs, but essential if driving, as there will always be diversions that appear simply to bamboozle you. If offering a lift to passengers, get them to sign a backseat driver's rights agreement. You drive – you decide. They are (preferably) silent and grateful.

Big bag address book

With all the numbers of those you would call in an emergency, for work, for pleasure, for romance, for practical assistance. If trying to save on space, these could be written into your notebook, but really essential ones should be committed to memory, or on speed dial in your mobile.

Diary/agenda

For all your important meetings and future dates.

Business cards

A good way to give out your details without appearing too forward/ desperate.

Spare pair of shoes and Band-Aids

This is clearly bag-size permitting, and plastic carrier bags (especially the supermarket brands) are to be avoided at all costs. But, sacrilegious as it sounds, something comfortable to accommodate any brushes with public transport or prolonged periods of walking, which ideally will have been discussed in advance, are a good idea. A new pair of shoes will always produce a blister somewhere. So think ahead.

Comb

Tissues

Aspirin

Mints

An evening bag can accommodate a fraction of the all-purpose, so go with the three essentials: lipstick, mobile, and keys.

How to
Walk in
High Heels

I don't know who invented the high heel,
but all women owe him a lot.
—*Marilyn Monroe*

How to select the heel

Rumor has it that the heel was invented by Leonardo da Vinci (1452–1519). But rumor has it he invented most things. Throughout history the heel has been enjoyed, by men and women, for its coquettish charm, as well as its height-helping inches. "High heels put your ass on a pedestal, where it belongs," says leggy supermodel Veronica Webb.

A good heel is like a flash car, or an incredible work of art. You don't *need* it, you covet it, savor it, worship it, and *have* to have it. A really good heel has been constructed to tilt you at the most flattering angle possible. Why go under the knife, or to the gym? A stiletto is the most effective instant slimmer.

Admittedly there is a certain level of discomfort to be endured, but they do hurt less the more you wear them. The only thing worse than a girl in cheap, chunky heels is a girl who can't walk in them. President Roosevelt coined the phrase, "You have to spend money to make money." Invest in a pair of Manolo Blahniks, the only stilettos that offer comfort on 5 inches, and watch the cocktails and dinner invitations come flooding in.

Before you even go near a shoe store, ensure that your feet are freshly pedicured and painted; yes, even if they'll be hidden in a closed toe. (See *How to do a home pedicure*, page 36.) It is NOT advisable ever to send loved ones to buy your heels. Size can vary according to cut, shape, and slant of heel – therefore you have to be prepared to try everything on before you purchase. Heels are tricky enough to master at the best of times, why add to your problems by having a pair that doesn't fit? All you will be able to use them for is as lethal weapons.

The thicker the heel the larger the surface area your weight has to spread over. The more wobbly you feel, the more millimeters you should add to the width. Wedges and platforms are excellent ways to achieve instant height and thinner thighs, but try to select a style that is reminiscent of Betty Boop, not Scary Spice.

It is worth bearing in mind that you assume different characters in different heights. Heights go from (yawn) 2 inches: practically flat; 3½ inches: day heel; 4 inches: foxy heel; 5 inches: the true pro aesthetic.

Walking in heels is like riding a bike – once you know how, you'll never forget. But just like a bike, the first time you ride without training wheels can be very precarious. Get the arches of your feet flexed and ready for some high-heel hints.

Who is Manolo Blahnik?

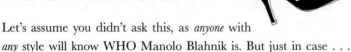

Let's assume you didn't ask this, as *anyone* with *any* style will know WHO Manolo Blahnik is. But just in case . . .

Manolo Blahnik is the patron saint of the stiletto, favored by the most important women in fashion, starting at the top with American *Vogue*'s Anna Wintour, a legend, as well as Carrie Bradshaw (Sarah Jessica Parker) in *Sex and the City*, Nicole Kidman, Amanda Harlech, Tina Chow, Paloma Picasso, and just about any stylish female you can think of who has worn shoes in the past three decades.

There are other shoe designers who are very successful, but this is my book, and therefore my bias. And my bias is Manolo Blahnik.

Born on November 27, 1942, in Santa Cruz de la Palma, Spain, Manolo Blahnik should be described as half sculptor and painter, half engineer. A combination of Picasso and Einstein, he's a magician and inventor.

The label started in 1971, after the then doyenne of American *Vogue*, Diana Vreeland, decreed: "Young man, do shoes." And so it was simple, he did. Since then he has collaborated with Ossie Clark, John Galliano, and Azzedine Alaia, amongst other names that would make you go weak at the knees. He personally carves, cuts, and sands his lasts (the term for the block from which the shoe is sculpted) by hand until he gets the precise shape he desires. His aesthetic and aerodynamics are such that his heels, though toweringly high, are perversely comfortable. Thus proving irresistible.

In 2003 the Design Museum celebrated thirty years of his London shop with an exhibition of his work. But really, for further information on Manolo Blahnik, the best thing to do is go and experience the shoes, by trying them on at any of his shops or major department stores. Or, if that sounds too scary, there is the Colin McDowell book, or his self-titled book of drawings, to help you build up to the Cinderella moment.

Should you wish to stray into the realms of other high-end "name" shoe designers, look out for red-soled Christian Louboutins, Jimmy Choo, and Gina. Hot on their heels are new, younger designers, including Olivia Morris, Pierre Hardy, or Georgina Goodman, who was actually taught by Mr. Blahnik. Other good names to consider for footwear come marching up the runways from the leading fashion brands, but these vary from season to season. The best ones to look at are Marc Jacobs, Miu Miu, Prada, YSL, Dior, Galliano, Gucci, and Louis Vuitton.

For more information on the history of the stiletto, see:

Shoes, Shoes, Shoes by Andy Warhol (Bulfinch, 1997).

Bag: A Lexicon of Style by Valerie Steele (Scriptum Editions, 2005).

Shoes: A Lexicon of Style by Valerie Steele (Scriptum Editions, 2005).

Manolo Blahnik by Colin McDowell (HarperCollins, 2000).

Manolo Blahnik Drawings (Thames and Hudson, 2003).

Stiletto by Caroline Cox (HarperCollins, 2004).

Sex and the City: The Complete Series DVD (http://store.hbo.com).

How to pick a shoe
by Manolo Blahnik, shoe designer

A good heel picks you. Don't follow trends – follow your-self, you have to stand tall and proud. Always go with your first choice, your gut reaction. This is what your soul says. You have to pick something that will make you look even more exciting, and feel even more adventurous than you did before.

My shoes are not fashion – they are moods and moments that want to come out to play. Every shoe must excite me, which is why I see every pair, every last, so if it doesn't delight me, it doesn't go through. I spend most of my time in the factory working. Don't let yourself get distracted by fashion; if you did you would have to change your wardrobe every four months and where's the sense in that? It would make your style schizophrenic. Be original, look at vintage, but do not copy for the sake of copying, have some of your own ideas. Right now, good Lord, every day, every-where I look I am blown away by something inspiring. I always have had an incredible appetite for luxury, and Russia. At the moment I am so excited by Russia, and have just been to Moscow. I had never been, apart from in books, through Tolstoy and the *Three Sisters*. I say always go to the source, always travel to find your inspi- ration, that's what all the great artists and romantics do.

I was always making shoes . . . even when it was subcon-scious. I know that sounds like a cliché, but it's true, even the lizards and dogs in the garden didn't escape when I was a child – I would take the Cadbury's chocolate bon-

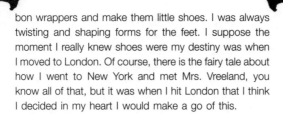

bon wrappers and make them little shoes. I was always twisting and shaping forms for the feet. I suppose the moment I really knew shoes were my destiny was when I moved to London. Of course, there is the fairy tale about how I went to New York and met Mrs. Vreeland, you know all of that, but it was when I hit London that I think I decided in my heart I would make a go of this.

I think you must always show some toe cleavage. Toe cleavage is very important as it gives sexuality to the shoe. But careful you only show the first two cracks, you don't want to give too much away, you're not that type of girl. . . . As for the heel, honey, it's got to be high. The transformation is INSTANT. It's a coup de théâtre. The height of a heel should depend on how dangerous you are feeling. High high high higher, I say! I am into comfort now: wear nothing less than 90mm. For me, the ultimate shoe would be a wonderful high court, in Spanish red patent. Something dangerous and provocative.

When you have heels you only need to pack two black dresses, and fill the case with twenty pairs of shoes. Let the heels do all the talking, and you'll be ready for anything.

I hope my shoes are comfortable. I have been working with craftsmen who have been studying traditions that go back for two hundred or so years and after all the time I have been doing it, I have learned a few tricks too. I don't wear them myself, I am not so into the cross-men-dressing – no, that is not for me – but I like to work on each creation so it is as comfortable as it can be. My shoes are for dancing, for living, for moving; you can't wear things that make you feel crippled, get them off! I

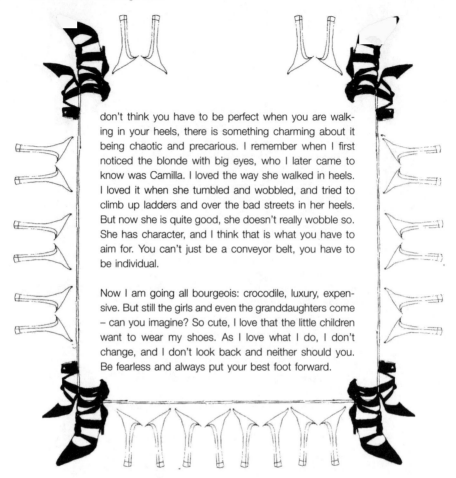

don't think you have to be perfect when you are walking in your heels, there is something charming about it being chaotic and precarious. I remember when I first noticed the blonde with big eyes, who I later came to know was Camilla. I loved the way she walked in heels. I loved it when she tumbled and wobbled, and tried to climb up ladders and over the bad streets in her heels. But now she is quite good, she doesn't really wobble so. She has character, and I think that is what you have to aim for. You can't just be a conveyor belt, you have to be individual.

Now I am going all bourgeois: crocodile, luxury, expensive. But still the girls and even the granddaughters come – can you imagine? So cute, I love that the little children want to wear my shoes. As I love what I do, I don't change, and I don't look back and neither should you. Be fearless and always put your best foot forward.

How to know when to wear a heel

High heels are NOT just for eveningwear. They work just as well with trousers, jeans, denim skirts, miniskirts, pajamas. You need to be adventurous.

Any aspiring Imelda Marcos needs to consider multiple locations and situations in order to ensure maximum and successful heel-wearing pleasure.

The weather

Suede, satins, and pale colors are OUT if there is the slightest hint of rain. No rain protector is worth the risk of losing a key shoe.

How deep is the carpet?

Dense shag pile = poor gripability. Heel height and width should vary accordingly.

Can you get from A to B? Taxi? Car? Escort?

Hitchhiking is out.

Hazards

Check for cobblestones, grass, grids, and grates. Also do you spy any toddling children? If there are stairs with no banister don't even attempt it. When going up stairs you should travel on the balls of the feet, when going down, sidestep slowly.

Dress codes

Dress codes are only for people who don't know what to wear or how to be chic. Remember: you can never be too glamorous or have too many heels. Every girl must have at least ten varieties of heels on hand at all times.

Short arse

If your escort is shorter than you in your highest heels, dump him immediately. Pointless. A pair of Manolos lasts a lifetime, and you shouldn't compromise style for love.

Hang the kittens

Don't let anyone, particularly not a "him," persuade you kitten heels are sexy. They equal chubby thighs and thick ankles if the truth were told. They are day shoes, they are practical, and they are a cop-out. Also, they are actually far more uncomfortable and quicker to cause pain to the lower back and arches than a proper pair of heels.

Know your realistic time limit

This can affect height and choice of style. Occasion and venue knowledge are essential for heel selection. For example, mules are good for dinner parties, but dancing requires straps of some sort.

Hitting the jackpot

A heel can make or break an outfit. High street becomes designer if dressed with good heels. Dress heels up and down.

Dress to impress

Bondage stilettos and skyscraper spikes are OUT for first meeting of prospective in-laws or vicars.

Always have a taxi number in your mobile

You look like a star so you can't be seen catching the bus. Public transport should be kept to a minimum, let heels justify your cab fetish.

Know your weaknesses

If cobblestone sidewalks are your Achilles' heel – walk in the road. If eight hours reduces you to tears, call it a day before this point.

Don't drink and teeter unless you have someone in mind to carry you home

Alcohol and heel coordination is tricky. Bad combination.

A heel symbolizes status and style

The thinner the heel, the higher the arch, the higher your status and situation. A Manolo Blahnik 10.5 spike heel, say crocodile, is the ultimate symbol of a lady – a vamp not a tramp, and should be approached with extreme caution.

Marilyn Monroe perfected the best wiggle in the business

How? She asked her cobbler to make one heel half an inch lower than the other so she'd always have a very exaggerated rear view. That's way too much. A more practical approach is to ask your cobbler to shave a few millimeters off one rubber-tip heel, and not the other. A cobbler can add years to the life of your heels, so if you find a good one, tip generously. Leather toecaps and rubber heels are essential regular maintenance.

Care for your Manolos

The man himself says, "Always have them on shoe trees, and stuffed with tissue so they keep their shape." You could also keep them safe in their boxes, and identify the contents with Polaroids stuck on the front.

A heel is worth the money

It is plastic surgery, therapy, and a glamour magnet all in one. Money very well spent.

Always give feet a day off

Tired feet may stop functioning altogether, and leave you unable to move. The only people who can stand in heels all day, every day, are mannequins, and they are plastic and have screw-off feet.

Stylish shoe trivia

- The patron saint of shoemakers is St. Crispin.
- Marie Antoinette had a servant whose only job was to take care of her shoes (all 500 pairs).
- In Europe it is a good luck charm to place a shoe inside a wall when building a house, just don't waste too good a pair.
- Cinderella's slippers are sadly unlikely to have been made of glass. More probably they were fur, but the story came about through mistranslation when the French for fur, *vair* was written as *verre* – glass.
- A horseshoe, as we all know, is a symbol of good luck.

How to put a heel on

Beginners should start with sturdier stilettos and choose a pair with straps that cross over the ankle and the bridge of the foot to hold it in.

Slingbacks and mules, with nothing more than luck to keep them on, are for the advanced classes only.

Best to have bare feet. If you really have to wear hosiery, try to wear fishnets. It is far easier to walk in heels if the flesh of the foot is in direct contact with the shoe. Not only can you feel every step, but – gross but true – the sweat helps stick the shoe and the foot together.

Sit on the edge of your chair, feet hip-width apart, flat on the floor, knees over the feet. Back should be straight, shoulders back, head held high.

Lift right foot, point toes as if you were a prima ballerina, arch foot, and slide into heel. Allow toes to wiggle and customize to new cramped feeling before lacing or tightening buckles.

Toes should now feel pushed forward, slightly clenched, and your weight should have moved from the feet and feel as if it is spreading up the leg and sitting on the hip. Calves should feel taut and ankles tight, as if you have found the biting point and are about to take the hand brake off. Now repeat the same process with the left foot.

While your toes are pushing forward, your ankles will try to push down and back. Let the two opposite ends of the feet jostle for balance and redistribute the weight as you fasten foot two.

Lean back, clench bottom, thigh, and stomach muscles, and slowly lift to stand.

Whoooah! Steady.

Hopefully you should, by now, be standing.

Place feet hip-distance apart and gently sway from side to side, like a pendulum, till you find a new center of gravity.

Your calves and knees should feel engaged as should the lower back.

Weight should be on heel tips and balls of feet.

Place the palms of your hands on your rear, one on each bottom cheek, and start to circle the room. This will help you check the angle of your hips, and develop a wiggle.

If you're tired, lean on one hip. This is not only a *very good look* – in a sultry kind of way – but it also rests one leg.

Practice leaning. Bend right leg slightly at the knee, and jut out left hip while keeping left leg taut and straight. Now reverse with right hip jutted and left leg bent. Now you are all loosened up you are ready to walk.

Best foot forward.

Lift right foot, clench toes, land weight on ball of foot, and spread to heel. When you push the weight to the ball to propel movement for the next step, it will also prevent your worst nightmare – heel snappage. Rock your weight between the two, and before you set out to stride like a super-model, remember: slow and sexy. Plus, smaller steps are easier to manage.

When you put your right foot down, land on the heel and instantly move weight forward. Don't lift the other foot until weight has been correctly repositioned. Tilt feet slightly out, at an angle, and almost curl your feet outward so they can lean away from each other. (This keeps the ankle at a more flattering angle and helps you pick up some speed.) Keep weight on the ball of the foot and the tilts will happen naturally. Remember: the lower the heel, the farther back you should throw your weight. Although you want your weight on the ball, you also need to push it into the heel – it's a delicate balance: too far back or too far forward and you will land either on your face or on your derrière – neither of which is a good look.

When walking, imagine that with each step your hips are doing a figure eight and that they are being pulled forward. Walk as if on a tightrope, straight and tall – and allow the hips to move first.

When stilettos start to feel like two portable cheese cutters, it's time to make an exit and change into your comfortable spare pair.

For accelerated learning, some may choose to practice in heels on treadmills, at the local gym. Mere mortals, however, who've spent a month's rent on the heel, can gain prowess with the much cheaper, and far more effective, aisle glide method.

How to aisle glide

When a *very* stylish lady sweeps into the room, as if she were walking on air – like Ginger Rogers herself – remember that they all started somewhere. Practice, practice, practice.

Once you've got the heel, tried it on, and know the basics it's time to take your new shoes to the nearest supermarket.

Fact: supermarket aisles are the perfect place to practice your glide. Not only do you get to stock up on all your groceries and *wow* the locals, but you can get up to twenty-four aisles' worth of runway-smooth surface to practice on, while being supported by a shopping cart, the ultimate stabilizer for the novice stiletto wearer.

Ignore any funny looks, they are either jealous they didn't think of this idea, or mystified why someone so glamorous doesn't have "hired help" to do their shopping.

Sneakers off – heels on. Clutch the cart handle bars and you're off! Right foot, left foot, right foot, left . . . a natural rhythm should be developing regardless of the tinny *Muzak*.

Use aisles as follows:

1–5: Establish your walk and your rhythm. Get comfortable and confident. If you put any relevant produce into your trolley, this is a real bonus.

6–10: Start to vary speeds, stops, and starts, perhaps even a corner – but NEVER let go of the trolley. Careful, let's not rush things.

11–16: Now you can practice developing wiggle and character steps, such as bends and turns and perhaps little heel kicks.

Final aisles: Be creative, and do a total routine, showcasing your new-found stiletto confidence. Queuing at the checkout can be a time to rest on the hips.

Packing your bags and getting them to the car? I would be very surprised if by now you didn't have a handful of drooling helpers on hand. But if not, don't worry, the bending will be good practice, too.

If things are going really well you could even try to walk to vehicle sans cart, using the bags as balance weights.

How to walk in heels on all surfaces

The trick is to *know what you are dealing with.*

Carpet

The deeper the pile, the greater the danger. Go for shallow patches and, like punting, stab the heel in good and deep for balance. BUT, if it's your carpet, put on a thicker heel; spikes can destroy a shag pile.

Pavements

In London, stay on the inside (near shop windows) and avoid the cracks. In Milan, it's the reverse. Walk on the outside, or risk getting heels trapped in the grating. In Paris, walk in the road and don't attempt picturesque cobbles. In New York, just hail a cab like everyone else.

Cobblestone sidewalks

The HORROR of all HORRORS. Uneven, small, and slippery, impossible to keep an even footing on. It is crucial to find your center of gravity. There is no easy way of doing them, and when it is wet and icy, forget it. Walking in roads is fine. Stopping traffic an added bonus.

Tarmac

Great in the winter, but sticky in high summer. When you're sticking, demand a piggyback, or radio for immediate backup.

Marble

TAKE CARE. One slip and you're floored, literally. It looks good, but in reality it's like a sheet of ice. If in doubt, go 'round the edges, near walls and objects you can casually cling to. If you decide a room crossing is really necessary, soles of shoes can be scored, rubbed with sandpaper, or scuffed to create a grip. If you don't want to do this, you can dab resin (wax used by cellists/violinists on their bows) or some seriously dry and spongy glue stick to the soles for added grip; just don't do this with really good Manolos on their maiden voyage. If in doubt, get a walker to cling to.

Wood slats

It's best to stick to the center as decaying wood tends to crumble from the outside first. Walk tall and fast, and in a straight line. Get your heel jammed in a gap and you could be there all night. When in Paris, avoid "romantic strolls" or shortcuts going across pedestrian wooden bridges, such as the Pont Neuf, unless you intend to carry your heels, in a nonchalant way, and risk splinters.

Grating

The smaller, the scarier the sidewalk becomes. Opt for a sedan chair, or perhaps the gentleman would lay his coat down for you to walk over? In these situations walk on the BALLS of your feet. The thinner the heel, the more wary you should be of gratings. Tiptoe and hope you can reach safer land quickly.

Escalators

The moving staircase is fine going up, as you can dangle your heels off the back, but going down is another matter. Harrods installed the first lifts in England, and smelling salts had to be handed out at either end. Things are not that bad now – you just need to hold on to the rail, go on tiptoes, and not allow the heel to sink between grooves.

Fire escapes and staircases in wrought metal

Time to cry. Demand a fireman's lift, and act very "damsel in distress," because if you attempt these stairs you will be one.

Rugs

A new-found foe. Rugs that move, or slide, are as easy as walking on flying saucers or ice. Clearly the person who has unsecured rugs scattered casually around their home wants to kill you. Aim to walk around them, and leave spiky marks on their carefully polished floor as your calling card. If you're a regular visitor, ask for the rugs to be nailed, glued, or stapled firmly into place before your next visit.

Airports

A deceptive amount of walking is required here. Now that shoes have to go through their own security checks and come on and off, it's sensible to pack highly complex, buckled, or bejeweled pairs. Instead go for footwear that is slouchy and soft, and leave the spikes off until you land.

Beach and *sur la plage*

Sand gets everywhere. Open toe it when near sand. Wedge it. Waterproof it. Carry it.

Dance floor

Here's where you need to diamanté and sparkle it up. Know all the right moves as well as your heels.

Cotton wool

A hidden stabilizer, cotton wool cushions toes in tight-pointing heels, and it can help the shoe keep its toe shape, despite the creases of age and walking. Squeeze toes so they are over the cotton wool, to increase the center of gravity on the ball of the foot. When walking on gratings, wiggle the cotton wool so it is no longer under the toes, but padding the ball of the foot, so you are angled even farther onto your tiptoes.

Travel heels

For subways, buses, and any mode of public transport, have ballet pumps or flats, either on your feet or in your bag. Any connoisseur will know the only real way to travel is by car or taxi. Live the fantasy, and write off taxi receipts for the obvious reason: SF (stiletto fatigue).

Driving heels

Bare feet or flats. Don't drive in heels. Any emergency stops or sudden braking and the heel could snap. Don't even try driving in platforms. You can't feel the brake or clutch, or gauge the biting point.

How to cope in a real emergency: when a heel breaks

New heels have steel rods inside the flesh of the heel so they shouldn't break, and if they do you are walking at a very strange angle.

If a heel breaks while you are out, improvise.

If it has snapped off altogether, retrieve it. If it is hanging off, try to wedge it back on (so the illusion is that it is still in place).

With both of the above, transfer all the weight to the balls of both feet instantly. Walk on tiptoes, find a seat, or lean in a stylish way against wall or prop.

If you are required to stand still, place weight on foot with heel still intact, but do not stand still for too long.

Do not draw attention to broken heel, you will be inviting ridicule and "oh, you should get a good solid pair of blah blah blah . . ."

Retire to replace shoes at soonest possible interval.

Now would be the time to call that cab/companion.

How to keep your seams straight

Be honest, can a gusset ever look attractive? If wearing heels, you need to set them off with the correct accompaniment.

Stockings with garter belts give stems far superior va va voom than regular tights do. Seams and stockings are those rarest of things: items that will always be in fashion and will always be sexy and seductive. However, there is nothing more unappealing than a stocking seam that wiggles and lurches up the thigh like a drunk trying to cross the deck. It will make viewers of your rear feel dizzy and nauseous. Definitely NOT the feelings you want to inspire.

Back when luxury was rationed, ladies had to "make do and mend" and went to great lengths to have a wiggle-free seam.

If, for some peculiar reason, you want to put yourself in the mind-set of our forebears and try to re-create this look, you'll need a bottle of Sally Hansen Airbrush Legs or some watered-down gravy. First ensure leg is exfoliated, hair-free, and moisturized. To achieve the perfect seam, take a ruler and carefully paint along one long edge. Then, similar to potato printing, place the inked edge of the ruler to the back of your leg and press. Repeat until you have traveled as far up the leg as you need to (I would suggest 15cm above the knee, and obviously on both legs). Allow to dry. The only danger of painting the leg is the slightly bizarre look you will be left with should you end up *in flagrante*.

Assuming you've sensibly decided to save the gravy for the roast and have a pair of stockings at the ready, roll each individual leg down so that it resembles a nylon bagel. The first rule of wearing seams is to wear stockings, and not tights. Anything with a built-in gusset will, when you do something as inconvenient as walk, perish the thought, twist the line out of place.

Dip your finger in some Vaseline and smear a thimble's worth up the back of the bare calves along the line where the seam will lie. This will help stick the seam in place. Do this operation one leg at a time as it can get rather sticky. Carefully roll one leg up to the knee, ensuring it is straight, and then smooth, stretch, and roll over the knee. Repeat the process with the other leg.

For added peace of mind, choose a garter belt, the chicest way to ensure the stockings stay in place. This way, if the stocking were to fall, you would at least feel a snap on your leg as warning, rather than the slow slide of the hold-up device down your thighs.

Footsie is really *not* a recommended sport to indulge in whilst in stocking hold-ups, as what rolls up may fall down.

Note: stockings are perfect with pencil skirts, split skirts, and evening attire. But no wardrobe would be complete without a pair of black opaque tights. Much more suited for microminis and windy days.

How to wear sheers with no ladder

Moisturize from tip to toe. Roll the sheer onto your leg and let it grip and cling. The thinner the denier, the higher the price you need to pay. Cheap tights snag, sometimes before you've even left the house.

The dressier the event, the thinner the hosiery. The same applies to heels.

Legs	Skirts	Shoes
Opaque	Micromini skirts	Flats
Fishnets	Knee-length	Kitten heels
40 denier	Above the knee	60-mm heel
15 denier	Split/on knee	90-mm heel
10 denier	Pencil skirt	105-mm heel
5 denier	Floating above knee	105-mm heel/slingback
Sandalfoot	Evening dress	Open-toe sandals

Glossary

- Denier: this is the unit for measuring the fineness of silk, rayon, and, most commonly, nylon. The higher the denier the thicker the coverage; 10 denier and lower are sheer.
- Sandalfoot: this is the illusion of being open-toed, no seam or "toe line." Ideal for wearing with sandals or mules, if you can't face going bare.
- Opaque: thick, non-see-through, opposite of sheer.
- Garters and garter belts: essential accessories, see Marilyn Monroe in *Some Like It Hot*. Her entrance, viewed from the rear, wiggling her way to the train, gave knee highs one of their greatest fashion moments.

How to Be Groomed

Know, first, who you are; and then adorn
yourself accordingly.
—*Epictetus*

How to do a home pedicure and first-aid maintenance for feet

Frequent heel wearing requires a fully maintained raw foot to work with. Just as you take your car to the garage, so must you have regular pedicures. Feet are the most overused and least appreciated form of transport. Love them.

Pedicure feet at least once a month. You should also have a friendly local podiatrist, for a six-monthly, degree-trained overhaul and general health check. If you don't have time to go to a professional, which can be claimed as "grooming" or "therapy," learn to DIY.

First remove any old nail polish. Soak feet in a basin of warm water, ideally for as long as it takes to drink a cup of tea.

Clip and file toenails *straight*.

Push back toe cuticles. They should be soft after soaking, but if not, use a cuticle moisturizer.

Use a loofah or pumice stone to smooth any hard skin.

Separate your toes. Do this by folding a tissue longways and twisting it in and out between each toe, or use a special pedicure foam separator, if you want to be flashy.

Apply clear base coat, and allow to dry. Usually takes the equivalent of one CD track. This is the perfect foundation, so don't skip this stage.

Apply polish, twice for deeper colors, and tidy up with a Q-tip dipped in nail varnish remover to wipe away any stray blips or mistakes.

Allow polish to dry thoroughly. This takes longer, allow three tracks of a CD to be sure.

Apply clear topcoat. Leave shoes off, or wear open-toed sandals for at least an hour to ensure they are really dry. Shroud them too soon and you risk messing up all your handiwork.

While you have all the products to hand it'd be silly not to do a manicure, too. Matching fresh nail color is essential. There is no point angling for a diamond ring if you don't have nice, well-groomed, kissable hands. Therefore, it is only sensible to paint them, and prime them, to their best advantage. Try to avoid painting finger tops as well as tips; for this reason it is best to get dark colors professionally applied. But remember, the longer they are the less easy it is to type or write, among other necessary functioning skills.

Nail varnish should be stored in the fridge. It makes it easier to apply and the varnish glides on thicker and smoother in fewer coats. It also adds a dash of decadence to your dairy product section.

A quick word on colors and their associations

Red is dangerous, vampy, sex siren. Think Marilyn Monroe, Liz Taylor.

Rouge Noir is vamp with a twist. Plum and poisonous. Immortalized by Uma Thurman in *Pulp Fiction*.

Pink is girly, dainty, pretty, and sweet. Grace Kelly.

Clear suggests a good girl and hard worker. Perhaps a little safe. Audrey Hepburn and Carolyn Bessette Kennedy spring to mind here.

Nude/cream means you're high maintenance, well groomed, and know a good manicurist.

French Manicure is when tips are white and a clear gloss is run over the tops. Super high maintenance, and that's just the glossing! But don't knock it till you try it.

Fashion colors, glitters, blacks, and blues are fine if you are on the runway or fifteen years old. But unacceptable otherwise.

How to cope with chipped nails

Chipped nails are far from ideal, but it does happen. That's life.

If wearing deep plum or red, always carry a bottle of the matching shade in your bag for emergency cover-ups.

File your nails while you assess the damage. A nail file should always be close to hand, whatever the length of your nails. Think: do you add more of the same colour? Take it all off? Or can you afford to splash out to the nearest manicurist?

Sometimes it can be easier to add than subtract. Add a fresh layer of varnish to dark colors rather than wipe it off. Softer shades last longer and are more chip proof because errors show less.

A slight chip is excusable (for half a day till you reunite with the bottle of polish). A chipped nail on your way out is not.

In addition to a nail file, always have nail varnish remover in your desk, your bathroom, your location.

Red, Rouge Noir, and glitter varnishes are hard to remove and require patience.

How to understand your silhouette

In my day, hot pants were something we had, not wore.
—*Bette Davis*

A body is like a cello. Your job is to work out how to play it.

Everyone comes in different shapes and sizes, and as much as we'd all like to have "the perfect A1 figure" that the magazines showcase, we don't. It's called individual character. We all have different features to work with. Know your body shape, or at least have an honest idea of what it is like without airbrushing and Lycra, and learn how to maintain it.

Unfortunately, some form of fitness or exercise is recommended, but it needn't be too ghastly – it can include dancing, yoga, and shopping.

To be able to accessorise and enhance what you have been born with, decide are you:

Waif
   Twiggy? Kate Moss?

Top heavy

Jayne Mansfield? Sophia Loren?

Hourglass

Monica Bellucci? Catherine Zeta-Jones?

Masculine

Marlene Dietrich?

Belle of the bottoms

Jennifer Lopez? Beyoncé?

Voluptuous

Marilyn Monroe? Bardot?

Statuesque

Nicole Kidman?

Petite

Kylie Minogue?

Stand in front of a full-length mirror, if not at home, in a private shop fitting room (don't torture yourself in the communal ones). Look and learn.

Work with the good bits. You've got underpinning and underwire bras, and underwear that can streamline and enhance your silhouette at your disposal, so make sure you build a good base to drape your designer labels on. Tailor around your finest assets, and draw attention to these rather than focusing on the negative.

As Sophia Loren said, "A woman's dress should be like a barbed-wire fence: serving its purpose without obstructing the view."

The most important thing is to be honest, as once you know your strengths, and any weaknesses, you can know what to hide and what to flaunt. "Keep your friends close, your enemies closer" is very true when understanding what you are left with when the lights go off.

If you have:

A tiny waist

Choose low slung skirts/pants. Knot shirts at waist. Cropped tops are not just for Britney, but they are for moments of extreme confidence and reckless abandon, aka holidays and special occasions.

Ample cleavage

Wear necklaces to draw the eye down. Open-necked shirts. Strappy tops are great so you don't look bound in or constricted, but only opt for the spaghetti option if you have enough support elsewhere.

Eye-catching cleavage

Pick V-neck sweaters, or again, dangling necklaces that draw the eye down. Padded uplift bras are a given if you haven't opted for a nip-and-tuck job.

Broad shoulders

Go easy on the shoulder pads, favor cardigans and soft open tops, or structured tailoring.

Chunky thighs

Wear loose palazzo pants. Flowing skirts.

Chicken arms

Cover shoulders, wear shawls, pashminas, or chiffon-capped sleeves.

Long legs

Lucky you. Wear minis – why hide them?

A shapely derrière

You need to show it off. Pencil skirts.

Big tummy

Wear baggy shirts over trousers, empire-line dresses, suit jackets, and nothing too fitted at the waist.

Big hips

Again, you can conceal with loose baggy tops, flowing feminine skirts, and highlighting another area.

Oversize proportions

Remember that big is beautiful. To streamline and slenderize, head-to-toe black works.

It is a fact that very few can look good in:

Horizontal stripes
White jeans
Flannel tracksuits

White tights
Blue lipstick
Wellington boots
Workmen's overalls

So wear at your own peril.

How to stick to a gym membership

When you join a gym, tell everyone. Not only will you get the credit for joining, there will also be the added worry that if you don't stick to it you will be ridiculed. Buy yourself some new gym clothes.

Ideally go with a friend. Depending on how your mind works, either go with a thin friend – who looks better than you and where the rivalry will encourage you to work twice as hard. Or – the easier option – go (alone) and seek out the overweight-woman corner of the room and work out there. That way even if you are going puce in the face with every weight you lift, you'll feel some camaraderie or (whisper it) relief that you are not alone.

If the OAP (old-age pensioner) group is more sprightly than you, it's time to double your visits.

Know what will scare you into action. Book to go on a bikini holiday, buy a little black dress that is one size too small, or know that the Christmas party/wedding is coming up. Whatever your Achilles' heel, use it as your motivation. But don't set unrealistic goals. Give yourself time to make it – gulp – pleasurable. A quick workout before a night out can be very ener-gizing, so they say.

How to wear the appropriate underwear

Underwear is like men: you have your top end, your dependables, and your trash. It is sod's law – lawrus sodimus – that the one time you can't find a matching set of bra and panties, or you chance it and go out in your granny underwear, will be the night they end up on show. Think Bridget Jones.

Repeat after me, there is NO such thing as lucky knickers. You do NOT need to have one pair in fast rotation, it was your personality, NOT your panties, that pulled.

General Rules

If you're planning on being seriously seductive, a matching set of bra and knickers is called for. If you want to go the whole hog, get a garter belt, too. It is a myth that only prostitutes wear coordinating and matching underwear. Anyone concentrating should.

Wear nudes if in chiffon sheers, or when invisible, blendable cover is needed.

HIDE panty lines and avoid VPL (visible panty line). When wearing a thong with jeans, tuck it lower, or purchase the hipster variety.

Boxers are good on Sundays, comfort days, and for traveling. Briefs are ideal with low-slung jeans; slips with trousers and, on serious days, spice things up with thongs, which are also the best option for frivolous floaty dresses and "invisible" undie days. Choose tummy and toning control underwear for LBD (little black dress) days, office parties, and dressing to impress.

The ultimate in small is the "rien," which is such a sparse piece of dental floss that the only place where the label fits is on the front. Ugh. Leave those for models and other people worth hating.

Avoid getting your knickers in a twist

It's a fact that very few bums actually look good in a *thong*, which looks better off than on. You need a perky, round, size 2 to 6 bottom for these to work beautifully, or months of working out, so it depends on your commitment to the thong cause.

The *French cut*, which is a half brief at the back, is certainly more flattering than the thong. This is good on a flat bottom of most sizes or a dainty, perky bum. Both the boy-leg short and the French cut are great alternatives to G-strings if you don't want a panty line showing under trousers.

The *very low-cut triangle brief* is an extremely sexy cut and is a brief at the back so it is good on most bums. But – danger – it can ride up on flat bums (which are better going for the French cut).

For extra control, face it, you want Spanx, for super-strength hold-ins that will take your breath away, quite literally.

Beautiful lingerie is an investment. The price will be forgotten, but the quality will always be remembered. Have as many colors as there are changes in the weather, and as many styles that suit you.

The best way to enhance your asset is to exercise it, wiggle it, move it, and work it. Dieting can make it saggy, so you don't have to stay away from those cream cakes.

Bras

Above all, work with what you've got. Yes, it is incredibly hard to find the perfect fit, so go to a professional, from Victoria's Secret to Bloomingdale's or Macy's, locate an assistant with a tape measure, and get it done for you.

A lot of women are wearing incorrect bra sizes, which makes the whole purchasing process expensive and pointless.

The under-bust measurement is represented by the number sequence: size 32, 34, 36, etc. The bust/cup size is represented by the letters A, B, C, D, etc. The higher the letter the bigger the bust.

If you are tiny around the back, but have a well-endowed bust, you could be a 32D. Similarly if a woman is largish around the back, and is fairly flat-chested she could be a 36A. The balconette style (low cut and straight across the bust) looks great on most busts, except DDs and Es. The soft-cup bra (no underwire) looks great on all small, perky sizes.

The best way to get the right size is to try them on. All bras fit slightly differently. To calculate your correct size, wrap a soft tape measure around your rib cage, just below the bust line, add five to this measurement in inches, and the result will be your band size measurement. Next, measure around the fullest part of the bust; this will tell you what cup size you need. Each inch difference from your band size is equal to one cup size. Less than 1 inch is an AA cup; 1 inch: an A cup; 2 inches: a B cup; 3 inches: a C cup, and so on.

A well-endowed bust is best in an underwire bra with triangle cut and full coverage. Large-busted women need to choose styles with thick elastic straps, otherwise they will get a lot of pain in their shoulders.

To pad or not to pad? Most busts look good in a well-shaped padded bra. It provides good support, refines the shape, and boosts the bosoms. Though a heavily padded bra is full of false promises.

The best way to tell when a bra is going to be supportive, and fit properly, is to check if the middle of the underwire sits against the body and does not stick out. Check to see that it's molded to your shape. Once the hook and eye is done up, bend over and wiggle your bosoms into the cups. Adjust the wire to get it just right under the bust, then stand up, et voilà!

Check the wiring when you buy a bra, as the more wiring the worse the fit can become. Ensure that the wire is not too tight in the wire casing, otherwise it's liable to break through and poke you.

Finally, before you make your purchase, look at the straps and ask yourself whether you would like them showing through garments.

Silk lingerie should be hand washed in cold water. Gentle machine wash is fine for synthetic, nylon, tulles, and cotton.

How to enhance your assets
by Heidi Klum

Lingerie doesn't have to be luxury in the sense that you need a special occasion to wear it. Pretty lingerie can make any woman feel sexier underneath even sweats – even if only she knows she's wearing it.

The rule for lingerie is pretty much the same as for clothes, hair, makeup, accessories – you just have to feel it. If you feel good in it, if it makes you radiate confidence, then go for it! Not everything has to be matchy-matchy all the time, although bra-and-panty sets definitely have their place. And no one style is best for every woman. Some women like the teeniest, tiniest underthings and other women like a bit more substance; some like the most over-the-top, lacy, ruffled numbers and others like the plainest cuts and materials, so I don't think there's any universal rule.

I'm not into visible panty lines, so I mostly go for thongs and seamless underwear, but beautiful lacy bras that peep out underneath blazers or tank tops are also good. Triangle bras and string bikini thongs are styles I find myself naturally gravitating toward. In terms of color, my personal lingerie wardrobe encompasses the entire rainbow, but black and nude are always classic.

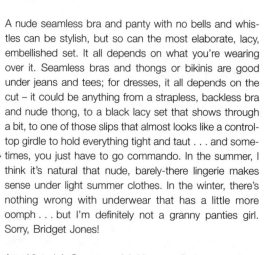

A nude seamless bra and panty with no bells and whistles can be stylish, but so can the most elaborate, lacy, embellished set. It all depends on what you're wearing over it. Seamless bras and thongs or bikinis are good under jeans and tees; for dresses, it all depends on the cut – it could be anything from a strapless, backless bra and nude thong, to a black lacy set that shows through a bit, to one of those slips that almost looks like a control-top girdle to hold everything tight and taut . . . and sometimes, you just have to go commando. In the summer, I think it's natural that nude, barely-there lingerie makes sense under light summer clothes. In the winter, there's nothing wrong with underwear that has a little more oomph . . . but I'm definitely not a granny panties girl. Sorry, Bridget Jones!

As a Victoria's Secret model, I have really too many bras and panties to count . . . but I think a nice drawer full of good underwear is sensible. And when things start stretching and snapping, then you know it's time to get more!

How to hide a spot

The world need not necessarily come to a grinding halt when you wake up to find you have been invaded and have a pimple. Think fast. Highlight another area. Today would be the day to wear red lipstick or smoky kohl-rimmed eyes. Wear your hair loose and flowing. It will not only be distract-ing, it will softly conceal the offending area and is far more subtle than opting to hide under a balaclava.

If the pimple is persistent and is an offending shade of Day-Glo that is ruining your day, do react. Dab a little extra concealer onto finger and apply to problem patch. Delicately apply powder to dry and cover it, but try not to cake it in makeup, as not only does this slow healing, it can make it even more noticeable.

If you can bear it, try when at home not to cover said imperfection in makeup. Cleanse skin and let it dry and heal au naturel. Do not pick it.

For DIRE blemish breakouts, book emergency facial, drink gallons of water, and stay in, with the curtains drawn, lights dimmed.

How to wear the right makeup

As ever, preparation is key. Cleanse, tone, and moisturize before you start applying makeup.

Confusingly, shades are not standard, so you always need to check an individual product. You need to see what color the makeup will look in a natural light. Place a sample of the foundation/makeup on the inside of your wrist or on the back of your hand. Half rub it in. Department stores have very harsh lighting, so get a few testers on your arm and go outside to consider, being careful not to smudge the product in question on cloth-ing or passing shoppers as foundation is a very stubborn stain.

Walking away from the stand will also give you time to consider your purchase instead of being rushed into a decision by a pushy sales rep who is, let's face it, not after your best interests, but their commission.

If the makeup looks invisible and blends in smoothly, you have the correct shade for you. If you can still see it, or it has a yellow/orange/pink hue shining through, try something else; you are not after a mask.

Liquid foundation moves with skin and looks healthier and younger. Powder is better for winter or close-ups, as it sets and closes the pores. But be careful how much you apply, as you don't want to look like a clown. In summer try to wear next to no foundation, or replace it with a tinted moisturizer. Year-round, a good sunscreen must be worked into your routine.

Makeup artist favorites to name-drop (therefore must be worth adding to your makeup bag) include:

- Laura Mercier for foundations and lipsticks.
- YSL for skincare and foundations, in addition to the must-have Touche Éclat.
- Nars for darker foundations and full color range for lips, eyes, and nail lacquers.
- MAC for lighter foundations, and super-jazzy color range.
- Chanel, fabulous for skincare and nail varnishes.
- Estée Lauder for skincare and foundations with supermodel endorsement.
- Dior for tasty flavored liped glosses, including meringue, and foundations. And for skincare and cleansing, you can never go too wrong using Lancôme, Kiehls, or Dermalogica.

If you could take only one piece of makeup onto a desert island, choose YSL's Touche Éclat; it is everything you need in a wand – magic.

If possible, keep skincare, makeup, and face packs in the fridge. They last longer and makeup stays fresh and elasticized, making it much easier and more pleasant to apply.

After you've achieved a flawless base, start working on the eyes. Begin with the eyeliner, then mascara, eye shadow, and more mascara.

Blushing

If applied sparingly, blusher freshens and can add a healthy glow to cheeks. Swirl a big brush on the blusher and sweep from cheekbone toward nose in a downward stroke. Repeat each side and blend.

Shades are like seasons, there are the trends, and there are also the perennial classics:

In autumn, go for orangey blush.
In spring, go for pinks and pastels.
In summer, go for golds and bronzer.
In winter, a classic look is warm reds with pallid alabaster skin. Warmer complexions can also turn up the volume on their lipstick colors for instant sophistication.

But be warned; Oscar Wilde once wrote: "She wore far too much rouge last night, and not quite enough clothes. That is always a sign of despair in a woman."

How to apply red lipstick and get it to stay

Always keep lips well moisturized and conditioned; a lip balm should always be near to hand or lurking in a handbag.

For extra durability, apply lipstick with a lip brush.

First line and rim lips with a matching-color lip pencil.

Apply color first to bottom then to top lip.

Rub your lips together to ensure even color stain.

Blot with tissue.

Softly kiss back of hand, and if it's still leaving a deep crimson stain, blot again, this time more firmly. You want the lips to be red, but you want it firmly in place so it does not wind up on your teeth.

Always check your teeth, and run your tongue or finger over them to wipe any lipstick away. Lipstick on teeth is a big faux pas.

Be aware that red lipstick will come off when you're kissing, drinking, and eating. Kiss-proof lipstick has yet to be patented, despite the claims of certain brands. Either be prepared to reapply, accept that it will leave lip blot stain, or consider a softer nude shade if you're anticipating action.

How to get a tan

Tanning is the fast and simple way to look better. The English rose look works fine for pre-1900s, Merchant Ivory films or Nicole Kidman, but for the majority of women a golden glow can work miracles. It makes you look healthier, improves skin, and slims. It is not, however, a sport to be taken to excess.

It was Coco Chanel in the 1920s who first turned tanning into a status symbol. It is said that she wore gloves and a veil while sunbathing, which must have caused some very bizarre tan lines.

Now that we're all wise to the dangers of the sun, it takes a lot of time, effort, and really cooperative weather to achieve a good look naturally. Take a moment to pause and praise the inventors of fake tan. And also do the math: faking it is so much cheaper than flying off for two weeks in the sun.

There are lots of products on the shelves and you should find one to suit you. To avoid the shame of tell-tale streaks, make sure you exfoliate and wash rigorously, scouring your ankles, knees, and elbow joints before you begin. Then, after moisturizing, apply tanning cream all over your body.

Immediately after, with all the paranoia of Lady Macbeth, wash your hands and be sure to go between your fingers. Toes and creases, such as elbows and knees and ears and ankles, are all problem patches to look out for. Take extra care and wipe around joints and creases with tissue to remove any excess tanning cream. Caution at this stage will minimize bizarre stripes that are hard to justify as "natural." Should stripes appear, a dab of nail varnish remover on the skin wipes away the tanning slip.

Don't wear deodorant or antiperspirant while "tanning." Rumor has it there could be a funny reaction and your underarms could go green – and that really would be a disaster.

Currently the two most popular options are:

St. Tropez self-tan is very popular with the contributing stars featured in the weekly magazines. It follows a similar process to that of basting a turkey. The dark treacle-like lotion is applied and the color change is almost immediate. This is far too tricky (and stainable) to do at home, so fall asleep on a dark-colored towel and let a professional slap it on. It produces a dark rich tan, too heavy and orangey for pale skins. Roughly the equivalent of two weeks in Cuba.

Spray Tan is ideal for the fairer skinned or first timer, and is the most effective and painless form of faking it. No greasy application or tedious procedures here. It's not a sun bed, it's an airbrush. What looks like a watered-down version of the St. Tropez treacle is sprayed in circular curls over the body. The tanning mist settles on the body, and the sun spray (DHA) works with the amino acids in the skin, causing a chemical reaction. You should exfoliate and moisturize the night before as once you are there you just strip, they squirt, and you (redress and) go.

If you do insist on being old-school and going au naturel, baste yourself in high factors, cautiously decreasing the factor as tan develops. Optimize tanning opportunities by running around scantily clad. Regularly top up the factor, remember to rub cream on toes, all 'round the neck and collar line, and don't forget those earlobes. Always ensure you have UVA/UVB filters in your cream, as this is the bit that protects you.

Leave conditioner in hair, so it doesn't get bleached and turn crispy. Or wear a hat. Better to have a straw hat than straw hair.

Whichever way you go, be it fake or natural, always go light and gentle on the face.

How to swim in shades

Not only does wearing shades mean you don't have to worry about your mascara, they aid vision and add glamour to the pool.

To avoid them becoming dislodged while you're in the water, wrap an elastic band around each arm of the shades. Twist and twist and then, just before the last twist is too tight to take any more, thread a strand of hair through the loop, like a miniponytail, only this one is a small piece hidden behind each ear. This will "superglue" the shades to your ears, and however high the waves and however often you tip off your inflatable, your shades will stay. Leaving you, in theory, looking like a modern-day Ursula Andress.

It's likely that they will get wet, so don't throw away one of your fave pairs on this. Every girl should have a few options: swim shades, beach shades, shopping shades, posing shades, morning-after shades, etc.

And most crucially, don't forget they are clamped on, as this makes lending them and taking them off quickly tricky. If you need to look over them, tip them down rather than remove them. Take them off in a changing room, or alone, as whimpering in pain may be the price you have to pay.

How to keep your color

Highlights show less regrowth than a full head of colored hair. The blonder you are, the darker the roots will grow. To make up for this, blondes show gray less than darker colors.

If you're going gray or white, go for tints that can color to the root.

Color should be refreshed every 6–8 weeks, or as required. Don't neglect it, the only person that really suffers is you. Blondes should use a purple/silver shampoo to get rid of the tacky brassiness.

In between salon visits, NEVER try touching up your color yourself. Similarly if your perm starts to dry or flop, get straight to the hairdressers.

To prolong color you should rinse hair in cold water to close the cuticles.

Fact: faux redheads require the most salon trips and maintenance.

How to look like you've just stepped out of a salon
by Sam McKnight, hairstylist

Never let a hair dryer be too hot or too close.

The greater the volume (you want) the bigger the brush (you need).

Hair longer than elbow length is too long.

When drying hair, always finish with a blast of cold air; this will seal cuticles and add shine. Don't buy a hair dryer without a cold air option.

The optimum styling time for hair is when it is 85 percent dry. Hair drying = hair volume + a groomed finish. Drying hair with a hair dryer lifts the hair from the roots, and gives added body. Natural drying promotes natural curls and wave. Don't fry, attack, or overdry your hair. LOVE your hair.

Don't overwash your hair. Excessive shampooing and styling strips the hair of its natural oils.

Even if you are growing your hair it still needs trims. Split ends lead to unhealthy, stunted growth and then where will you be?

To give hair added luxury and shine, always do the final rinse using bottled water. That sounds decadent, but tap water around the world has a variety of different pH levels and some harm the hair. Using bottled water ensures a neutral/balanced pH level. Within a month your hair will have a natural shine and improved lustre.

Build a rapport with your hairdresser. Pop in every time you are passing.

My four unsung hair heroes

1. For instant lift, roll three huge Velcro rollers on the crown of the head, spray, and blast with the dryer. Untwist for "salon finish" styling.

2. Soft-bristle round brushes are the tool of the trade, and a dressing table essential.

3. Dry shampoo is perfect for reviving bangs, which will get greasier faster as they are rubbed against makeup and forehead. Apply a quick squirt, comb, and have fresh hair that lasts all night.

4. For instant extra inches, try *backcombing*. Ensure hair is dry. Spray with a holding spray, if desired. Turn head upside down – so that your head is swinging between your knees. But think long term: a comb will destroy your hair, a brush is softer. Take a brush and stroke through hair.

Starting at the back of the head, closest to scalp, take a section of hair and rather than combing forward, start to stroke the comb, or better still, the brush, backward. It is like stroking a cat backward; the hair follicles try to resist going in the wrong direction and within seconds the hair has clumped together.

After repeating with a few sections, the hair starts to gather together nicely.

Flick yourself up the right way and marvel at the volume and the height.

Comb over the top layer, being careful not to comb out the backcombing.

Lift a section on one side of the parting and backcomb under this to give extra volume and height on the crown. Repeat on other side. Very Barbarella.

Tips for the hair salon experience

1. However long you thought you would be – DOUBLE it.

2. Always dress to impress when you go to the hairdressers. You want a trendy style? Give them something to work with. Inspire them.

3. Be prepared. You will have to look at yourself for hours and hours and HOURS. Bring a book, magazine, or temporary blindness, because, under the unforgiving light and uninterrupted scrutiny, even the most vain will tire of the sight of themselves and start to see faults that no one else notices.

4. Do not opt for a style that you need to have a degree in cutting and hairdressing to re-create each morning unless you are, or live with, a hairdresser.

5. Never say "Do what you fancy." They will scalp you or, worse, get "creative." It will take months for your hair, along with your confidence, to grow back.

6. Know what style suits your face and stick with it. Be cautious about following trends.

7. Assess the conversational skills of your hairdresser. Do you need a) a book – no interaction; b) magazine – occasional smile and comment, "Ugh! You're not going too short, are you?"; c) neither – you have a comedian cutting/drying your hair and you enjoy the banter.

8. Never chat when they are cutting your bangs, they could have your eye out. Or you could end up with hair in your mouth. Most unpleasant.

9. It is hard to hear when the dryer is on, so get past the punch line of the story before then.

10. Be aware of the weather. What is the point of getting a "do" done and then stepping out into a hurricane or downpour? It is common sense ALWAYS to have a brolly with you.

For further reading, but perhaps not at the salon, where you have weeks' worth of back issues of *US Weekly* and so on to devour, have a look at:

Heads: Hair by Guido (Booth-Clibborn Editions, 2000).

Bad Hair by James Innes-Smith and Henrietta Webb (Bloomsbury, 2002). Photographs of hairdos that should never have been allowed and nothing to let your hairdresser get inspired by.

How to deal with bad hair days

by Jacquetta Wheeler, model and trainee milliner

When wearing a hat, be prepared to get more attention than usual.

However, and be sure about this, different shapes suit different faces. You might look like a clown in a trilby but look fantastic in a flat cap, or vice versa. Try on a few styles before ruling a hat out forever.

Hats are good for clothes crises and bad hair days. Wear a fabulous Stephen Jones with jeans and a T-shirt and you've got an outfit, problem solved. Hats ARE outfits!

If you feel too smart, funk yourself up a little with a cap from the market.

If you feel too pretty, wear a masculine hat, a trilby, or a cap.

If you feel too plain, wear a hat, be it decadent, frivolous, or evocative.

If you feel too masculine, wear a girly cloche hat and add a flower.

If you feel too boring, wear a hat, give your look a twist of eccentricity.

If you want to make your eyes look bigger and sparkle, wear a hat with a veil.

If you want to feel special, wear a hat.

If you want to look individual, wear a hat.

Whatever you are wearing, make sure your hat fits well. If it's too small it will sit too high on your head, and you'll look like a fool, or it will give you a headache. On the other hand, if it's too big, it's in danger of falling off and exposing your flattened, mangled hairstyle . . .

How to wear a hat

by Stephen Jones, milliner

Wear it: with confidence, with nonchalance, with humor, with drama, with frequency . . . and many, many more times.

One must remember that milliners or *modistes* were once responsible for the outward appearance of not only hats but dresses, too. *Couturières* were responsible for the undercarriage and the construction, therefore, at its roots, a hat is just a trim and completely ephemeral. High art? Rubbish, more the clothing equivalent of *People* magazine and should be worn as such. The simplest black beret worn with attitude is more dramatic than most haute couture.

If clothing was a radio, a hat is the volume control!

Disregard the pushy sales staff who want to make you look as though you are going to Ascot when all you want is something to wear to work on a February Monday morning. As Edith Sitwell said, "If you are a greyhound, what is the point of trying to look like a Chihuahua?" Leave the frills and veil for others. Conversely, if you are five foot nothing and want to wear a wide-brimmed cloche, you may look like an animated mushroom, but if you feel like a willowy creature of mystery, so be it!

Wear the hat at home first, so you can get used to it: will it stay firm or should you change your hair? Experiment with the angle (remember Marlene Dietrich's 45-degree allure), pin on a brooch, silk sweet peas, a veil, try it on back to front, upside down; there now, it looks like you!

If you have a long face try a beret, and whilst putting it on, pull it out at the sides for extra width. Try a gardenia tucked behind your ear, à la Billie Holiday, and you'll smell gorgeous, too.

For a square face, try veiling or feathers to soften and add femininity.

If milady has a round face, suck in your cheeks and look ingénue in an asymmetric hat.

Spectacles suit upturned brims.

Big nose/no chin? Join Central Casting.

Now, wear your hat outside and the world really will be a different place.

How to achieve perfection

Whether you are born with beauty or not, you have to maintain yourself. Appearances are everything, and so ensuring you perform regular maintenance is an essential part of being a lady, or not, case depending.

There are necessary, unmentionable evils, starting with wax. Waxing hurts, but ensures finer regrowth and lasts longer than shaving. Gives smoother, more feminine feel. Exfoliate at least two days before you go for your waxing appointment. It frees follicles, ensuring hair is pulled from roots, and makes it less painful. Taking painkillers is another option.

Don't attempt to do home waxing unless you are a professional beautician or suicidal. Waxing also needs to be planned in advance, as you need to allow a day or two for skin to calm and stop resembling that of a freshly plucked chicken.

You budget for the upkeep of your house, regularly service your car, so why cut corners on yourself?

Copy this schedule into the front page of your diary/planner and ensure you keep the system smooth and purring.

The Bare Essential Ladies' Checklist

Bikini line:
Deep breath: a Brazilian, every 2–3 weeks. Note: before we leave this topic, which we will very soon, be wise, and never shave here.

Underarms
Either wax – every 2–3 weeks – or shave every other day. You sweat more in summer so there is faster regrowth. Go for whichever option you can stomach or budget.

Legs
Wax every 3–4 weeks or shave as required. Go for a half leg in winter, full leg in summer. Darker hair may need more attention. Waxing and salon methods are more effective than the razor.

Eyebrows

Get plucked, waxed, or threaded, whatever you wish. (Threading is a beauty technique from India where twisted cotton is rolled and twisted over the skin to remove the hair from the follicle. Totally painful, but your choice.) Whatever you decide, it is advised you do it once a month. But you can keep tidy by plucking (cautiously) at home.

Facial

The stresses of modern society mean it is recommended you have a salon facial every six weeks to purify and detox skin.

Pedicure/manicure

Once a month to maintain shape and color.

Lip hair

If you have it, deal with it. Wax once a month or as necessary. Bleaching is utterly pointless. You might think you want electrolysis, but your pain tolerance barrier has to be sky high to go for this option on your lip.

These are the basic no-frills essentials. Alarming but true. Ideally everything should be done in a salon. You would not attempt to maintain your own car, or operate on yourself, so why on earth would you let anyone other than a professional work with your body and on your face? Individuals should assess the need and budget accordingly. For holidays, weddings (particularly your own), and special occasions, salon trips are highly recommended. Do not forget hair/color maintenance and regular dental appointments. Hair 6–8 weeks. Dentist every 6–12 months.

How to Have Perfect Vision

Beauty is in the eye of the beholder.
—*Proverb*

How to wear contact lenses

Assuming the world only has eyes for you, you should make sure that you are able to view it with equal clarity. If you do not have 20/20 vision, spectacles are very becoming and give an air of intellect to a person. But if they are not your bag, and life is a blur, you need to get to grips with contact lenses.

If you can get them in, contact lenses are the non-laser-surgery option to achieve "natural vision," without having to wear specs. They also give you the option to change your eye color.

That said, they are not great for hay fever or allergy sufferers who are prone to watery eyes, for people who are squeamish, or who are generally babyish about touching their eyeballs.

If you hate wearing glasses, are "beauty conscious," sporty, or have a non-glasses-friendly occupation, contact lenses are great. Also, a science bit here: if you suffer from moderate to serious refractive error and need vision correction all the time, this is the option for you.

WARNING: You have to be motivated, methodical, and hygienic to get over the initial discomfort and maintenance hassle that comes with wearing lenses.

Myths and legends

It is impossible to get a contact lens stuck behind your eye.

They can break – but they don't tend to shatter in your eye.

You cannot lose them in your eye, they are in there somewhere; or you did indeed drop them on the floor, so mind where you step . . .

The main types of contact lenses

Rigid Gas Permeable (RGP)

Also known as *Oxygen Permeable Contact Lenses*. These are made of breathable, flexible plastic that allows more oxygen to pass through than a normal "soft lens." They are also easier to clean as they don't contain water. RGP lenses are custom made for the individual so are often the most comfortable option as they are really tailored to fit.

Conventional

The daily-wear soft lens that is designed to be replaced yearly. As you would expect they require cleaning and disinfecting daily after use, and you should review with an annual eye test.

Daily disposable

These lenses are designed for single, one-day use, and are to be discarded at the end of it. The benefit of this is that they do not require cleaning with fiddly solutions. You will be assured of fresh, clean new lenses every morning.

Disposables (weekly/monthly)

These are designed with a specific expiry date, depending on your prescription, but are usually weekly or monthly. Good choice for those who suffer from allergies as it prevents build-up of dirt particles or too much eye irritation.

Extended wear

If you are thinking of going out to a party and wearing your contact lens overnight, this is the lens for you. They are made of a highly permeable silicone hydrogel that allows oxygen to pass through to the cornea, much more than a soft lens does, so you can wear these for up to thirty days and nights without worry. This eliminates the drama of inserting, removing, cleaning, and so on, and for a month you can pretend you have 20/20 vision. Also a good option for Miss Allergy.

Toric

If you suffer from "double vision" (when sober), you will need this lens as it is fitted to correct this astigmatism, which is caused by the irregular shape of the cornea. The Toric lens corrects the refractive error by creating a single focus point for the retina so you don't have to. Toric lenses have two special features: one for astigmatism, the other for "myopia" or "hyperopia," but let your optician tell you about this.

Bifocal

This is what you need for the "aging eye," or the presbyopia, usually for people aged forty or above (think gold-rimmed, half-moon glasses, usually on a string, worn by librarian or granddad in toffee advertisements). You need these when the crystalline lens of the eye grows harder and thicker and loses its elasticity. With age the eye-muscle control decreases, and it becomes difficult for the person to focus on near objects. Multifocal lenses contain over two kinds of correction to correct near and distant vision simultaneously.

Colored

A jazzy "fashion" option that changes the color of your eye with a variety of lens types. It does the same focal correction as above, but turns your brown eyes blue, or whatever your particular iris pleasure. Dior is offering lenses in gold.

Other useful extras worth investing in include:

Visibility tint

This doesn't change your eye color but is an aid to help you find the wretched lenses if you should drop them.

Light-filtering tint

Developed with the sportsman in mind. They enhance certain colors – e.g. yellow, so tennis ball stands out – so good for pool, golf, and other games but not necessary for the odd game of baseball.

Enhancement tint

This is a solid, yet translucent, tint that enhances the existing eye color, a bit like getting streaks in your hair. This is especially good if your eye color is very light.

Opaque color tint

A solid color that can change the hue of someone's eye (iris) dramatically, from hazel to blue and so forth. Ideal for actors, going undercover, or Halloween parties.

How to fit contact lenses

Soft lenses are the easier and more comfortable option to insert, so go for these if you can. Application of Gas Permeable lenses is a whole other ball game – below is how to fit soft lenses.

1. Wash, rinse, and dry hands thoroughly.

Note: it is very, VERY important not to let water near your lenses. A wet finger could cause a soft lens to flatten. Avoid using fingernails when handling the lenses as this can scratch them. Keep nails short.

2. Learn and perfect a routine, then stick to it. Always insert and apply in the same order to prevent confusion, or skipping a vital part of ritual.

3. Pour the lens from container, with the storage fluid, into the palm.

4. Using mirror, examine the eyes for any debris, tears or excessive watering before insertion. Also check contact lens is intact, and not chipped or buckled. Do not insert if contact lens is damaged.

5. Is the lens the right side up? Sounds obvious, but this is like putting the shoe on the wrong foot, so it's worth checking. While it isn't dangerous if you do end up wearing it inside out, it will be a bit uncomfortable and will be harder to get out. So, to check it's the right side up, place the lens on your forefinger or your thumb, whichever is steadiest. The lens should have a bowl shape. If it's inside out the edges will bow out, if it's the right way up it will sit like a little hat on your fingertip. To turn it the right way 'round,

simply pop it back in the solution and fish it out the other way. Alternatively you can gently squeeze the lens between your thumb and forefinger. If it's the right way up, the edges should turn inward.

Once you're a real pro you'll be able to open the case and position your index finger on the lens to remove. Place the lens in your eye using the thumb of same hand holding lens to pull bottom lid down, whilst index finger of opposite hand is pulling upper lid up. Sounds too much? If you are wearing them every day it will become second nature.

6. The actual insertion. Until now it's been all talk:

a) Hold the upper eyelid open to stop it blinking shut, which will be its involuntary action.

b) Use the thumb to pull the lower eyelid down.

c) Look upward at the ceiling and with finger place the lens onto the white part of the eye. (With more practice you will eventually just put lens directly onto the center of eye.) It will wiggle the lens naturally in a wink of an eye, literally, into the right position.

d) Try NOT to panic, squirm, or make any sudden movement – it will prolong the procedure. Be cool, calm, and collected.

e) Remove the finger – well, obviously, that's not going to stay there – and try not to blink. Allow the lens to fix into position by looking down. Allow the lens to swim 'round the eye to find the correct position.

7. Relax and close eyes for a moment, and when you open your eyes every-thing should be crystal clear.

8. If the eye feels dry, use one or two drops of lubricant.

But don't rejoice yet. What? It's not over yet? NO. Unless of course you are a Cyclops, normal people tend to need to repeat the procedure for the other eye. Wearing one contact lens will leave you feeling very off balance.

How to remove contact lenses

Don't panic. If you got it in your eye, it is only logical that you will be able to get it out.

Approach the situation calmly.

Always ensure hands are clean and dry, and have no scratchy unfiled nails.

Look up – or to the side – and position the contact lens on the white part of the eye, sliding it across using the forefinger.

Pinch contact lens gently between the thumb and the forefinger. (This is why long nails could be a liability.)

It should come out easily . . . but practice makes perfect and do anticipate a few pokes in the eye in the early days.

Place lens on tray to be cleaned and repeat process for other lens, then give eyes a chance to recover. Maybe lie down and close eyes, or cry. Depends what you have time for.

How to shape your eyebrows

Eyebrows can make your face, as they frame and enlarge your eye. A bit of shaping can change the way you look. They can hide your flaws and enhance your beauty spots.

The beginning of the eyebrow should be in line with the inner corner of the eye, and should end just beyond the eye. A perfect arch.

The greater the distance between the two eyebrows the wider your nose will look.

Tweeze hairs on nose bridge (if any) immediately, too unsightly.

Remove hairs that are obviously outside the natural shape.

When tweezing, remove a few hairs from one eye, then alternate to other brow. Yo-yo back and forth. This eliminates overtweezing and helps achieve a more balanced look.

Pluck from under arch up. Never destroy natural top arch of brow, as this will cause chaotic regrowth.

If a few hairs are missing, draw in each hair with a kohl pencil using a feather-light touch. Begin at bottom and draw upward, following hair direction.

The finishing touch: coat eyebrows with clear mascara, which holds it all in place.

How to Deal with Unpleasant Situations

Courage is grace under pressure.
—*Ernest Hemingway*

How to have a good bedside manner

Plump up their pillows, draw their curtains, get them a fresh glass of water and a cup of tea. Ask them if there is *anything* that you can get them, and indeed what their symptoms are.

If they seem really unwell, you can offer to take their temperature, get them a cold washcloth or hot-water bottle. If they seem contagious, it might be worth trying to keep the window open so that the room is ventilated, and the germs can easily escape.

Have a medical book to hand, listen to your patient, and ask them to describe their symptoms. See if you can locate what is wrong in the index. But know the three stages of illness. One – you can cure. Two – a doctor should see it. Three – call an ambulance.

Make sure you understand how to tell a heart attack from wind. And perhaps you might ask the casualty what health insurance they have.

Remember: be as nice and considerate and soothing to them as you would expect them to be to you. If you have a good bedside manner, then when you are sick they will want to fuss over you.

How to avoid flu fast and fashionably

Stay away from people with flu. Avoid sneezing, coughing, and sniffing friends.

Keep your hands clean, and keep them away from your eyes, nose, and mouth to avoid spreading any germs you may have accidentally made contact with.

Drink lots of water and eat plenty of healthy food. However much you crave chocolate cake, throw some fruit into the mix. Aim to drink eight glasses of water and eat five pieces of fruit or vegetables a day.

If you are worried that you are coming down with something, increase your vitamin intake.

Do as your mother always wanted: eat your greens, join a gym and exercise, be it walking, stretching, running, swimming; there must be something that you can do/tolerate.

How to care for yourself if you have the flu

Keep yourself warm, wrap up, and stay in. There is no point going out with a red and runny nose.

If you are losing your voice, try gargling, either with a little bit of salt or some soluble aspirin.

Hot showers and hot drinks: these will not only comfort you but help you sweat the fever out. If you are feverish, drink lots and lots of water, even more water than a supermodel, as you will dehydrate faster than usual.

Soup, either lovingly homemade or Campbell's. Tomato for comfort and chicken for mucus. Euugh. No, really. It has an amino acid in it called cysteine that will help clear it.

Cut out dairy products as they will cause gridlock in your sinuses. Replace with hot water and lemon.

Go easy on the cough sweets as they mask the cough and you need to cough it out.

Stay in bed and try to rest.

Try not to get wound up by work, as if you are stressed you will take longer to get better.

Herbal remedies
- To prevent a cold, try echinacea and garlic and zinc.
- For headaches, take 1 tablespoon of lavender, betony, marjoram, and rose petals. Put into a cloth sachet bag, add boiling water, and drink.
- For coughs and colds, you want honey and glycerine.
- For sore throats, add 2 tablespoons of dried rosemary to a pint of boiling water and drink.
- For indigestion or an upset stomach, try peppermint tea, and to relieve fatigue add a few drops of lavender oil to your bath.

If you are still sick after forty-eight hours, get to a doctor. Beg for some antibiotics, and if they say it's "just flu," feel free to cry.

How to hold court from your sick bed

Depending on your symptoms, you do not have to disappear from society. You can still have visitors bring you magazines, flowers, and news from the outside world. Depending on how contagious you are, you might consider sending packages of Airborne along with your invitation.

Put on a nice, covering nightie; negligees are not suitable for receiving when sick. Light a scented candle, because even if you can smell nothing you always have to think of others, and the flickering dim light of a candle can add to the overall effect of your sick setting. Prop yourself, or get help, up on your pillows, have tissues, Vicks, and blankets within reach.

Keep your guests at a slight distance, as you don't want to pass on the flu, nor do you want them to see how red your nose is.

Limit visits to no more than twenty minutes if truly sick, but if you are simply bored and it's a leg-in-a-cast, can't-move-type scenario, get them over to watch a DVD or something to keep you company.

How to stock your first-aid kit

A workman needs his tools, so minimize the amount of blood staining your carpet and general hysteria by having your own in-house pharmacy in the bathroom cupboard. You can buy ready-made first-aid boxes, but filling your own plastic lunch box is better as it will help you be aware of the remedies to cure snake bites, witches' spells for headaches, and potions that are at your disposal.

You absolutely must have:

- A packet of antiseptic wipes to clean a wound easily.
- A packet of Band-Aids in a variety of sizes.
- Antiseptic cream.
- Painkillers.
- Bandages, gauzes, cotton wool, plus bandage tape, safety pins, and scissors. (Yes, you do need seperate first-aid scissors as you'll never find your other pair in times of need.)
- Tweezers for removal of splinters, gravel, and so on.
- Eyedrops
- Packet of tissues to dry any tears.
- A flashlight (well, what if you are injured in a power outage?).
- Packet of sweets (good for distraction and shock, have enough for both you and the wounded).
- Emergency contact number list.

How to apply adhesive bandages

Paper cuts are a very nasty hazard and unspoken danger of the workplace. They most certainly deserve a Band-Aid. They are well worth investing in and come in all shapes and sizes, including ones shaped like butterflies that can curl around your fingertip. Check that the wound is clean and is not bleeding too much, then curl bandage 'round, and kiss better.

How to deal with wasp stings

As with most things, you need to know what you are allergic to – and avoid it. Bees and wasps can be avoided, but sometimes they are determined, so if you are allergic to them always have the appropriate antidote with you to prevent things from getting serious.

If it is just one sting you can deal with it. Hopefully they will sting and buzz off (wasp) or die (bee), but right now this is not your main concern. You need to remove the stinger without the poison going farther into the skin or blood system. Do not try to pluck it out – this could release the venom. Instead get tweezers or a blunt knife (note "blunt" here) and try to scrape the stinger out. Then once it's been removed, wash the wound and if there is swelling or pain, place packet of frozen peas on the wound. Apply antiseptic cream, and if still in pain, take a painkiller.

If you get stung in the mouth or throat it's a serious problem; head to the ER. Likewise, more than one sting may lead to anaphylactic shock, which is really bad.

How to be stylish in a sling

First of all, you need to know how to style a sling or, in layman's terms, how to knot it on. Take a triangular bandage, or fold a square one in half, and sit down. You will need help doing this if you are the wounded. Support your broken wing with the opposite hand, so that only you are manhandling the battered arm. Hold gently across your chest and forward enough to enable your assistant to slip one side of the triangle underneath. They should then take one tip of the triangle up to the neck and fold the other behind the elbow and up to the neck on the other side. Knot as comfortably and as tightly as possible. Finish off with a little safety pin to tuck the arm safely in at the elbow, so it feels supported and safe.

Do not feel restricted to using cream-colored and hospital-regulation slings – silk scarves also work, especially if it's an evening function. An arm in a cast is no reason to neglect your label commitments. The choices are endless: treat yourself, or ask to be treated, to Dior, Burberry, Gucci, Pucci, and, if you are feeling really sorry for yourself, the ultimate, Hermès. But finds from your travels can be equally fabulous as long as they are highly patterned, silky, and stylish.

If you are suffering in a sling, opt for halter-neck tops, button-up shirts, and cardigans. Adapt your wardrobe and explore new ways to dress to make the most of your sling status.

How to walk with crutches

Before you leave the hospital in your cast, get some instructions and road test your crutches. Make sure that you have the correct size and height so that you are as comfortable as possible. Position under both arms and lean forward. Unfortunately the footwear will have to stoop to sneakers, and only on one foot; this is the only time you should abandon heels as there is no point wearing down one side. Check that the padding feels comfortable around the hands, and don't try to walk too far on your first trip – the armpits will ache.

Take small steps at first, and aim to have someone close by in case you topple over.

Rest as much as needed, but try to move around as much as you can bear to because this will aid the healing process. You need to keep your strength up so try to exercise the muscles, otherwise you will be as stiff as a cream cracker and feel dreadful when the plaster cast comes off. And while your foot/leg is in plaster, don't forget to wiggle your toes and treat them to a good pedicure – they will be feeling really stressed out.

How to use toilets at concert venues

If you are rock chick enough to go to Glastonbury or some other outdoor concert and you need to make a call of nature, be prepared.

If you simply cannot keep your legs crossed for another six hours, you will have to venture into a scary Portaloo situation.

First try to blag your way backstage into the VIP enclosure, saying that you are an A&R scout, a backing singer, a girlfriend, their PR, whatever fits your look, and use the facilities there. The groups tend to have their own fancy trailers with all mod cons attached so theirs will be up to department store standard.

If this doesn't work, there is nothing else for it than to join the queue.

Take a friend with you as you may be gone hours. If you are worried about physical contact with the door, you could bring along your marigolds (rubber gloves).

Take a deep breath, open the door, and do not breathe in.

Touch NOTHING; ideally get your friend to lean/stand in front of the door so you do not have to lock it and risk getting trapped in the toxic coffin for the afternoon.

Go prepared. Take tissues with you, and antibacterial wipes.

As unladylike as this sounds, in a venue like this there is no choice but to squat and pray and, as you are not breathing in here, be as quick as possible.

If going at night you will definitely want your friend to come, perhaps equipped with a flashlight for some illumination.

As you leave and disinfect yourself, squirt yourself with a dab of your signature perfume, and slip your shades over your eyes as you recover from this dignity loss. Pretend it never happened.

How to change a diaper

There is one key tip here: do it quickly. This is another hold-your-breath moment, but first of all have a sniff around the derrière region and be sure it is absolutely necessary to change before you unleash the odor of the devil. Diapers are only your responsibility if it is your child. Do not volunteer unless a blood relative. Cloth diapers may look cute, but washing and recycling nappies is a commitment that only the greenest should take on.

Lay your little gurgler on their back on a mat, unbutton so that you can get to said diaper. Have all your equipment to hand: bin, wet wipes, fresh diaper, and peg for nose.

Tickle their tummy to distract them while you get the front two stickers open, and then, taking a deep breath, whip the mini baby legs up in the air with one hand and pull the diaper off with the other.

Throw the horror – diaper, not child – immediately into trash bin.

Wipe them down, and reseal water leak with fresh diaper, quickly.

You can always practice on Tiny Tears dolls, or alternatively employ a nanny and catch up with your child once they are potty trained, or collecting their degree.

How to pick up dog doo with style

It is not a naturally easy thing to do with style, but if you have a dog it will become necessary. Cats would be absolutely horrified if you got involved with their toilet habits, whereas man's best friend feels happiest with you by their side through every aspect of the relationship.

When the inevitable situation occurs, try not to pull a sour face, but whip out a plastic bag. A supermarket bag is ideal here, see-through is clearly not good, and paper ones, despite having superior labels, don't scrunch up as well. With the bag inside out, your hand inside the plastic like a glove, knees together and head high, stoop down, place hand over poop, and as you grab it flick the plastic bag 'round it, tie knot, and get to the nearest rubbish bin to dispose. Quickly. However much fun the walk is, you do not want to be wandering around with this for long.

How to Perform

How kind of you to let me come.
—*Eliza Doolittle (Audrey Hepburn), in* My Fair Lady

How to survive an occasion: weddings, funerals, and birthdays

There are the good, the bad, and the downright ugly, but however hard you try to avoid them you can never escape them.

Birthdays are fairly predictable and there is the comfort that everyone there has shared the same experience. Funerals, though not a merry gathering, are also straightforward and an equally shared ground.

The hardest thing to navigate is the wedding.

Weddings

Marriage is a wonderful invention; but then again, so is a bicycle repair kit.
—*Billy Connolly*

Weddings are the happiest day of the white-dress-wearer's life, so it stands to reason that for a truly joyous union there has to be misery and stress somewhere.

To avoid Lady Luck picking you as the unhappy person, follow this fail-safe guide.

What to wear

Comparatively simple for the bride, utter nightmare for everyone else.

Ascertain what color the bridesmaids are wearing, or what the color theme is of the flowers or wedding. This should influence your palette – no point clashing with the focal characters in the official photos.

A good tip is to stock up in the January sales on summer/evening dresses and rotate them around the summer weddings. You'll be amazed, it's like buses: you wait for years, and then three (weddings) happen at once.

Go for pretty, delicate, non-slutty, unaggressive styles, and comfortable heels, as you will be on your feet all day, all night, and most likely will have to deal with grass, cobblestones, stairs, and all the major heel-wearing hazards.

Play fair – it is considered very bad form to upstage the bride at her own bash. It is not fair to give the groom doubts.

You can wear white and you can wear black at a wedding . . . if you have to. But far better to avoid these colors altogether, unless you are trying to make a *statement.* Not wearing white is obvious good manners, unless you intend to jilt the bride at the last minute. As for black, Mary, Queen of Scots wore this to her wedding and all her subsequent misfortune has been attributed to it. But that's the English for you; in many parts of America wearing black or black tie is embraced at weddings, so just be location sensitive.

Hats

You don't have to wear a hat to a wedding, but it is a good excuse to. (See *How to wear a hat,* page 59.)

RSVP

You *have* to RSVP promptly and politely to wedding invitations, ideally on the cards supplied, whether you can attend or can't think of anything worse. (But don't say this to them.)

When replying to the invite casually call and find out the program, religion, and any additional points to navigate. Pot roast/buffet style? Any unwelcome surprises – i.e., nightmare scenarios far better to have advance warning of? Try to uncover these NOW. This will influence dress and shoe code, e.g., outdoors will need shawl and heels that can cope with grass stains, potential rain, and chilly relatives.

If an overnight stay is required, RSVP really early. If the couple suggests a hotel, it is usually good sense to opt for this as it should be in close proximity to the event, and shows willingness on your part. Proposed venue should have arranged a special rate for wedding guests.

Wedding registries

If they have a wedding list, go for it. Give them what they want, and save yourself hours of agony. If all you can afford is a sugar-bowl lid, so be it.

Food

Have a big breakfast that morning, as you may not see food for a very long time. There is the service, the photos, the line-up, and all manner of rituals and alcoholic moments to get through before you taste a morsel. Line your stomach.

Being single

You can still breathe, walk, talk, and live as a single person, however thoroughly inadequate days like today make you feel. Everyone there has been single at one point or another. Remember this from nine-times married Zsa Zsa Gabor: "Husbands are like fires. They go out when unattended." At least you don't have that to worry about.

NEVER go alone. Tradition says that this is THE place to meet your future beloved, and if this is the case you don't need anyone cramping your style. Rubbish. If you get invited to a wedding, take someone. If you don't have a partner, pay someone or drag along a "best boy friend." Gay boyfriends are the best option here, but do remember to ask in advance if you can bring a guest. Seating and head counts are major wedding headaches, so uninvited guests are a real no-no, and an ambiguous hint of a possible plus one will buy you some time to shop around the singles market.

A friend will make you seem much more approachable, and you can have a partner in crime for the day's antics. If you were alone you would simply have to nurse the obligatory flute of champagne, while standing with a glazed fixed smile on your face, wondering silently why that woman chose headgear that looks like a vegetable.

Think of others

If you do see someone on their own, go up and say something to them, compliment their dress, or (if they look too ghastly to go there) say how wonderful the wedding/cake/weather is. Compassion.

Jive bunny

You are not meant to hit the dance floor until after the newlyweds have had the first dance, even if you are a far superior dancer.

Exits

Know when to leave. It is considered bad luck to leave before the cutting of the cake, or indeed until the bride has tossed the bouquet, especially if you intend to catch it.

Always prebook a cab. Why do you think Cinderella caused such a sensation at the ball? She left early. Always leave people wanting more. If you arrive knowing when you are leaving, you can calculate how long you mingle, how long you drink, how long you turn on the charm, and so on.

Share and share alike

Don't hog the bride or groom in conversation. They have to circulate, meet, and greet.

What to say

In case you get tongue tied, have glazed over, or are really quite inebriated, have a prepared conversation opener in mind:

Bride – You look beautiful, who made your dress?
Groom – She looks beautiful, where did you get her (ring)?
Best man – Great speech . . . got any friends?
In-laws bride side – You must be very proud.
In-laws groom side – You must be very relieved.

Get your best side

Always be nice to the wedding photographer. (See *How to look good in a photo*, page 275.)

And finally . . . you may not slap the wandering hands of a lecherous drunken relative; your parents will never let you live it down.

Funerals

"The only way you can become a legend is in your coffin," said Bette Davis. Katharine Hepburn took an equally cynical line: "Death will be a relief. No more interviews."

A solemn, sad, and much more straightforward event.

Wear black daywear, not eveningwear, and never too tarty. Think demure rather than black widow. Think soft makeup, waterproof mascara.

Hats, or, better still, a black tulle veil.

Think Jackie Kennedy at JFK's funeral, Princess Diana at Gianni Versace's funeral.

Sombre yet chic.

Take tissues; if you don't need them, someone will. Handkerchiefs are unhygienic and horrid to share.

Preorder flowers to arrive at the funeral with message of condolence.

NEVER be late. Bad karma.

Wakes. You have to go – but not for long.

Respect the wishes of the immediate family.

Don't mention money or settling old scores, not today.

Birthdays

Men may carelessly forget them, while women try to and cannot. Birthdays herald another year has passed, another wrinkle, another wealth of experience, another chapter in life's rich tapestry, and another *distinct lack* of marriage proposals.

On your birthday, write a list of things you want to achieve in the coming year – and review it on your next birthday to see where life has taken you.

Write all friends' birthdays in your *address book* so as not to forget the date when diaries get updated.

Say it with diamonds, say it with flowers, say it with cake, say it with gift-wrap, but say it with meaning. And don't forget to call.

Anyone can remember Christmas. Birthdays are for the individual so that day must be special for them. It must not be forgotten.

Stick with the motto, If you can't say anything nice don't say anything at all. Tell them tomorrow how stupid they are to have a face-lift.

'Tis better to give than to receive. Set high standards for yourself and try to give something unique that reflects how you feel. You will get as much out of giving as they will in getting. It also raises the stakes when you are on the receiving end.

Cakes and candles, whatever the age, are essential. When you are fifteen you wish you were sixteen, when you are seventeen – eighteen. When you are twenty-one you long to be thought of as an adult. When you wish you were getting younger, you are getting on. Have as many great memories as you have candles on your cake.

Other than the early years, eighteen, twenty-one, thirty, forty, fifty, and sixty are the only birthdays that really "matter," the only real milestones that require big hoopla.

You are forty only once, ONCE. Make a note of anyone who invites you to their fortieth birthday party three years in succession, and deplete gift accordingly.

Only the Queen of England can have two birthdays. Everyone else has one, once a year.

How to survive New Year's Eve

It is a fact that few people care to admit, but New Year's Eve is one of the most overrated and stress-inducing dates in the calendar. The only way to be able to survive it is with forward planning. Spontaneity collapses on New Year's Eve as most drinking holes and clubs have cottoned on to this "event" and sell tickets in advance.

There are a few options you can go for:

Plan ahead and get all your friends to buy tickets for the same place on the night and go together. Or avoid hassle and debates by giving them all tickets to the venue that you want to go to for Christmas.
If you are feeling energetic, throw a dinner party.
Book a country cottage or B&B or go abroad.
Or you can watch the obligatory reruns on television, make a list of New Year's Resolutions, stay up to watch the ball drop, and go to bed sober.

Wake up fresh as a daisy and ready to start the New Year as you mean to go on: hitting the sales.

How to be astrologically in tune

You can tell a lot about someone's personality if you know his star sign. Take Jesus, born on December 25. Fed the five thousand, walked on water – typical Capricorn.
—*Harry Hill*

Astrology is one of the oldest and most mystical methods of predicting the future, and the horoscope page is by far the most essential page in a newspaper.

If you can't decide whether you should risk getting out of bed and going to work, what you should wear, and need to know which are the days you are destined to fall in love, this is the thing for you. Astrology looks to the stars and hints at what action to take.

Astrology does have a science bit, but like most things, you can ignore this. It's a daily update on "will they or won't they," "should you or can you." There are twelve signs of the zodiac divided not monthly – no, that would be far too simple – but, according to your birth date and the phases of the moon, they predict your daily destiny and fate . . . which is always handy.

Find a publication that you like, and more importantly trust – as in "get favorable results from," and you have your morning solace with your cornflakes. You can even have your stars texted directly to your mobile (but be slightly wary of the hidden $$ sting this has). You know a relationship is getting serious when you start scouring the papers for what your partner's stars say.

Go to *www.astrologyzone.com*. The forecasts of Susan Miller are so popular that the site is usually jammed on the first of each month. Proof that she is good. She can tell you who you should be with, and what signs are really worth avoiding.

Try to read just the positive and not the negative, and definitely ignore any flowery hippie language. Don't forget: you make your own luck.

Aries—March 21–April 19

Symbol Ram

Ruling planet Mars

Element Fire

Not to be coupled with Taurus, Virgo, Scorpio, Pisces

People under this sign are said to be active, ambitious, bold, and impulsive. They dress this way, too. They are confident and more often than not are the trendsetters that inspire the room. They are charmers and like sexy styles that draw a crowd.

Taurus—April 20–May 20

Symbol Bull

Ruling planet Mercury

Element Earth

Not good with Gemini, Libra, Sagittarius, Aries

This is the person who will buy the most expensive designer clothes, and still hoard their thrift shop finds. They tend to be of a muscular build and suit earthy colors. They think with their hearts rather than their heads, but have strong willpower and integrity and seldom buy on impulse.

Gemini—May 21–June 21

Symbol Twins

Ruling planet Venus

Element Air

Disaster with Taurus, Cancer, Scorpio, Capricorn

Blessed with intelligence and innovative qualities, this is the sign of a true multitasker. They are decisive shoppers and good listeners. They do not need to make fashion statements and can keep their looks constantly updated by mastering the art of classics with a twist. They are witty and alluring, but there is a danger that they may be a little too blunt. The perfect shopping partner.

Cancer—June 22–July 22
Symbol Crab
Ruling planet Moon
Element Water
Best to avoid Leo, Sagittarius, Gemini, Aquarius

These are sentimental souls who are fond of traveling, as long as it's 'round the home. They love tactile materials, luxury, and have sharp memories. They are very independent, with tricky-to-predict moods, and dress accordingly, black for melancholy and bright colors for a lighter mood. They are the star sign best suited to silks and embroidery, cottons and jazzy motifs.

Leo—July 23–August 22
Symbol Lion
Ruling planet Sun
Element Fire
Shouldn't shake with Virgo, Capricorn, Pisces, Cancer

The most extrovert and, generally speaking, the most noble of signs, which can sometimes come across as arrogant. They tend to be big-hearted and magnanimous, but never like to settle down. They live life to the full and in style. They like well-cut clothes that demand attention. They like the bold and the beautiful and tend to radiate confidence. They are the magnets in a room. But don't push your luck as the roar is best avoided.

Virgo—August 23–September 22
Symbol Virgin
Ruling planet Mercury
Element Earth
No go with Libra, Leo, Aquarius, Aries

Fond of frequent changes, yet at the same time they are methodical and thorough. They can wear the most revealing number one minute, the primmest thing the next. They are a mass of contradiction – keen to save money and get rich, only then to spend it as fast as possible. But underneath all this bravado there is a deep-buried sentimental soul.

Libra—September 23–October 22
Symbol Balancing scales
Ruling planet Venus
Element Air
Best to avoid Pisces, Taurus, Virgo, Scorpio

This sign has a fertile imagination and does well in the creative industry. They value peace and friendship and are renowned for being level headed. They tend to be beauty-conscious and look (the females, that is) their most alluring in dresses, as these set off their flirtatious and graceful charm.

Scorpio—October 23–November 21
Symbol Scorpion
Ruling planet Mars
Element Water
Clash with Aries, Gemini, Libra, Sagittarius

These are demanding, high-maintenance creatures who tend to prefer to crush rather than move obstacles. That said, if you ignore the sting in the tail this is a very sexy sign, and they are very keen to show this off. They are adventurous dressers, yet are happiest in black and well-structured looks. They are volatile and volcanic, and at the same time intoxicating. Think the Addams Family meets Jessica Rabbit.

Sagittarius—November 22–December 21
Symbol Archer
Ruling planet Jupiter
Element Fire
Steer clear of Scorpio, Capricorn, Taurus, Cancer

A fiery, independent sign that does not follow fashion; they would rather create it. They are the trailblazers. They are not afraid to experiment, and are boldly passionate and full of fun. You can never predict what "look" this sign will turn up in, but whatever they do, it will be an adventure.

Capricorn—December 22–January 19

Symbol Goat

Ruling planet Saturn

Element Earth

Don't go with Aquarius, Gemini, Leo, Virgo

This sign likes to dress casually – until it's time to shine in the spotlight. They can sometimes come across as aloof, but really they are big worriers. They like classical and sophisticated styles for romantic evenings and take some dragging out of their shell.

Aquarius—January 20–February 18

Symbol Water bearer

Ruling Planet Saturn

Element Air

Bad news with Cancer, Pisces, Capricorn, Virgo

They love to dress unconventionally for that "shock" value and look sensational in dark colors, geometric patterns, and asymmetric cuts. They can be wild and unpredictable one minute and meek and mild the next. They have a tendency to overlook the obvious, but can charm their way out of trouble.

Pisces—February 19–March 20

Symbol Fish

Ruling planet Jupiter

Element Water

Complete catastrophe with Aries, Leo, Libra, Aquarius

An agile sign with exceptional decisive power, a gift for sales time. They like clothes that reflect their personality. For them clothes are an extension of their sensitive and compassionate soul. They are unfazed by trends and favor instead old faithfuls. They are the sign that loves a good handbag above all else.

How to impress the in-laws

Charm is essential

You might actually be blessed with lovely in-laws, but even the loveliest will initially question whether you are good enough for their precious baby. Most will subject you to a trial by fire to prove your worth.

On a first meeting with the prospective in-laws, *never* attempt to cook – unless of course you are a famous celebrity chef.

Choose (with the guidance of your beloved) a favorite restaurant, try not to go anywhere too flashy. That will make you look irresponsible with money. Hope/assume they will be nervous, too.

Dress to impress – but not terrify

First impressions matter.

Even if corsets and bondage are the height of fashion, save them for another occasion. The hooker look may instantly get the dad on your side; a "high-fashion" label may win over the trend-conscious sister, the matron/schoolteacher with a string of pearls, the mother. But don't dress for them. You have to be yourself (albeit toned down). Instead of vampy nails go clean, and consider giving your Wonderbra a day off.

Do your homework

Know some current affairs, be up to date on all soap operas, and scan national newspapers for a week before so you have general knowledge of world events.

Likewise, learn all the dramas of your beloved's family dynasty: divorces, births, deaths and marriages, as well as family feuds.

On the day

Keep your mobile OFF.

Do not drink to excess

You will be nervous so it could go to your head dangerously fast. Be responsible but not a kill-joy.

Rebuff his father if he dares to make any naughty advances; politely, yet firmly, put him in his place with something like, "Oh cheeky, just shows how young-looking your WIFE is . . ." Also take a good hard look at the father, as this is the wrinkly version of what you may end up with. As before, slapping someone in the face or throwing wine over them won't help with the harmonious unity of your families.

Be prepared

As with a job interview, know answers for the following frequently asked questions:

How did you meet?

Do you like children? Want any? Have any?

Are you planning on getting married?

Are you a gold digger?

Have you got a criminal record?

Do you moonlight as a pole dancer?

Avoid

It is generally wise to steer clear of subjects such as:

Bikini-waxing horror stories.

Exes and lurid one-night stands.

Debauchery and favorite swear words.

Showing where your latest tattoo is going.

Stick with

Keep on the positive side and stay with topics like:

How much you like the restaurant. Proof that you are not anorexic.

How much you like living in this neighborhood. Proof that you are not suddenly going to elope to the other side of the globe.

How much you love being with whoever. Refrain from using pet names in public, particularly in front of either set of parents; it is nauseating.

Touch on where you grew up, studied, your family. Paint an idyllic picture of family bliss and wholesome education, aka Brady Bunch. Leave expulsion stories and so forth for later.

Emphasize your own career, that you are your own person, with your own aspirations, and how they complement his. This shows you are independent, intelligent, and an asset to the relationship and their family.

Talk about home purchase and investments. This shows you appreciate the cost of living and are not the gold-digging hussy they dread.

Get the parents on your side, get the blessing and the engagement ring, and
wedding planning will improve. And if you think things are going badly for
you, watch *Meet the Parents* and you will feel heaps better.

How to rebuff unwanted advances

Obviously when one is young and lovely, and has a magnetic personality,
one will receive many unwanted advances.

Bizarrely the less attention you pay someone, the more persistent they
become.

A swift, short, sharp rebuff MUST come sooner rather than later.

Never make fun of a love-struck fool because one day it could be you.

Treat as you wish to be treated, and never date out of sympathy.

Tempting as it is to keep your options open, don't give false hope and
don't be a tease.

Hard as it is, you have to be honest. There is no nice way to let someone
down. "Let's just be friends" or "I value our friendship too much to have
a relationship with you" are cowardly, inexcusable, and, frankly, insulting.
Unless you mean it, and then you have to be cruel to be kind.

Always do the deed face-to-face or, if they are likely to be completely
hysterical and irrational, on the telephone. Talk it through. Dumping
someone via text or e-mail is pathetic.

The direct approach is definitely favored by Vivienne Westwood. Bella
Freud witnessed her classy rebuff. In a club a man who used to hold a torch
for Vivienne came bounding over, but she just lifted her arms in the air and
drew a circle around herself. When asked what she was doing, she replied,
"I am rubbing you out, sir." Beat that.

Remember: from Jane Austen to *When Harry Met Sally*, the fact that men and women cannot simply be "just friends" has been amply illustrated.

How to dance and decline with etiquette

"It is a truth universally acknowledged, that a single man in possession of a good fortune, must be in want of a wife," wrote Jane Austen, in *Pride and Prejudice* in 1813. True before, true then, true today.

It should, however, also be written: "It is a truth universally acknowledged, that a single woman in possession of a good heel, must be in want of a dance partner."

Thanks to fashion and the modern world, the gentleman with his top hat and white tie and tails ready to whisk you off your feet has become somewhat extinct. But should the situation arise, you need to know how to deal with it.

Dancing is a way to show off your finest assets. Like a presenter on the shopping channel, you have the duration of one track (averaging three minutes) to show off and sell the merchandise. So no pressure. Always have a miniroutine in mind.

General dancing tips, be it disco or ballroom, are:

1. Stand facing your partner. If you don't have a partner, do the first number solo and aim to find one.

2. Make eye contact. This is key, as you can assess in a moment whether they actually know how to dance and will be able to take the pressure off you. Depending on the tempo and genre of music you have several options, whether to wiggle, hold hands, and so on. You may have to try out a lot of dance partners, but view it like finding the perfect fit of jeans or shoes.

You have to go through a lot of "nearlys" and "not quite rights" before you find perfect harmony and happiness.

Remember, dancing is 10 percent skill, and 90 percent confidence.

Always have icons in mind. Icons don't fall (over).

Men should aspire to Fred Astaire, John Travolta, and Gene Kelly.

Women should think Ginger Rogers, Madonna, Kylie Minogue, Jennifer Lopez, Beyoncé Knowles, and a sexy pole dancer.

Dutch courage is often necessary, but do the math first:

- Where are you? Who are you with?
- Is there anyone you want/need to impress?
- Anyone who you work with there?
- How many staircases are in the club?
- Where did you leave your coat?
- How dance-friendly is your bag and your look?
- Above all: what shoes are you wearing? It is crucial to calculate the shoe-to-alcohol ratio.

A few basic tips to keep you in time

Invest in VH1 and MTV – watch the videos and learn.

Doing the Time Warp or Birdie Song will never, EVER look cool.

If you lack coordination, shimmy on the sidelines.

If you really want to dance, wear shoes you can dance in. Never go barefoot – unless on a private beach – too many hazards, such as broken glass, to avoid.

Take lessons, and don't be shy; you have to learn to drive, so what is the shame in learning to dance?

Do not neglect the classics in your studies. Just as in music and art, you have at least to nod to the masters to know how it's done.

Nights in can become essential research evenings. Watching in your leotard, try *Fame* or *Flashdance* for frenetic moves, any Fred and Ginger or

Singin' in the Rain for tapping tips, *Strictly Ballroom* for your waltzing, and *Dirty Dancing* for your wooing, or should that be wowing?

Decline with etiquette

Just as we are no longer in corsets, it is now somewhat easier to decline a dance without totally wounding someone. Dance cards may have been abolished, but do not let the polite panache of courtship go with it.

If a hip-shaking Lothario shimmies over and starts to dance with you, it's good manners to endure a split second to assess whether this is friend or foe. Then, either turn firmly away, with a smile, or perhaps do the opposite.

Quick getaways include:

- Sudden and extreme dehydration. An urgent call of nature can't be argued with.
- "Oh my *god*! My top has *just* gone out of fashion, must dash."
- A sudden need to find a missing friend; or you have just spotted your long-lost fiancé over on the other side of the room.
- "Sorry, dancing has *just* gone off trend – gotta fly."
- You urgently need to call your office – in Rome. Thank God the way he grabbed you reminded you.
- Your heel has suddenly twinged; it's about to snap. Curses.

All are highly effective and plausible, but develop your own and keep them a closely guarded secret.

How to tango your way in and out of trouble

Heaven – I'm in heaven – and my heart, beats so that I can hardly speak; and I seem to find the happiness I seek, when we're out together, dancing cheek to cheek.

—"Cheek to Cheek," music and lyrics by Irving Berlin, sung by Fred Astaire in *Top Hat*

They weren't tangoing – but the lyrics still apply. Tango is a fusion of South American roots and flaming Spanish passion. Originating in Buenos Aires, the music comes first, then the rhythm, then the moves. It is an intimate dance, not for the faint-hearted, but classier than the hip-gyrating salsa moves.

Being the most sensual of all partner dances it is only fitting that this is the glamorous tool you should use to dance your way out of a situation. Not enough people do this nowadays.

A brief history

In the early 1900s around two million immigrants arrived in Buenos Aires to make their fortunes in Argentina or Uruguay. Many were single men, hoping to earn enough to return to Europe. They had nothing and were penniless; it was all fairly desolate and bleak – but in the brothels and gangster-run streets they restored their male pride and danced their troubles away.

The dance is a blend of influences from Europe as well as South America. It takes traditional polkas, waltzes, and mazurkas and mixes them with the Cuban *milonga* dance.

Rumor has it that in the first brothels men were picked by the women for their dancing skills and they only had three dances to prove themselves . . .

When dancing

Partners should be too close to see each other, and your feet should mingle into one. You should be so close that you can feel the beat of your partner's heart. Try not to fret if this is the first time you have met him, this is the pulse for the rhythm of your dance. The woman needs to be submissive, "the follower," and is led by the male, who is called "the leader." He basically twists and turns the follower as he desires, but shows her off to great advantage.

Don't look at each other, and definitely no talking; you need to concentrate. Feel, trust, and anticipate each other as you glide your way across the floor. This is why you have to find a strong and capable male leader to dance with, as it's his fault if things go wrong.

Wear leather or more ideally suede-soled shoes; one distinct plus with this dance is that women HAVE to wear heels. These are a special purchase, so check your dedication levels before you buy. Okay, they are not Manolos (those would snap with these moves), but they are heels, albeit small square ones.

You must never lift your feet. You have to slide them across the floor as if they are attached with elastic to your partner's, toes to toes, and you are drawing shapes on the floor, as if skating. Keep knees soft and slightly bent, unless you reach the "cross" position, which is left leg crossed behind right at the end of a move. Try not to bob up and down, keep shoulders level and in line with his.

When your partner grabs you it doesn't matter if he is pretty, rich, poor, fat, or thin, all that matters is that you dance. The better the dancer, invariably the better looking he becomes.

So enough with the romance, you need to master the practicalities.

Step and pause, and seductively mirror your partner's moves, and spin across the dance floor.

Drop your partner a deep curtsy. Admittedly this might throw him, if you are in a bar or the line at the local supermarket, but, if you assume life is like the movies, he will be making a slow, stiff, yet refined bow to you and will ask, "Shall we dance?"

Ballroom tango is very different to Argentinian tango. One is sherry,

the other is red wine swigged from a bottle. It all depends on your preference. But learn one and it can easily be applied to the other; it all depends
on your taste in men.

*Must you dance every dance with the same fortunate man? You have danced with him
since the music began. Won't you change partners and dance with me?*
> —"Change Partners," music and lyrics by Irving Berlin,
> Fred Astaire to Ginger Rogers in *Carefree*

The basic steps of ballroom tango

Gentleman

1. Slide left foot forward – slow.

2. Slide the right foot forward – slow.

3. Glide left foot forward, so it is in front of the right foot – quick.

4. Move right foot to the side, and slightly forward – quick.

5. Draw left foot to close, next to the right foot – slow.

Lady

1. Stretch right foot backward – slow.

2. Glide left foot back to join – slow.

3. Slip right foot backward, behind the left foot – quick.

4. Then the left foot to the side, and slightly backward – quick.

5. Slide right foot close to the left foot – slow.

    To these basic steps you now add the rhythm.

Simplified this is: slow, slow, quick, quick, slow, but for this you need more than imagination – you need music.

Clap: slow, slow, quick, quick, slow. Now substitute as follows: tea, tea, cof-fee, tea. ("Coffee" being the two quick steps and "tea" the slow. This will give you an idea of the rhythm.)

Let the steps and turns transport you far from the problem. Surely by the end of the dance, when you drop a curtsy, and he takes your hand to kiss it, he will have totally forgotten what you were quarreling over.

It could be worth trying out on traffic cops.

If, however, you want to try the real, authentic thing, you need to learn the original Argentinian tango. Be warned. This is how to tango your way *into* trouble.

You could get the popcorn and let Al Pacino teach you in *that* scene from *Scent of a Woman*.

For further information, and other dances, true aficionados should look no further than Fred Astaire and the MGM dance greats.

How to serenade someone special

Serenading someone you love is something everyone should do at least once. As Orsino said in *Twelfth Night*: "If music be the food of love – play on." Shakespeare, no less.

Making yourself horribly vulnerable and risking humiliation is one of the most dangerous yet potentially rewarding things you can do. Really. As such, it is usually reserved for fools in love.

Note: only serenade someone if you are really in love with them as this is one stage shy of a proposal. (Just hope to goodness that they serenade you or propose first.)

Questions (seriously) to ask yourself:

1.   Will you sing or will you get someone else? You HAVE to be HONEST here: CAN YOU SING? Or are you going to suffer horrible embarrassment?

2.   Where will you do this? Public or private? Think. How fond of public displays of emotion is the recipient? Will they be delighted or demented? Once you have decided the above, you are ready to proceed.

If you are singing, practice, and maybe even do a demo to a close and honest friend.

If you are hiring, say, a cute little string quartet, can you choose that "special" song? What do they specialize in?

String quartet? Spanish guitar? Tinkling piano?

Will you be a capella (unaccompanied) or accompanied? Classical or pop?

Do you know any musicians or anyone who has done this and can recommend someone? If not, search Internet and local music stores/schools and ask for demo tapes and prices.

Think what style you want and what your budget is.

Decide whether the object of your affection has friendly neighbors, or a picturesque balcony they can lean off. Indeed, would you prefer to go for it in a restaurant?

Don't send a string quartet to an office; imagine if the shoe was on the other foot. You would be mortified. Flowers are the only acceptable nonwork thing to send to an office (and this is to be encouraged on a regular basis).

The final thing you need to be sure of is whether it's going to have the desired effect. If you think this extravagant show will have them running for the door, or changing their number, think again. Test the water. You have a good excuse to watch *Pretty in Pink* again, and see if their toes curl when Molly Ringwald is serenaded in the record shop. Use it as a barometer to gauge whether you should or should not go ahead.

How to meet the Queen of England

Should you be invited to a garden party at Buckingham Palace, or the royal family pops by for a cup of tea (well, they are terribly keen on "meeting the public" these days), you should know what to do. The English are terribly proud of their traditions; the royal family, and the protocol that goes with it, is just one example of this.

Buckingham Palace does not issue a strict dress code as Her Majesty does not want her guests to stress, or feel obliged to go out and buy a new outfit for the occasion. Which is very kind, but let's face it, you get an invite to the palace, you go and buy a new outfit. And some gloves. And a hat, but don't buy one with too large a brim, as you'll spoil the view for others.

If there is a specific dress code it will appear on the invitation. If you are invited by a member of the royal family to an event, you have to go. Treat it as a command. They have stopped chopping heads off, but it would be extraordinarily bad manners to decline the monarchy.

You can wear black when meeting royalty, but ladies seldom do, as royalty tend to wear this only at state funerals and when in official mourning.

For state banquets, it is white tie.

For an investiture or garden party, it's normally morning dress, national costume if applicable.

Take a small handbag and clear out any clutter, such as old sweets and pens minus lids. There will be a security check. Cameras are not allowed, and mobile phones are likely to be a liability.

Be punctual. You must arrive before the members of the royal family. If your car breaks down or there is an act of God which delays you, slip in as discreetly as possible.

Do not charge up to the queen. Make yourself approachable and wait for her to come to you.

If you are addressed by the queen your reply should start with "Your Majesty . . ." and continue with "ma'am." For other members of the royal household, begin with "Your Royal Highness . . ." moving on to sir/ma'am as appropriate.

You may not sit down to dinner, tuck in, or make any dramatic executive decisions until after the member of the royal family has entered, sat down, and gotten themselves settled. The same applies to leaving – you do nothing till they have made their move.

Try to relax, the royals are the most socially skilled family in the world. They are trained to put mere mortals at ease. Don't go there looking for love, this only worked for Cinderella.

Being Socially Adept

All the world's a stage,
And all the men and women merely players:
They have their exits and their entrances;
And one man in his time plays many parts.
—Shakespeare, *As You Like It*

How to
Play Games

Homer: Your mother has this crazy idea that gambling is wrong. Even though they say it's okay in the Bible.

Lisa: Really? Where?

Homer: Uh . . . somewhere in the back . . .

—*The Simpsons*

How to play poker

Thanks to the bright lights and casinos of Las Vegas, the glamour of gambling is *tout le rage*. Think Al Capone or Humphrey Bogart, and their diamond-drenched molls; Monroe or Sharon Stone are good starters. This is the ideal place for martini sipping, playing the glamour puss, and eyeing any potential sugar daddies or James Bond types. "Hey big spender, spend a little time with me . . ."

A brief history

Poker is the most played and popular of all card games. It can be traced back as far as China in 900 AD, although others say it is derived from a five-player Persian game that requires a deck of twenty-five cards with five suits. Another theory is that it comes from the French "poque" and became popular in New Orleans in the seventeenth century, where it was introduced by French immigrants. It traveled up the Mississippi and Ohio rivers, and then via wagon and train across America. This is also said to be where the original use of decks consisting of spades, diamonds, clubs, and hearts originated. In 1875 the joker, or wild card, was introduced.

Today poker is cautiously regulated by gambling casinos, yet remains the most addictive of all card games. As well as at tournaments and in casinos, it is now one of the most popular interactive games on the Internet.

Learning the basics

Although very dependent on the hand you are dealt, poker is essentially a game of skill. And instead of scoring points, you win cash.

But before you strap on the green visor, disappear under a fog of cigar smoke, and throw down your life's savings, you're going to have to learn when to "hold 'em" and when to "fold 'em."

There are countless versions and they can be quite complex, so focus on five-card draw, as it is the easiest to learn.

Understanding basic mathematical principles of probability are helpful – yikees – but the most essential skills are psychological. Women should win at *this* hands down.

Poker is played with a standard deck of fifty-two playing cards. The cards are ranked from high to low in the following order: ace, king, queen, jack, 10, 9, 8, 7, 6, 5, 4, 3, 2. Aces are ALWAYS high. Aces are worth more than the kings, which are worth more than the queens, which are worth more than the jacks, and so on . . .

The cards are also separated into four "suits." The suits are: clubs, spades, hearts, and diamonds. These suits here have nothing to do with tailoring and are all of equal value.

To start, each player is dealt five cards.

The object of the game is to end up with the highest-valued hand. From best to worst, hands are ranked in the following order:

Royal flush

The most valuable of all hands. It's composed of 10, jack, queen, king, and ace, all of the same suit. It is virtually impossible to get this hand, but this is the one to aim for.

Straight flush

This is comprised of five cards in numerical order, again all of the same suit. You're not allowed to "wrap around," e.g., Q-K-A-2-3. This is also very rare. If you get two of these in a row, you are cheating. If there are two straight flushes at the table, whichever hand's straight flush reaches the highest card value wins.

If you are already getting confused, why not start your poker career by playing with a partner. Two heads are better than one.

Four of a kind

Four cards of the same numerical rank, and another random card. If there are two or more hands that qualify, the hand with the highest-ranking four of a kind wins.

Full house

This is when of the five cards in your hand, three have the same numerical rank, and the two remaining cards also have the same numerical rank. Ties are broken first by the three of a kind, then the pair. So K-K-K-3-3 beats Q-Q-Q-A-A, which beats Q-Q-Q-7-7.

Still with me?

Flush

Nothing to do with excessive blushing, although poker can make you feel very hot and bothered. This is when you have five cards of the same suit, regardless of their numerical rank. In a tie, whoever has the highest-ranking card wins.

Straight

Five cards in numerical order, regardless of their suits. As with the straight flush, a straight cannot "wrap around." In a tie, whoever's straight goes to a higher-ranking card wins.

Three of a kind

Three cards of the same numerical rank, and two random cards that are not a pair.

Two pair

Two sets of pairs, and another random card.

One pair

One pair and three random cards. If more than one person has a one pair, then the person with the highest-ranking pair wins.

High card

If none of the players has anything of value, the player holding the highest-valued card wins, with the 2 as the lowest card, and the ace as the highest. In the case of a tie, you move to the next highest card, and continue.

Now you know what it takes to win. Gather a group, dim the lights, and shuffle the cards.

Unlike bridge, poker is almost always played for cash, not cards. But before the game begins, collectively agree on a betting limit. A betting limit keeps the game friendly, and prevents people from gambling away Manolos, diamonds, or happiness.

Getting started

Shall we begin?

1. Each player places an ante or "token bet" into the pot before the cards are dealt. The ante can be anything from ten cents to thousands and gets the thing going, but also sets the tone and gives you an idea of what stakes you are playing for. Remember: it is a game, so try not to get too competitive.

You do need an ante because it guarantees that someone will win on each hand, and hopefully that someone is you.

2. Once everyone has placed their ante/guarantee, the dealer deals the cards, facedown, around the table, starting with the player to their left and continuing clockwise. The dealer (if playing) always deals to themselves last. The "dealer" is the person who either knows what they are doing or is good at shuffling cards. The dealer gives everyone their first card, then goes back around the circle to deal the second, and so on. As soon as everyone has five cards, the remainder of the deck is placed in the middle of the table, facedown, and play begins.

3. Look at your cards, spread them into a fan shape so only you can see them. The first player places a bet. There are several ways of deciding who bets first, but when starting, keep it simple and let the player directly to the left of the dealer make the first bet. Then on the next hand, the person to his left will bet first, and so on around the table for each new hand. Play with poker equality and etiquette.

4. Players have several options as far as the first round of betting goes. If no one has made a bet yet, you now have two choices:

Open: If no betting has begun when your turn comes, you may "open" the pot. This simply means that you make the first bet.

Check: The opportunity to "check" occurs only if no one has yet opened the betting when it comes time for you to decide what to do. Decide if your cards are strong enough to stand up to the stress.

When betting begins you have three choices:

See: When you "see" another player, it means that you match their bet.

Raise: When you "raise" it requires you first to "see" the previous bet, and then increase the bet.

Fold: When someone else opens, you can always jump ship and cut your losses, in other words, you "fold." The act of folding is to give up, place your cards facedown on the table, and lose whatever you've bet so far.

You need to concentrate because if it wasn't already, this is where it gets complicated.

5. All the players who haven't folded are allowed to get rid of the cards they don't want and take some new cards. A player is permitted to get rid of up to three unwanted cards and receive up to three new ones from the deck (as long as the player always has five cards in total). No one sees what anyone else has "discarded" (thrown away) or "drawn" (got as a new card). It's all done facedown.

6. Once every player has drawn 0–3 new cards, the betting begins all over again. You have the option of "opening" or "checking," and once someone opens, you can "see," "raise," or "fold." The game ends when there are no more raises, or everybody folds.

7. At this point it's time for everyone to turn their cards over and see how they fared.

8. The player with the highest hand wins the pot.

And then you start the whole thing all over again. Poker nights are heavy, late, long nights.

Poker face

Basically the only way to stay in the game is not to fold. If you have terrible cards, or a "bad hand" and want out, you should seriously consider folding, because you'll need more than beginner's luck, you'll need a miracle. But if you think you have what could be a good or even an outstanding hand, then of course you should play on. The trick is not to give away what you are thinking or intending to do. You need to be able to "bluff" and avoid the "tell."

Bluffing is pretending to have better cards than you actually have. It is a fundamental strategy of the game.

A "tell" is a weakness; that's bad, you don't want one of them. A "tell" is a mannerism that you inadvertently repeat and that lets the other players know how good your hand is. No one ever wants other people to know their tell, but everyone has one. When you lie, you inadvertently give little clues. A player may mop his brow when he has a good hand, while another player may grit her teeth and mumble when she has a low hand. Whatever it is, you should always try to learn the other players' tells, as well as try to hide your own. Learn this skill as it can also be handy for work and dating.

Don't be scared to fold. Keep focused and concentrate.

Know when to quit, and never lose control. Bet with your head, not over it. This is the slogan for Gamblers Anonymous, and it couldn't be more accurate. Betting within your means will allow the game to remain fun. Remember: very few people make their fortunes playing poker. A lot more lose theirs.

If this has whetted your appetite, you should read Al Alvarez's classic *Poker: Bets, Bluffs and Bad Beats* (published by Bloomsbury, 2001), which is the definitive book for players, or pick up *The Big Blind* by Louise Wener (published by Hodder and Stoughton, 2003) with its poker-playing heroine.

How to place a bet

One very stylish way to make some money is "to have a flutter on the gee-gees" (horses). Not only the Ascot in Britain, there is the Kentucky Derby in the States; both races are not only *very* good reasons to get a lovely wide-brimmed hat, and deck yourself out à la Audrey Hepburn in *My Fair Lady*, there is a chance that you could make some pennies.

Try to ignore the men in the tweed coats who flap their arms about as if trying to prevent frostbite. This is apparently a code with tips on who to back, but often it's better to pass on this.

Most tracks have a minimum wager. Best to stick with this as there is no point getting greedy till you have mastered the ropes. At the racetracks you are betting against all the other people there – so as you win, someone else will lose. The track gets to keep a percentage of everyone's winnings, so they are always happy.

Before placing your bet, purchase a program and see if any of the candidates grab your fancy.

You can either use women's intuition or get expert opinions from more seasoned betters and see who is the favorite, who is the 10 to 1, or 2 to 1. Obviously the more likely they are to win the less of a gamble and the less you will win. But if you throw caution to the wind and back a wild card, simply because he shares a name with your nursery school teacher/first pet, and he romps in first, well, you will be in the money, honey.

So what to do:

1.   Make your selection. Know the name of your horse, its number, and have your cash at the ready as you approach the counter. You do not want to get flustered by hecklers and impatient queuers into making the wrong choice. Have all the information written down and be ready to bet. You have to get the official horse number from the program, so make sure you jot this down correctly, this is your lottery number!

2. Pick your wager. Ignore all the complex options, go with the easiest – a show bet, which means if your horse runs in first, second- or third you win, too.

3. Stick to your guns. Know your glass ceiling and do not be tempted to bet beyond this. Strong willpower. Check that you are in the right queue; some windows are for million-dollar bets – you should not stand in this one.

4. When it is your turn, tell the "teller," who is the bet-taking person, the name of the horse you are going to put a wager on, the horse number and the race number, and then finally how much you are going to put on it to win. If you want to bet on more than one race, make a list and do all your bets in one trip as you won't be able to show off your outfit to its best advantage standing in a muddy queue.

5. Get your ticket – proof of your bet – and put it somewhere safe, as you cannot collect any winnings without it.

6. Get a glass of Champagne and go and watch the race.

Betting terms to know

Abandoned: A race that has been canceled so all bets are refunded.
Accumulator: A multiple bet where you make simultaneous selections on two or more races. But be warned: all sections must win before you win.
All out: Ahh – the horse is going all out, giving it his best shot and galloping his heart out for you.
Allowance: Weight concession the horse is given to compensate for rider's inexperience.
ART: Artificial turf.
AWT: All-weather track.
Back: To bet or wager.
Banker: The one expected to win.
Bar price: Refers to the odds of the runners, nothing to do with drinks.

Blind bet: Not your bet, but a bet made by another racetrack bookmaker to throw you off the winning scent.

Blinders: The eye masks the horses wear.

Bolt: A bolt from the blue, an unexpected veering from the straight course.

Daily double: Type of wager where you select the winners of two consecutive races.

Dam: Mother of the horse.

Dead heat: A tie, two horses finishing at the exact same time.

Favorite: The most popular horse in the race.

Filly: Female horse four years old or younger.

Fixed odds: Your return and odds are fixed when you place the bet.

Green: An inexperienced horse.

Handful: Slang for odds of 5 to 1.

Heinz: Consists of fifty-seven bets – six selections in different events.

In the frame: This is when your horse finishes in the top three.

Late double: A second daily double offered during the latter part of the program.

Lay: To take a bet on.

Maiden: A horse or rider that has not won a race, or a female that has never bred.

Mare: Female horse five or more years old.

Monkey rider: A rider who is great at the money races.

Morning glory: A horse that performs well in the morning.

Nailed on: The selection that is considered to be a certainty.

Odds: The chance or likelihood of a horse winning.

Odds-against: The stakes against it winning.

Odds-on: Odds of less than even money, where you have to put down more than you win. Seems nuts.

On the nose: Betting a horse to win only – forget second and third.

Paddock: The area where horses are saddled and kept before the race.

Single: Most common and simplest form of betting. One wager, one bet.

Tips: What the experts tell you to go for.

Underdog: The horse bookies think has the least chance of being the winner.

Wager: A bet.

How to play chess

Chess is like the game of life.

Each move you take has to be carefully considered and thought through. Grown men agonize for hours over what direction their next move should be – while the young just play, and to hell with the consequences.

A brief history

Voltaire said that chess was "the game that reflects most honor on human wit." The game evolved in the fifth century AD in northwest India. Despite the rumor that it was played in ancient Egypt, no proof or pieces have yet been found.

In the sixth century it spread from India to Persia and later the Arabs took up the game. Chess entered Europe around the tenth century, probably picked up on a crusade.

The first English chess-playing monarch was Edward I (1239–1307).

The first book on chess in English was Caxton's *The Game and Playe of the Chesse*, published in 1474.

Today's rules date back to the seventeenth century.

Learning the basics

If you are a good chess player, people will respect you and think that you're smart. Great chess players are seen as being among the intellectual giants of the planet, along with nuclear physicists and brain surgeons. This status has been awarded because chess involves concentration, simultaneous use of strategy, mathematics and risk analysis, and because the game itself has so many rules it's really, really complicated to learn, let alone play.

Essentially it's black versus white. Ebony and ivory. One-on-one combat.

The general idea is that you have two battlelines pitted one side against the other and the object of the game is to get the opponent's king. First you send out the cavalry (the pawns) to start the attack. Crank up the drama by using the knights, bishops, and the castles/rooks, the latter being best employed to slide up and down and protect the monarchs. Then when it's all hands on deck, royalty get involved for the final skirmish.

The pieces

They consist of eight pawns, two rooks, two knights, two bishops, one queen, and one king.

The pawns are the smallest pieces, the cavalry.

The rooks look like castles with jagged edges along the top.

The knights look like horse heads.

The bishops are the things with balls on the top of their bishop hats.

The queen wears a crown.

The king is the tallest piece and has a cross on top of his crown.

Laying out the board

No chic dwelling should be without a chess set. What the game involves is two people sitting on opposite sides of a chessboard. One side has black pieces, one side white, or a trendy variant depending on the type of board you pick.

1. First select the color/team/side you are going to be.

2. Put your rooks on the two outside corners of the first row.

3. Next to each rook, put a knight.

4. Next to each knight, a bishop.

5. The queen goes on the first row on the same color box as the color of your pieces. (In English, if you are the black pieces,

put the queen on the remaining black, on the first row, and put the king on the remaining white square. If you are the white pieces, put the queen on the remaining white square and the king on black.)

6. Line up all your pawns on the second row.

Confused? It sounds worse than it is. Basically, the pieces get taller as you move inwards, and the queen goes on her own color. Your queen will always face your opponent's queen, just as the king will face the king.

The moves and the grooves

Every piece has different rules about how it can move. Only one piece can ever be in a square at a time. If you want to put your piece in a square that already has a piece in it, you have two options:

1. If the piece in the square is yours, first you have to move it out of the way before your new piece can go there.

2. If the piece in the square is your opponent's, then you can "capture" his piece. That piece is now out of play forever.

Hopefully it is more often option 2, as there is no point destroying your defense in the attack.

The pawn
The first line of defense. You have an army of eight, but an individual pawn is relatively worthless. They can move only one space forward. That's it. Three exceptions to this rule:

1. As the game begins, when the pawn is coming out of its box for the first time, you have the option to move it either one or two spaces forward.

2.   When a pawn captures another piece, it can capture it ONLY by moving one box forward in a diagonal. It can't capture a piece head-on.

3.   If your pawn makes it to the opposite end of the board, it gets a "promotion." This means that it can become any piece it wants to be, getting that piece's rules and powers. A word to the wise: promote your pawn into a queen, don't mess around with any other option.

The rook/castle
Moves up and down, or side to side.
The bishop
Moves in a diagonal line for as many spaces as it likes until something blocks it.

Note: they'll always stay on the same color square that they started on.
The knight
The complex one. The knight can only move in an L-shape. This means that it moves a total of three boxes: 2 straight 1 sideways, or 1 straight 2 sideways. It can go left or right as desired. But an advantage of mastering his moves is that the knight is the only piece that is allowed to jump over other pieces to land in an empty square.
The royal family
The queen: Once her royal highness gets going she charges around, and can move as much, or as little, as she likes. She is a combination of the rook and the bishop, moving as many spaces as she likes along a rank, file, or diagonal. She is the most powerful and useful piece in the game. A real catastrophe if she is beheaded. BUT typically it's the bumbling king – who can only move one step at a time – who has the final say. He can move in any direction, but only one box at a time.
Check mate is crunch time
This is when a piece lands on the square facing the opposing king. Nightmare. Game over if the king is taken.

Learn your tactics well; to quote Tammy Wynette, always "stand by your man," and don't let any other hussy come along and take him.

Chess etiquette

You are not meant to refer to the rows and columns on a chessboard as a "row" and a "column," that's baby talk. You must refer to them as a "rank" and a "file." And just in case things weren't complicated enough, each rank has a number and each file has a letter, so that everybody can follow what's going on. For example, your knight is in box b1 (you have another one in h1). But, frankly, avoid theorizing as this is an added headache; you just want to play, not revisit a mathematics exam.

How to be Filled with the Sound of Music

Extraordinary how potent cheap music is.
—*Noël Coward*

How to choose the correct music

Music is a great scene setter, seducer, and room warmer. *But* you have to know *what* music is appropriate *when*. Make sure that you have a wide repertoire of CDs – classical through to pop trash – at your well-manicured fingertips. Know just what to reach for in any given situation.

To stop yourself from having a crisis when you can't find the right tune for the moment, have this list of moods pinned to the lid of your CD player, and fill in your favorites. For example:

Mood	Suggestion
Uplifters	Diana Ross and the Supremes "Baby Love"
Relaxers	Mozart Piano Concerto No. 21 in C major K.467
What's up with them?	Stevie Wonder "Lately"
The bills have just arrived	Tchaikovsky 1812 Overture
Getting ready	Destiny's Child "Independent Woman"
Put those dancing shoes on	Michael Jackson "Billie Jean"
Getting undressed	Donna Summer "Love to Love You Baby"
Evening in with pizza	Eartha Kitt "Let's Do It"
Hitting the town	Roy Orbison "Pretty Woman"
Working too hard	Dolly Parton "Working Nine to Five"
He's just called	Louis Armstrong "What a Wonderful World"
Exercise/vacuuming	Olivia Newton John "Let's Get Physical"
Cocktail mixers	Frank Sinatra "I've Got You Under My Skin"
Harry Met Sally moment	Harry Connick Jr. "It Had to Be You"
Missing you	Stevie Wonder "I Just Called to Say I Love You"
Dusting	Saint-Saëns "The Swan"
Feeling blue	Patsy Cline "Crazy"

You are FABULOUS	Tom Jones or Prince "Kiss"
Anti-men	Aretha Franklin "Respect"
Seducers	Marvin Gaye "Let's Get It On"
Breakups	Wham "Careless Whisper"
Melancholy evening	Yves Montand "La Vie en Rose"
Don't want to go on, but will	Frank Sinatra "My Way"
Predinner party drinks	Mozart "Eine Kleine Nacht Musik"
Impromptu party at home	ABBA "Dancing Queen"
Bubble bathing	Glenn Miller "Moonlight Serenade"
Preproposal setting	Nat "King" Cole "Stardust"
Hellfire and damnations	Holst "The Planets – Mars"
You're going to confront him	Beethoven opening to Symphony No. 5
You're going to kill him	Mozart's Requiem

How to sing and know all the words

One of life's mysteries is how some people hear a song for the first time, and, by the end of the first phrase, can be singing along as if they had known it all their life.

But with practice you can, too.

Keep up to date with who is who. Know who is number one, as the popular songs are the ones you are most likely to have to join in with. Listen to the radio, have it on while you have your breakfast, tea, or are driving. Get acquainted with what is "in."

Always have a repertoire of songs you DO know and which will come on the radio at some point in the day. Likewise refresh seasonal songs as appropriate.

If you are tone deaf – know it. Don't sing, don't hum, don't try. You must have other gifts. It is recommended that you include whistling, crooning, and everything other than talking on the list of don'ts. There is a lot to be said for being a mute backing singer – look at the Alaia-clad foxy ladies in Robert Palmer's "Addicted to Love" video. Do something like this.

If you don't know the words sing *hmmmm* or *lala* in a kind of carefree tra-la-la way. Meanwhile, LEARN the words (having downloaded the lyrics from the Internet).

How to enjoy karaoke

Either you love it or hate it, but karaoke is bound to happen to you sooner or later, so it's best to be prepared.

A brief history

The word comes from two Japanese words, *kara* meaning "empty" (a karate empty hand) and *oke* (short for *okesutora*) meaning "orchestra." So the orchestra is your personal backing, albeit on tape; grab a mic and you're on.

The origin of actual karaoke is less defined. It is believed to have started in the 1970s in Kobe, Japan. The best story is that a performer for a small snack bar fell ill, so the owner of the establishment prepared tapes of the backing music and got his guests to sing along instead. Others argue that it started in the 1950s and 1960s in America with the sing-alongs, using lyrics that bounced along the bottom of the screen.

Whatever is true, it is now a widespread problem, with systems popping up in pubs, clubs, rentals, and even specially dedicated bars all over the world. In Japan it is a national obsession; see Bill Murray struggling with his karaoke moment in *Lost in Translation*, or Harry Burns trying it out in a store in *When Harry Met Sally*.

If you love it, don't hog the microphone, go up for lots of songs, go in groups, as well as solo. If you are nervous and not sure how you ended up there, go in pairs, or join groups and build up your confidence. Practice in the shower, or in the privacy of your own home.

Have a decent repertoire at the ready

Veto boring songs. FACT: no one can make Jimmy Nail's "Crocodile Shoes" entertaining to listen to.

Always aim for SLOW songs – it is easier to look good while performing these, and remember that you have to perform. No point being bashful; it makes it even more painful to view.

Here are some examples of songs you can karaoke with class to:

For the boys

Stevie Wonder	"I Just Called to Say I Love You" (guaranteed result)
	"Lately"
Frank Sinatra	"I've Got You Under My Skin"
Lionel Richie	"Hello, Is It Me You're Looking For?"
Elton John	"Your Song" (and most of his other slow ones work)
Leo Sayer	"You Make Me Feel Like Dancing"

For the girls

Diana Ross	"Baby Love"
	"You Are Everything"
Tammy Wynette	"Stand by Your Man" (with irony)
Sister Sledge	"Sisters Are Doing It for Themselves"
Gloria Gaynor	"I Will Survive" (with the girls)
Lady Marmalade	"Voulez Vous Coucher avec Moi (Ce Soir)"

Kylie Minogue, the Bangles, All Saints, Destiny's Child, and other chart "girl" groups are also worth investigating, and don't forget their older equivalents, such as the Nolans.

In a couple

Frank and Nancy Sinatra   "Something Stupid"
Sonny and Cher   "I Got You Babe"
The Carpenters   "Close to You"

Be careful not to choose anything too saccharine as the other patrons will be leaving in droves.

Had one too many

The Beatles   "Yesterday"
               "Hey Jude"

Several too many

Grease   A full medley, obviously in girl and boy groups

Foolhardy

ABBA   "Dancing Queen"
        "Waterloo"
        "Mamma Mia"
        "Money Money Money"

Despite everyone knowing all the words to these, they are actually very hard. Only to be attempted when entire room is paralytic. The ABBA girls had trained, almost operatic, voices. You may not.

Ones to avoid AT ALL COSTS

Aretha: Sorry forget it! You will have no R-E-S-P-E-C-T if you attempt this.

Marvin Gaye: "I Heard It Through the Grapevine," a deceptive killer.

Diana Ross: NO to the screeching ones.

Likewise NO Mariah Carey, NO Celine Dion, NO Christina Aguilera. Britney Spears is surprisingly difficult; see if you can do Madonna instead. Avoid anything with too many vocal Olympics.

How to Be an Art Lover

A woman is fascinated not by art but
the noise made by those in the field.
—*Anton Chekhov*

How to enjoy modern art

Ever been to a gallery and, even with your eyes half shut, it still looks like a load of childish scribble? Worse still, you are at some pretentious installation which looks as creative as the emperor's new clothes, and frankly you haven't a clue what people are rhapsodizing about? You need to understand and appreciate modern art. Or at least know the right noises to make. But remember Andy Warhol's words: "If you look at a thing for long enough it loses all meaning." So no need to stand there all day.

Try to view the picture with an open mind. Always go to a gallery free of any preconceived ideas. An art gallery can be more soothing than the most rewarding of yoga sessions as, when it touches your soul, it can lift you out of reality.

And according to David Hockney, "Art has to move you and design does not, unless it's a good design for a bus."

Modern art itself is not intimidating and scary, it just gets a kick out of being exclusive, and attracts a few condescending morons who put you off the whole thing, just like a members' only bar. But with a few well-dropped lines you can easily be on the guest list.

Start by learning the history, and getting a feel for things with the classics and the old masters. Once you are satisfied that you are proficient in your da Vincis and Titians you can travel from Manet to Van Gogh via Degas and Monet with a brief pit stop at the Pre-Raphaelites. Then to Picasso, Bauhaus, Rothko, and Warhol, careering your way ever closer to the modern day. You will notice that a lot of ideas that seem so modern are actually reworkings of things that have gone before. Turner and Constable were once considered modern, while now they are more likely to be adorning notebooks and umbrellas. Da Vinci was at least four hundred years ahead of his time, Picasso caused an uproar equal to the anarchy of the Sex Pistols, and Andy Warhol practically caused the establishment to have a breakdown. So people being outraged by modern art is nothing new. Artists such as Peter Blake, David Hockney, Gilbert and George, Anthony Caro and Anthony Gormley, Frank

Auerbach, and Lucien Freud are now very much part of the establishment and are part of the Royal Academy crew. Proof indeed that artists these days do not need to die impoverished, unrecognized, or, like Van Gogh, have only one ear.

If at a loss when contemplating art, and asked for an opinion, key areas to talk about include: color, mood, texture, and technique.

Remember how you used to dissect poetry at school? Finding meaning that the writer clearly had never intended? This is what you are doing with art; all you need to do is talk with conviction. To do so it is always useful to have some pretentious-sounding phrases at your disposal. You might choose to admire the "juxtaposition" of the work (how it is hung or set against something) or mention how the "Dionysian" feel (sensual, wild, unrestrained) moves you.

But also remember that one man's meat is another man's poison, so do not inflict your tastes on someone, nor allow yourself to be subjected to one type of art, when really your passion is for another.

How to know which names to drop

The London gallery owners

In London, the main players are Saatchi, Serota, Joplin, and Sadie Coles. And now the New York gallery owner Gagosian have also come over.

Charles Saatchi

Collector and owner of the Saatchi Gallery. A keen and passionate promoter of contemporary talent, he was one of the first to buy

Damien Hirst. He also is a megasuccessful advertising guru and is married to celebrity chef Nigella Lawson. He is considered to be the modern-day Medici, or John Soane, in terms of his patronage of art.

Sir Nicholas Serota

The current director of the Tate. Serota was appointed to the role in 1988, and under him the gallery has undergone its most dramatic era of expansion and thrown its door open to record numbers of new visitors. Previously director of the Museum of Modern Art in Oxford then the Whitechapel Art Gallery, after moving to the Tate, Serota opened Tate St. Ives in 1993, followed by Tate Modern in 2000, as well as relaunching Tate Britain.

Jay Joplin

Director of the White Cube, and married to artist Sam Taylor Wood. The ruling King and Queen of Cool in the London art world.

Sadie Coles

The trendy collector and owner of self-named Sadie Coles Gallery. Supporter and scout of many of the newest and coolest names in London art.

"Go Go" Larry Gagosian

The archetypal New York private-gallery owner, who was the first to represent Damien Hirst Stateside, recently opened his own gallery in London's King's Cross area.

The artists

For artists you should name, check either side of the pond, and include:

Lucien Freud

English painter, specializing in portraits. He has painted Kate Moss and Jerry Hall in the nude, among others who queue to peel off for him. His children include Bella Freud, fashion designer, and Esther Freud, writer, whose work includes *Hideous Kinky*, which became a film starring Kate Winslet.

Peter Blake

Often seen front row at Stella McCartney's fashion shows, a family friend since doing the Beatles' *Sergeant Pepper's Lonely Hearts Club Band* LP cover for her dad. The British 1960s Pop Art veteran has gone from LPs to the Royal Academy.

Damien Hirst

Put a twelve-foot stuffed shark in a tank, pickled a calf and cow, and opened a restaurant called Pharmacy. He also directed the video to Blur's "Country House." Incidentally, *Portraits of Blur*, by Julian Opie, hang in the National Portrait Gallery. As Hirst said on winning the Turner Prize, "It's amazing what you can do with an E in A-level art, a twisted imagination, and a chainsaw."

Andy Warhol

Always a good name to drop. Studio 54 was his club, and he was the leader of the hedonistic New York scene. His Pop Art featuring Monroe, Elvis, Jackie Kennedy, and Elizabeth Taylor is always in fashion, and his Campbell soup prints are a stylish addition to any kitchen. He was shot, but not fatally, by Valerie Solanas, a disgruntled member of his Factory studio scene who was the founder of SCUM (Society for Cutting Up Men). Warhol far outlived his fifteen minutes of fame. He said, "If you want to know everything about me, just take a look at the surface of my paintings, it's all there, there's nothing more."

Julian Schnabel

Achingly cool New York–based artist who you would simply die to have your portrait done by, and has daughters you would love to hang out with. He is friends with the legendary Azzedine Alaia and has painted fashion designer Roberto Cavalli, as well as having exhibitions and collaborating in hotel design worldwide.

Tracey Emin

Rose to fame with her notorious installation of an unmade bed, and is now a model for Vivienne Westwood, and has designed luggage for Longchamp. She has helped rejuvenate the UK art scene and brought a certain sexiness to cool Britannia. Her *All the People I Have Ever Slept With*, a tent listing names of those she has been intimate with, was destroyed in a fire along with much of Saatchi's collection.

The Chapman Brothers

Jake and Dinos are also benefactors of Saatchi's patronage. They are labeled the bad boys of the art world. First gained critical acclaim with their sculpture of tiny figurines, re-enacting scenes from Goya's *Disasters of War*. They went on to take part in the Sensation exhibition (1997–99) and Apocalypse (2000) and were one of several artists to illustrate Kate Moss for *Vogue*, when one of them was dating her. Jake is now married to model Rosemary Ferguson.

Nan Goldin

She is recognized as one of the leading art photographers. Her images are raw, frank, and intimate. When she contracted HIV she decided to use her camera to document the lives and loves of those who she came into contact with, including transsexuals and prostitutes. In 2001 the Georges Pompidou Centre, Paris, was the first stage of a major touring survey of her work.

Sam Taylor Wood

Specializes in photographic and film work that is distinguished by ironic and subversive use of media. Began in 1995 with series of photos entitled *Five Revolutionary Seconds*, panoramic audio photographs that rotated 360 degrees. Her self-portrait hangs in the National Portrait Gallery, alongside the infamous *Beckham Sleeping* picture of the soccer star. Her husband is Jay Joplin, curator of White Cube.

In the States, names to know include:

Pace Wildenstein, Barbara Gladstone, Gavin Brown, and the recent winner of the Hugo Boss Art Prize: Rirkrit Tiravanija. For dealers and names to know there is also Feigen, Mary Boone, and Gagosian for the most expensive art in NYC and Deitch Projects, which is changing the art market with large-scale installations, fashion shows, and dance. Wrong Gallery, Exit Art, Mary Ryan, and Jan Krugier are also names to drop with a loaded hint at your insider artsy knowledge. Confidence is key here.

Reena Spauling is a name to know, but not to be confused by. There is actually no such person as Reena Spauling – she is a fictional art-world "It" girl, portrayed by artists Emily Sundblad, John Kelsey, and others, and the pseudonymous star was included in the artists' showcase at the Whitney Biennial.

Prizes and Prestige Names to Know

The Turner Prize is the most prestigious award in the UK art world. It is given to "British artists under the age of fifty for an outstanding exhibition or other presentation of their work over the last twelve months." The prize was established in the UK in 1984, and winners have included Howard Hodgkin, Gilbert and George, Rachel Whiteread, and Damien Hirst. In the States the Hugo Boss Art Prize is called the Turner equivalent, but art-worldy types have concluded that getting picked up by the Whitney Biennial is really the ultimate in prestige.

If you are considering adding any new artists to your "artists' names to know" repertoire, in New York City "It" boy Ryan McGuiness is famed for being the youngest ever person to have his own show at the Whitney (featuring mostly pictures of his friends' intoxicated revelry) and is totally the name to drop to sound NYC art savvy.

Jeffery Deitch, owner of Deitch Projects, lists his most art-world insider, in-the-know, cutting-edge galleries below. These are the names the art cognoscenti drop to impress their fellows and are clearly the ones we were going to say, too:

Green Naftali
Rivington Arms (small LES gallery with three 2006 Whitney biennialists)
Andrew Kreps

Daniel Reich

Zach Feuer

Nicole Clogsburns

It doesn't matter if they don't mean anything to you now; they will.

Galleries to go to

Really to appreciate art and understand it you have to experience it firsthand, go to exhibitions, and visit new and national galleries. Don't let anyone tell you what you like, go and try it for yourself. Modern art is like sushi. Once you've tried it, if you get the taste for it, you'll want to have it again. And then once you realize you weren't poisoned you get braver, maybe even try sashimi; and in this way your taste advances, as well as expands.

As for galleries to go to stateside, you are even more spoiled for inspiration.

Everyone knows the real way to see a city and appreciate its culture is to go there and ask a local. However handy the *Time Out* guides are that cover the "here and the now and shut on the day you are in town," in every destination it is the insider opinions that really help you pinpoint the bold, the brave, and the wow. I found an angel at a fashion show one season, a student from Columbia University overbrimming with ideas and enthusiasm, and this is not the sort of thing that usually happens.

She has turned out to be my indispensable guide of how to hang out in the right places stateside, and is on hand to offer some advice on how to get cultural.

Sarah Maslin Nir, a student far too wise for her years, advises these things to do at museums and galleries:

- Those in the know do the "gallery pub-crawl" in New York. It is on Thursday evenings from 6:00 P.M. to 8:00 P.M. starting in Chelsea. At least a quarter of the galleries here have openings at this time in which they serve free glasses of red and white wine. Hipsters and art students walk up and down the blocks from Twentieth to Twenty-eighth streets between Tenth and Eleventh avenues going from gallery to gallery and glass to glass . . .

- Fridays in New York mean a date with the Metropolitan Museum, where a classical quartet serenades a small restaurant that springs up for the day around the Great Hall Balcony, on the second floor. Waiters serve wine and cheese and assorted tapas as they navigate the small tables that displace the collection of Chinese vases from ancient dynasties. Make a reservation at *http://www.metmuseum.org/visitor/dining_balcony.asp.* But if you don't have time for something this fancy, all of the museum's cafeterias were overhauled this year and are now gourmet and delicious.

  Members of the museum can enjoy a private dining room that serves a classic English afternoon tea, served with tiered platters of sandwiches and crumpets.

- Located in the basement of New York's Whitney Museum is an offshoot of the famed brunch venue *Sarabeth's*. Come Sunday, there are lines 'round the block at the Upper East Side original restaurant while the offshoot at the Whitney serves the same goodies, homemade jam, and is rather less crowded and nestled in culture: *http://www.sarabeth.com/*

- Works and Process at the Guggenheim, New York is where you can see snippets of the city's upcoming theatrical, dance, and performance works that are sold out, and stay for discussions with the celebrities, authors, and musicians that the art world clamors for. Log onto *http://www.guggen heim.org/education/worksandprocess/index.html* to see when your hero is in town.

As well as daytime things to do, there is also the after dark art world of parties:

- The Guggenheim Young Collectors' Ball is THE fashion-arts-jet-set scene for the younger set. The Metropolitan Costume Institute Gala is

a periodic gala celebrating big Costume Institute events, such as the
Chanel or Anglomania exhibit opening, attended by a Who's Who of the
fashion and art worlds. Then of course there is the Whitney Biennial,
"the nation's signature survey of contemporary art."

- Art Basel Miami Beach is the premier art fair, modeled after the famous
Art Basel in Switzerland. It is a weeklong fashion party/art extravaganza.
Their website explains: "[It's] a new type of cultural event, combining
an international art show with an exciting program of special exhibitions,
parties, and crossover events including music, film, and architecture. An
exclusive selection of 195 leading art galleries from North America, Latin
America, Europe, Africa, and Asia will exhibit 20th- and 21st-century art
works by over two thousand artists." Go to *http://www.artbaselmiami
beach.com/ca/cc/ss/?lang=eng.*

- The Smithsonian Institution (*http://www.si.edu/*) is composed of eighteen
museums, most of which are located in the Washington, D.C. area. It is
worth mentioning as a whole, but the most innovative of its museums is
the Cooper-Hewitt National Design Museum located in New York City
(*http://ndm.si.edu/*), and is the only museum in the nation devoted exclusively to historic and contemporary design.

Its other institutions include arts and nonarts museums of varying
degrees of importance:

- African Art Museum
- Air and Space Museum and Udvar-Hazy Center
- American Art Museum and its Renwick Gallery
- American History Museum
- American Indian Museum
- Anacostia Museum
- Arts and Industries Building
- Freer and Sackler Galleries
- Hirshhorn Museum and Sculpture Garden
- National Zoo

- Natural History Museum
- Portrait Gallery
- Postal Museum
- Smithsonian Institution Building, the Castle

Other places to buy postcards across America include

L.A.'s J. Paul Getty Museum: *http://www.getty.edu/*
New York City's Metropolitan Museum of Art: *http://www.metmuseum.org/*
Washington, D.C.'s National Gallery of Art: *http://www.nga.gov/*
Boston's Museum of Fine Arts: *http://www.mfa.org/*
New York City's Frick Collection: *http://www.frick.org/*

Best galleries in Britain

Brighton Museum and Art Gallery: *www.virtualmuseum.info*
Edinburgh, National Gallery of Scotland: *www.natgalscot.ac.uk*
Glasgow, Centre for Contemporary Arts: *www.cca-glasgow.com*
Liverpool, Tate Liverpool: *www.tate.org.uk/liverpool*
Manchester Art Gallery: *www.manchestergalleries.org*
Newcastle, Laing Art Gallery: *www.twmuseums.org.uk/laing*

Best galleries in London

Design Museum: *www.designmuseum.org.uk*
National Gallery: *www.nationalgallery.org.uk*
National Portrait Gallery: *www.npg.org.uk*
Royal Academy of Arts: *www.royalacademy.org.uk*
Saatchi Gallery: *www.saatchigallery.org.uk*

Serpentine Gallery: *www.serpentinegallery.org*
Sir John Soane's Gallery: *www.soane.org*
Tate Britain: *www.tate.org.uk*
Tate Modern: *www.tate.org.uk*
And of course, Victoria and Albert Museum: *www.vam.ac.uk*

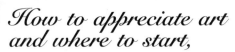

How to appreciate art and where to start,
by Vivienne Westwood, fashion designer

Lady Bracknell to Ernest: "Young people either know everything or nothing. Which do you know?"

At the age of seventeen I knew nothing. Yet I thirsted for knowledge and I wanted to understand the world I live in. I have always thought it extremely important to form my opinions from facts and to have some responsibility for my actions. There is such a thing as cause and effect. Look before you leap.

Don't waste your time with conceptual or abstract art: there is nothing to see in it except what you invent.

One of the things that art teaches us is that others have thought differently, and there are other ways to understand the world. Knowledge is relevant, and once we acquire the taste for it nothing will stop our curiosity.

I send my fashion students in Berlin to the art galleries. I tell them: imagine which painting you would save if the room was on fire. Eventually they will choose a different one because of their developing judgment.

Look at seventeenth-century Dutch painting; in the history of art there is nothing more strikingly original. Each painter

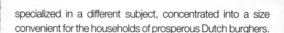

specialized in a different subject, concentrated into a size convenient for the households of prosperous Dutch burghers.

Go to the National Gallery, in London; there is a still life you must see by Willem Kalf. I think he always has a half-peeled lemon in the foreground. The design is of a disordered table with a great red lobster and a drinking horn with an elaborate silver mount. These decorative vessels were often completely invented by the painter.

Genre scenes of social life, particularly tavern scenes, were another speciality. You can do no better than look at Adriaen Brouwer. Gerhard ter Borch shares with Vermeer the subject matter of a woman in a private room, sometimes playing music or drinking with one or two men. One of my favorites, in the Louvre, in Paris, is of a large man, a cavalier, offering money to a woman. I like his expression, a combination of desire and appreciation, as he waits for her response. The Wallace Collection, in London, also has a fine ter Borch of a woman reading a letter. However, my favorite Dutch painting in the Wallace Collection is *A Winter Scene,* by Aert van der Neer, who specialized in capturing moonlit scenes.

Salomon van Ruysdael and Jan van Goyen were particularly prolific painters of seascapes and landscapes, but the greatest landscape painter of them all was Jacob van Ruïsdael. His skies are unequaled, and you feel you could inhabit the view, follow the stream, be the young woman cutting through the undergrowth of the wood.

There are many more Dutch painters of these perfect works. For example, there is Hercules Seghers, an engraver and painter of the first landscapes (but his works are few). These small landscapes are so concentrated that looking at them I feel as if somebody gave me a piece of time to hold.

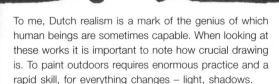

To me, Dutch realism is a mark of the genius of which human beings are sometimes capable. When looking at these works it is important to note how crucial drawing is. To paint outdoors requires enormous practice and a rapid skill, for everything changes – light, shadows.

We are so lucky in England to have the Wallace Collection, which houses the eighteenth-century French art which survived the Revolution. It was collected by Lord Hertford along with furniture, porcelain, clocks, and snuff boxes.

I also love the nineteenth-century French landscape painter Corot. He was enormously prolific, thanks to an inheritance which gave him the autonomy to paint even though this was counter to his father's wishes. Corot is associated with the Barbizan School, and other members Daubigny, Rousseau, and Boudin are all well represented in the National Gallery.

Watteau was a prodigious talent. His paintings, known as *Fêtes Galantes,* revealed theatrical scenes which captured the imagination of the century. Watteau's genius was in the way his paintings were "drawn." People say he draws color. What was so new is the sketchiness of his paintings.

He is followed by Boucher and Fragonard, Boucher's pupil, who both paint in this sketchy way. There is a lightness and air grounded in the most rigorous anatomical objectivity. Boucher invented an unending stream of compositions out of his head – nude and clothed, without the use of a model. Fragonard (after all that practice) said he could paint with his arsehole.

Finally, you get out what you put in. In cultivating your taste, by comparing, building your judgment, you are acquiring objectivity: this is knowledge.

How to Have Good Manners

Eric: We went out for a special meal one night. It was very posh. Just to impress the wife, I ordered the whole meal in French. Even the waiter was surprised.

Ernie: Really?

Eric: Yes – it was a Chinese restaurant.

—*Morecambe and Wise*

How to complain with class

There are some people who are never satisfied and who kick off at every opportunity. Then there are those who are as silent as a stealth bomber but when they blow – wow – they really lose their rag.

Always try to be the latter. If you cry wolf too often people won't listen to you when there's a real emergency.

First, stop. Count to ten. Do you have grounds for complaint? Be very friendly, present the problem, and ask what they can do to assist you. You don't want to alienate your target. Get them to empathize.

Always complain in a slow, low voice. If you start in a screech you will have nothing to crescendo up to.

Always aim to have a captive audience, evidence, a witness, and an alibi, and a packet of tissues – for any dramatic eye dabbing.

They should immediately seize the offending garment or dish (if in a restaurant) and offer a full and immediate replacement or refund.

Remember: never get too irate and don't lose sight of the fact that YOU are the victim.

Never throw food at the waiter – you lose the evidence and it weakens your case.

Always get the name of the idiot who is not assisting you, and assure them you will contact their boss.

Promise also to contact the press, do an exposé, call the police, lawyers, *America's Most Wanted* or *Oprah*, etc. Voice could perhaps waver at this point.

If all else fails, get your coat and entourage and LEAVE IMMEDI-ATELY.

Never back down, or apologize if they are in the wrong.

Don't look over your shoulder.

You can make counterattacks via phone/letter from the safety of your home, with the advantage of time, clarity, and distance on your side.

Always make sure your opinion is heard.

How to behave stylishly when dining out

When eating out, it is vital to observe a few extra rules of etiquette, in addition to your general good manners.

1.   Try to make a reservation in advance. This always impresses and endears you to the staff.

2.   If bringing children, ensure they are on their BEST (quiet and non-food-throwing) behavior. Warn restaurants in advance when making a reservation if bringing little ones, as it could be distracting and distressing to other diners when they get a meatball smeared on their leg. Advance warning also applies to blind grannies and deaf uncles.

3.   When the maître d' offers to take your coat, try to see how secure it will be on the coat stand rather than ask if they have ever been convicted of a felony. The general policy is, if you have worn a bulky coat, yes, hang it. If you are wearing vintage/a one-off/borrowed/next season's couture, decline. Say you're feeling a little chilly, and you want to keep it with you. You can drape it over your shoulders or the back of your chair, which is to be advised if wearing low-cut bottoms. The art of slipping clothes on and off in public can be very alluring.

4.   If you don't know what something is on a menu, ask. Nicely. You want to get the best possible from the menu, so flatter them. You don't want them to spit in your food.

5.   When ordering crocodile, locust, scorpion, or any rare and exotic dish, it is worth remembering it is *not* going to kill you. Restaurants don't aim to poison their diners. If in doubt, stick to a creature, crustacean, or plant that you have seen sold in a supermarket.

6.   Less is more. Always leave enough room for dessert. No one likes some-

one who peaks too early. When on a date, eat light and seductive bites. If it's a good date you should have butterflies in your stomach, which will keep the dining dainty.

7.   If you have any allergies, take extra care when ordering – and do not feel shy about asking how it's cooked and how you would like it. You can get away with murder if you do it with a smile. Think of how ordering totally *a la carte* changed Meg Ryan's entire career, and made ordering an art form.

Dishes and scenarios to avoid on a first date

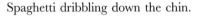

Spaghetti dribbling down the chin.
Slurpy soup.
A sauce-drenched rack of ribs.
Corn on the cob.
Snails and potential flying objects.
Blood-dripping meat – particularly not good if date is vegetarian.
Baguettes, bananas, and anything that could be construed as a double entendre.

Don't speak with your mouth full. Chew, swallow, speak. Nothing will be that urgent that you need to slobber with a full mouth. Likewise, don't put too much in your mouth at one time. Cut food into small, manageable pieces. It will make conversation more pleasant.

Lips

When dining out, consider the lipstick. Red lipstick stains on a glass can be, in a movie, attractive; lipstick on teeth and smearing up your cheek is carnivorous and slutty. Also keep an eye on teeth, avoid getting bits stuck. Go to the ladies' room and check.

Double Dutch

Always try to go Dutch. Hopefully they will refuse. Try to remain independent. If they insist on paying, offer to get them an after-dinner drink, if you can stand it.

How to eat tricky foods

"After all the trouble you go to, you get about as much actual 'food' out of eating an artichoke as you would from licking thirty or forty postage stamps," says Miss Piggy.

Artichokes are one problem dish, and unless you have a violent allergy to seafood/shellfish, there are two other slippery suckers you should get to grips with.

Oysters

Of the two, oysters are the more "acquired" taste, though as Eddie Murphy says, "Anything you have to acquire a taste for was not meant to be eaten." That said, they are reputed to be a most potent aphrodisiac. So swallow.

First hurdle with an oyster is to open it.

If it's a restaurant that values their whitewashed walls, and other diners, hopefully the chef has done this job for you.

Pick up the oyster in its shell. Give it a gentle wobble; it should be like jelly on a plate.

Hold to your mouth, tilt your head back, open your lips, and tip. A *real* pro will look at their dining partner as it slips out of the shell, confident the damn thing won't slide down their chin. This allows their captive audience to see it slide carefully into their mouth – the aim is that it does not touch the teeth – and, with a swallow, move down the throat, past the Adam's apple.

When dining on oysters, insist on eating only at the best places. The most glamorous are the Rialto Market, Venice; Grand Central Terminal Oyster Bar, New York; Wiltons, London; and in front of a log fire, by candlelight.

Lobsters

Assuming that all you have to do is consume and not cook the wretched beast, half the battle is already won.

Lobsters are an impressive dish to be served and most decadent to order. Plus, you have really to fight and wrestle to get to the meat, so you will build up an appetite.

First, allow it to cool enough so you can touch it. Perhaps slip off a few of your diamonds while you wait, as you don't want these getting fleshy meat and shell stuck in them.

Treat lobsters like giant prawns.

Twist the two great big claws off first – take away the weapons.

Crack the claws. The chef should provide a tool for this; it's the same process as cracking walnuts.

Bend the body back from the tail; this will crack and reveal more meat.

If this is all sounding too brutal, and not for you, ask the kitchen to prepare it. Many restaurants serve it in an easy-access way so you don't feel like you are doing a postmortem on the poor creature.

Ease meat out of the cracked shell, remove and discard black vein in tail, dip meat in melted butter, and enjoy.

True addicts can delve deeper and find the liver, but, if you're trying simultaneously to sustain a conversation, I would pass on the next stage of the lobotomy.

Dip fingertips into lemony finger bowl.

Dry on napkin.

Replace jewelry.

Order dessert.

How to eat alone in a restaurant

"I just vant to be aaallone," sighed Greta Garbo. Sometimes this is true of everybody, she just coined the phrase. It can be very chic to be alone, and have some quality time with yourself. You just need to know how to manage Garbo situations.

You can, if the mood takes you, book, but eating alone suits being more of a lost soul or free spirit, wandering into wherever fate has led you.

When asking for a table for one, try to opt for a quiet table. This can be done with a simple bat of your eyelashes and a glance from your big, doleful eyes. The blink of your eyes will say to the waitress: table for one, somewhere quiet and soothing, please.

It's hard enough to do this whole "eating out alone" thing, but *really* to be put next to a boisterous laddish table, or, even *worse*, a courting couple, would be more than you should have to bear.

You WANT to be alone. You're not going to be:

a) Sobbing into your appetizer.

b) Moving to outer space.

c) Talking to yourself.

If dining alone you should always have a book, a notebook, a magazine, and a mobile phone in your bag. You may be able to gaze off into the sunset quite happily, but always have tools of distraction in case someone tries to break the spell.

Books are infinitely the most interesting, but when eating, especially maneuvering chopsticks, it can be tricky to keep the page open. There is nothing more frustrating than a piece of flying sticky rice concealing a vital bit of vocab.

This is why the book is for preorder and prefood only.

While eating, the magazine or paper is to be absorbed. It also acts as a shield protecting you from wanderers who may want to catch your eye and try to engage you in conversation. Magazines/papers are ideal because they lie flat on the table, stay open all of their own accord, as well as being easy to turn and stare at, and it's not too disastrous if food splashes on them, well, unless it's a collector's issue.

Notebooks can come out between courses, as if something has inspired and delighted you.

Mobiles should be kept in bags. Constantly looking at a mobile – willing it to ring – will inevitably cause the reverse. Leave it on, but on silent, so you can see if you have missed a call. A mobile on view will only fuel the rumor racing round the restaurant that some cad has stood you up.

Not true. They haven't. (Well, even if you have been, don't let on.) You simply had so many offers and so much to do, you needed to have dinner *toute seule* to regroup.

Try not to drink too much. It is a horrid sight to see a lonesome diner losing clarity. Always maintain dignity and poise. If you must drink yourself into oblivion, do it at home in front of the telly.

How to Deal with Affairs of the Heart

If you want to sacrifice the admiration of many men, for the criticism of one, go ahead, get married.
—*Katharine Hepburn*

How to hide a broken heart

At sometime or another it is a cross we will all have to bear. It is at times like these that you need the Bee Gees, and a box of tissues.

There is no telling how you will get over a broken heart, or if indeed you ever will. Different people, different ways. There is no fixed time frame, either. Sorry.

The best thing to do is to allow a few days to wallow, to see if they come back on a white horse with flowers, apology, and ring.

Be wary of wallowing alone, it is very unhealthy. For every night of wallow, prescribe three nights out.

Lines not to fall for

"Let's just be friends." Impossible if they broke your heart. Why prolong the agony? Say you'll think about it, and call them, maybe, in a few years.

"I value our friendship too much to date you." Bastard. They don't love you, never have, don't even find you attractive. Move on. They'll prevent you from meeting *the one* – and make you miserable in the process.

"I love you, but I can't be with you." A coward. Walk away; even if you paid for them to see a shrink, it is still an impossible and exhausting situation.

"You'll always have a piece of my heart." True. Save the violins, stamp on it. Let them regret losing you.

"It just was the wrong time, wrong place." The *only* "it was wrong time/place" was in *Casablanca*, which does not apply here. Poor excuse.

"I'm sorry. Can we try again?" How many times have you heard this before? Be honest. Once? Shame on them. Twice or more? Shame on you.

Some things are just not meant to be. Sometimes you grow apart, move on. You've tried, it didn't work, learn and leave. Try to find someone who will appreciate you. Don't kill each other's chances of happiness and waste years on something that will never happen.

Be honest. Be tough. Ask yourself: where do I see myself in ten years? What do I want to have achieved? What kind of person do I want to be with? What kind of person will encourage me to be the kind of person I most want to be?

Anyway, you think you've got problems, pick up *Romeo and Juliet* and their dire situation makes everything pale in comparison. Take comfort in the fact that falling in and out of love is never out of fashion.

Above all, believe in true love and know that men are like shoes. A couple is like a left and a right foot, and out there is your perfect fit. Sometimes you need to change styles and shop around to find it. Sometimes you have to break styles in, sometimes you feel like something that is unstylish but comfortable, and sometimes a style – as much as you like it – just doesn't suit you and will never fit.

Literary quotes may help, such as:

" 'Tis better to have loved and lost than never to have loved at all," from Tennyson, or the less literary ones of Miss Piggy: "Only time can heal your broken heart, just as only time can heal his broken arms and legs."

Take solace in slushy movies from *Sleepless in Seattle* to *Wuthering Heights*. Distract yourself, and learn all the words to Gloria Gaynor's "I Will Survive." If all this doesn't drive you out of the house, nothing will.

But all the best fairy-tale stories end "they all lived happily ever after . . ." And so will yours; and if not, you can buy yourself an awful lot of Manolos while trying.

Depending on your circumstances you could always, in extreme cases, consider:

Moving countries; Paris nearly worked for Audrey Hepburn in *Sabrina*.
Changing phone number.

Deleting the details or locking all contact info of the offending party in a secure, hidden case.

Changing jobs.

Changing hairstyles.

Rearranging the flat. If you shared, change the locks.

Removing every trace of them from view so you are not living with constant reminders.

Booking a holiday.

Starting a new hobby.

Joining a gym, or starting to go to the gym you are member of.

Doing things you *never* did with them.

Going to new areas or places of interest.

Rationing yourself to thinking of them for only twenty minutes a day, and gradually decreasing.

Banning yourself from talking about them to friends.

Not dwelling on the past.

And if all else fails: therapy – retail therapy.

How to make the first move

Ideally you will get swept off your feet, but, if you fear that you may be reaching your pension date sooner than dating the object of your affection, pluck up the courage to get things going.

Finding Prince Charming involves some strategic planning, but also some logic. If you despise bowling, why go to a singles night there? You could end up with a world champion, and you would have to spend a lifetime looking at those gross shoes.

There is no set law on who needs to make the first move. It does not make you seem desperate or indicate the biological clock is chiming; it shows initiative and that you are a free-thinking modern woman, albeit a single one.

(And if that scares them off, then really, what were you thinking of dating them for?)

If you have wasted a month's worth of great lip gloss, broken in some extrovert heels, and created some inventive fashion looks and still there is no date, while you have casually, for the fourth time that week, been propped at the end of their favorite bar, it's time to take control.

You can e-mail or text if shy – although this would involve some initial connection. Contrive a dinner party, or something where your life depends on an escort – them.

If there's been no contact, except the eye variety, it is time to extend this to a smile and walk over to introduce yourself. You have to introduce yourself to all sorts of horrid, dull people at work, shopping, traveling, so why should it be any harder when someone has a magnetic aura around them and their smile makes you weak at the knees?

How to love the right type

Well, this is impossible, and the more you try to love the right type – they will inevitably become the opposite. The more fabulous you are, the harder it is to find someone who can compete. Not to worry: you can meet them halfway. Once you have paired off, you need to run a few essential preliminary tests before eloping or introducing him to the parents and booking the church.

1. Does he make you laugh?√

2. Does he listen to and respect you?

3. Who does he like more: you or your address book?

4. Does he have ambition or a job?

If he passes all of these to your satisfaction, you move to phase two:

1. Does he love fashion? Does he want to work in it?

2. Does he take longer than you to get ready?

3. Does he express too much of his feminine side?

4. Does he dye/bleach/perm his hair?

5. Does he have a more extensive beauty regime than you?

If you think there would be a YES to more than three of the above, chances are he could be gay. You might want to check this with him sooner rather than later. There is nothing more fabulous as an accessory or girl's best friend than a stylish gay man, but he is not going to be marriage material. Sadly. Yes, they are more faithful, more amusing, generally far more creative, but you will share the same taste in boys, and will not be able to have the fairy-tale ending . . .

So before you open the joint checking account:

a) Are they truly single? Wife? Girlfriend? Skeletons?

b) Do they have children? Pets or a peg leg?

c) Do they have a criminal record or season tickets, and to which team?

How not to become a character rivalling Glenn Close in <u>*Fatal Attraction*</u>

Even the sanest people sometimes become as loopy as a bunny boiler – a term of endearment first coined to describe Glenn Close's character in *Fatal Attraction* – such are the complexities of affairs of the heart. Try never to have it attached to you. Never become overclingy or a wet rag, otherwise, quite understandably, they will forget what they ever saw in you. And although this gets far less publicity, men can also be bunny boilers, and in fact are twice as scary.

First assess who is playing the role of lunatic, and who is the perplexed and besieged. A second opinion may be necessary, but always try to assess objectively whether they have caused you to lose your marbles, or are being emotionally cruel, or indeed, are you scaring the socks off them by turning up at work with possible wedding locations? When is enough enough?

Sometimes you have to be cruel to be kind. If you have left over ten voice-mails, sent a casual five e-mails, and twenty text messages and got no reply, perhaps you should TAKE A HINT. Chances are if they had been in a dreadful accident you would have heard about it.

If they ask you to stop calling, do. Do not beg. If you ask them to stop calling, do not return their teary messages. In both cases, if the undesired persists, think how feasible it is to change your number or get pest control, and tell them firmly to STOP.

If you have not spoken to your sweetheart for over three months or had any form of communication, and there is no valid reason, it may be best to put the wedding plans on hold. Move on and let them realize the folly of their ways.

Some guys are bad news; like shoes, you need a sexy yet comfy pair that enhances you, not cripples you. If these shoes have erratic mood swings or ever hurt you, dump in trash immediately.

If it does do a nosedive, make sure there are none of your possessions left behind that they could turn into a voodoo doll of you, or use to build a shrine.

If you are the deranged one, think. Isn't less more? If they suddenly have to work late, avoid your calls and so forth, wake up and smell the coffee – Glenn Close got shot at the end of that film . . .

How to Wear an Apron with Style

Everything you see, I owe to spaghetti.
—*Sophia Loren*

How to eat in

As with everything, food is subject to fashion tastes and trends. The prawn cocktail, the height of chic in 1970s suburbia, was reviled a decade later. Nouvelle cuisine went the same way as the 1980s came to an end. The 1990s saw an unprecedented rise in fashionable cooking in England, with pin-up chefs like Nigella Lawson and Jamie Oliver encouraging you to throw things around in the kitchen. On the other hand, the rise in sushi and other such delicacies, microwave meals, and gourmet grocery takeout make it very easy to avoid ever needing to step into the kitchen for anything longer than the time it takes to boil a kettle.

Before you convert the kitchen into a spare guest room, remember that home cooking can be a great way to lure people over to your abode. You can also showcase your Fendi baguette, vintage Schiaparelli lobster-print dress, or even a Chloé banana bag as a nod to culinary couture. Cute.

The best way to make entertaining as stress-free as possible is to have a couple of simple signature dishes up your cashmere sleeve, and remember that presentation is EVERYTHING.

If all the stirring and chopping really leaves you cold, make decorating the table the way you'll demonstrate your creative flair. (To prevent a headache, see *How to decorate a table*, page 181.)

How to master home cooking: the shortcuts

While you might not have any desire to take on Martha Stewart's mantle, sometimes it is necessary to have a level of domestic whiz, or be able to create the illusion of competence and culinary charm.

First step, dash around to your nearest gourmet food shop and grab all the ready-made meals you can carry. Could always have some in the freezer as emergency backup.

Cook in microwave as instructed and lay these out on your best plates.

Bin all evidence, in black trash bags. Take trash bags out – if a stray wrapper surfaces while guests are around, look disgusted, and obviously deny all knowledge and recognition.

For a real homemade feel, warm the bread in the oven and always have fresh coffee percolating for the essence of domestic goddess.

How to fake it: fail-safe, idiot-proof dishes

As with the perfect little black dress, always have a few key dishes on standby that you can rustle up in extreme emergencies, such as unexpected visitors appearing. Failing this, always keep trusty takeout menus and delivery service numbers at hand. And don't forget there is nearly always a new restaurant worth trying nearby. Eating out is not a cop-out, in fact it is very cosmopolitan and social.

But as long as you have a toaster and microwave in your home you will never go hungry. Toast: a meal in itself, an accompaniment or foundation for numerous dishes, beloved to the British, and second only to tea. Perfect with soup, cheese, jam. Also invaluable when diced: as croutons for a Caesar salad; or sliced: as soldiers for dipping in a soft-boiled egg. And don't give me that excuse of "I can only eat wheat-free." Most supermarkets cater to the allergy neurotic so you can still have toast.

If in doubt, consult a trusty cookbook, or speed-dial your mom, the fairy godmother of culinary crises. Remember also that cookbooks are great props to add to the kitchen, even if they are purely for decoration.

The full English

All British citizens should be prepared, and able, to cook a full English breakfast. You may not be a British citizen, but as with a good cup of tea, its appeal is universal.

For the full English you need to master: toast, fried and scrambled eggs. Both are easy, so add to your résumé.

To fry

Heat oil in a frying pan, pour raw egg into pan, heat, and "spoon" hot oil over yolk and white till it appears suitably solidified. Remember not to overcook – egg yolk should remain runny and dip-able.

To scramble

To get a softer, fluffier egg, you need to crack three eggs into a bowl, add a splash of milk and seasoning, then beat with a fork until mixture is an evenly blended pale yellow. Melt knob of butter in pan, then pour in egg mixture. Stir slowly and continually in a figure-eight pattern. You can let the egg begin to set before you start to stir, but the trick of scrambling eggs is to do it on a low heat and slowly. Continue this method until the eggs are the consistency you like. Soft scrambled eggs are the creamiest and most comforting, and trickiest to perfect.

Best served with . . .

Grilled bacon, sausage, and tomato

Generously pierce and put under grill, and flip when they look done.

Optional extras

Baked beans

These can be microwaved or, better, simmered in pan; add a knob of butter.

Mushrooms

Grill or, if adventurous, and for high cholesterol, fry (for real indulgence, fry bread, as well).

Doing the continental

Continental breakfasts are even EASIER and far preferable if offering breakfast in bed.

Open a carton of orange or apple juice, as preferred. Get either bakery-fresh or packets of croissants and *pain au chocolat*. Toss some fresh fruit into a bowl for a token health thing, and fill the gaps on the table or tray with newspapers and a cereal option.

Have kettle ready to serve coffee or tea and you will have people queuing up to stay over.

Lunch

More often than not eaten on the run or eaten out . . . it's come nightfall when it's your turn to get back in the kitchen . . .

Some simple starters

Appetizers are essentially stallers. They can be easily skipped if you so wish, or used as a time delay for the main. Don't let your guests totally fill up on these. This is just the introduction.

For chic starters, why not serve:

Parma ham and melon
   Pretty self-explanatory.
Salad
   Choose a prepacked bag of leaves (though there is only 15 percent of the goodness in prepacked stuff so, if you can be bothered, buy lettuce and wash and chop yourself), chop fresh tomato to toss in. Garnish with chopped, cooked bacon or chicken and salad dressing.
Tomato mozzarella salad (avocado an optional extra)
   Basically this is slices of tomato and slices of mozzarella. Serve with dressing and a sprinkle of fresh basil, if desired. No cooking or complicated timing issues and the colors work wonderfully.

Baked Camembert

Take small whole Camembert and place in rustic ovenproof dish and heat at about 350 degrees until melting and creamy inside. This will only need to be heated for about five minutes. Serve with fresh French bread and salad – fantastic.

Manageable mains

Risotto

Rice plus anything in cupboard.

Shows you can rustle up anything; good for impromptu entertaining and impressing new friends. This, however, requires a lot of stirring, so not good if you're planning on multitasking, or are prone to tennis elbow. Great if you have a guest that you need to keep still and can put to good use while you pour the wine, get ready, and do the whole hostess thing.

Bangers and mash

Is what the Brits call sausages and mashed potatoes. Ideal for nights in front of the telly/slobbing out – the perfect "not-trying-too-hard" dish. Adding a splash of milk or knob of butter while mashing generally improves things enormously, but for a really delicious mash tip try crème fraîche and a little bit of oil, which is less fattening than lots of butter, but always make sure you mash thoroughly.

The all-in omelette

Eggs and anything in the fridge. This is similar, at the start, to scrambling; you beat the raw eggs in a bowl. For a plain omelette, pour the mixture into a frying pan and treat egg mixture as you would if you were cooking a pancake, which surely everyone knows how to do. Cook on medium to high as you need enough heat for it to cook, but not too much as you need time to prepare toppings – so stay in control and don't let the stove rush you. Either sprinkle toppings on once it is cooked, or you can add after one side is done. For cheese you should cook one side, then fold over and sprinkle grated cheese on the top. Alternatively you have the option of shoving pan and all under a hot broiler until it browns. Note: the ultimate omelette is Spanish. Fry diced potato and onion in your pan. Pour the beaten egg over this and let the mixture cook on one side. Turn the omelette onto a dinner plate (do not attempt to toss or flip this heavy thing) and put it back in the pan on the reverse side. This can then be served hot or cold.

Spag Bol

Spaghetti and minced meat. Easy and impressive, shows you know your way 'round the kitchen, but are too busy to fuss. Fry some chopped onions, add the mince and once it's brown add tinned tomatoes and tomato purée. Stir and leave to simmer. Boil water and follow cooking instructions for spaghetti; this should be one of the few useful lessons that the Girl Scouts taught you.

And as for the summer or healthy moments? Salad. Why make life complicated?

Desserts you don't need a degree to dish up

Sometimes the best ideas are the simplest. Ice cream accompanied by fresh fruit or berries. Chic patisseries and cake shops are there for a reason: simply no one should attempt to make choux pastry. But of course if you have the resources, a homemade apple pie, crumble, cake, or tart can be charming.

But above all a dessert you have invented is a perfect way to showcase your imagination in the culinary department. If there is a story behind the invention, it gives you the perfect opportunity to introduce an anecdote that shows you in an interesting or amusing light.

One of my signature dishes is *Crêpes à la Toblerone*. And how did I come up with this taste sensation? Since you ask, it was inspired by the view from my window: the Eiffel Tower.

1. Take ready-made crêpe, fold, and place on plate.

2. Take four triangles of Toblerone and roll crêpe 'round the chocolate.

3.   Put in microwave on high for a minute and a half, or until you see triangles start to sink.

4. Sprinkle with instant hot-chocolate drinking powder.

5.   Serve with cream or ice cream as preferred. Job done.

How to produce a fabulous three-course dinner (and still be able to make pleasant conversation at the end)

Okay, you should be a bit warmed-up by now. You're ready for the ultimate culinary challenge: the dinner party. Remember to check the following with your guests: are they vegetarian? Are they allergic to anything? Do they have any faddy diets? Is there anything they cannot eat? Are they definitely able to come? Do they want to bring one of the courses?

Assuming you are aiming for your guests to arrive at 8:00 P.M. and eat by 8:30 P.M., this handy step-by-step guide will ensure everything runs smoothly.

The Menu
Avocado with mint and lime vinaigrette

****

Mushroom risotto

Green salad and dressing

*****

Snow Queen with fresh raspberries

******

Coffee and chocolates

Dinner parties require as much planning as an outfit. After work the day before the dinner party, go to the supermarket and purchase all fresh items. Get a cart, it's too heavy a shop for a mere basket. Also, carts leave you with hands free to cross off lists, the balance you need to think, and break in the new heels you have purchased for the occasion.

For dinner for four, you will need:

2 ripe avocados
1 lime
3 large onions
1 clove of garlic
1 packet of mixed-leaf salad
1 packet of green salad
1 packet of watercress
1 packet of fresh mint
Vinaigrette dressing
1 box of mushrooms (big ones, NOT button ones)
2 boxes of fresh raspberries
Boullion stock
8oz. packet of Arborio (risotto) rice
1oz. packet of dried porcini mushrooms
12 meringue cookies
$\frac{1}{2}$ cup superfine sugar
1 pint whipping cream
fresh Parmesan
3 willing guests

Don't forget to pick up wine, tea, coffee, bottled water, and a couple of bunches of flowers. Twenty-four hours to go and regretting it? Check that all the guests are coming, and fill any gaps that may have appeared at the table. The night before – make Snow Queen (don't panic, see page 171 for recipe) and put in freezer. So if your soirée is during the week, preparing what you can in advance will mean you avoid a cooking frenzy after a day at the office. If you've had to skip this stage you can adlib on the day and just do a raspberries, meringue, and cream thing. But aim high.

Also the night before – tidy/vacuum/polish. Get all odd jobs done in advance. This will avoid any early guests seeing you performing unsightly chores.

Synchronize your watch: timing on the day

6:00 P.M. Lay table – decorate with appropriate festive decorations, placements, candles, and put people in strategic positions. Why else have a dinner party unless it has match-making potential.

6:30 Cook risotto – main stirring section here; if really rushed you could consider doing this night before or morning of . . . once cooked, transfer to ovenproof dish and set aside.

7:00 Change into glad rags. Hair, makeup. Acetominophen (See *How to get dressed in five minutes*, page 3.)

7:40 Put out nibbles, olives, and set up carefully selected, appropriate CDs. (See *How to choose the correct music*, page 124.)

7:45 Get all dinner plates ready; have appetizer ready to chop.

7:55 Light all candles, press play on CD, squirt yourself with perfume.

8:00 Guests arrive, welcome, offer glass of wine.

8:15 Disown any friend still to arrive.

8:20 Get guests to sit down at table.

8:25 Bolt front door – any latecomers not to be admitted now.

8:26 Go to kitchen, chop avocado, and serve immediately.

8:30 The appetizer.

8:40 Slip into kitchen to put risotto in medium oven and, if not already, throw salad into a bowl. Remove dessert from freezer.

9:00 Clear appetizer plates, invite guests to have more wine, carry through fresh plates and salad.

9:05 The arrival of your risotto.

9:15 While people are enjoying the risotto, slip into kitchen to turn dessert out of container onto plate – how does it look?

9:30 Remove main course dishes and offer guests slight pause, perhaps change CD now.

9:35 In kitchen, sprinkle fresh fruits and decorate Snow Queen ready to serve.

9:40 Dessert through to table.

10:00 Suggest all retire to sitting room/leave table, carrying plates through to kitchen.

10:30 Serve coffee and chocolates.

11:00 Hope guests have enjoyed meal but want to leave soon.

11:30 Ask guests (nicely) if they think it might be time (yawn) to leave.

11:45 Start clearing up/washing up. Note: do it that night, it is horrid to wake up to.

12:30 Bath and fall into bed.

e menu and the moves: the appetizer

This is an easy dish, but should not be done until the very, very last minute as the avocado will turn brown and look horrid. Halve, destone, and peel avocados.

Place each half facedown on plate and sprinkle with mint, dressing, and garnish with slice of lime.

Or, half fill the avocado with dressing, where stone was, and place on plate garnished and decorated with the above.

The main course

The wine and happy banter should have distracted everyone nicely, but you have to worry about the main course, which is why if this is one of your first forays as an all-cooking, all-performing hostess it's best to keep it simple by having it simmering before the first guest even rings the doorbell.

That is why risotto is a masterful choice: it is filling to eat – and essentially only involves stirring to make. But don't forget the stirring. To do this you need to have your biggest saucepan on the stovetop on medium heat, and stir and stir and stir continuously for twenty minutes while you mix in all the ingredients. This recipe is for mushroom risotto, but you can substitute anything you fancy for the mushrooms. Once it is ready, transfer to a chic ceramic dish, well buttered, and put to one side. Twenty minutes before you want to eat it, reheat in a moderate oven.

1. Chop $1\frac{1}{2}$ onions and gently fry in a tablespoon of oil and some butter.

2. Add your 8 oz. Arborio rice

3. Stir continually.

4. Gradually stir in stock (made from the bouillon), a little at a time, until completely absorbed.

5. Add mushrooms.

6. Keep stirring. Don't let it dry. You may need more stock. It should be like creamy porridge.

Snow Queen

This should be prepared the night before at the latest, as it needs freezing.

1. Whip cream until stiff, with whisk, then fold in the sugar. ("Fold in" means use a metal spoon and stir in trying not to lose the air.)

2. At this point you can add a dash of brandy if you want to pep up the taste.

3. Crush the meringues.

4. Mix meringues into cream mixture with spoon.

5. Either leave in mixing bowl or transfer to nicely shaped bowl.

6. Freeze overnight.

To serve

Take the meringue and cream mixture out of the freezer and leave to temper on serving plate UPSIDE DOWN for about thirty minutes. Hopefully, with a gentle prod, the mixture will slip out, like an oversize crème caramel.

Serve with a sprinkling of raspberries over and around pudding, and if you like, garnish with marshmallows.

Serve immediately.

 *The aftermath*

Not as glamorous as the presentation but, if you can face it, all Cinderellas are advised at least to rinse the plates before they stagger to bed. Washing up will seem a lot less traumatic if this initial gesture is made. If your guests offer to do the washing up more than once, accept gracefully, unless of course you are trying to woo them . . . remember to blow out the candles – unless of course you are still wooing.

If you are a guest
You have been very lucky, and very privileged, especially if you have escaped not only wanting seconds but avoiding food poisoning. You must write a thank-you note. The hassle of finding a card, a stamp, and uniting them with a post box will be nothing compared to the trouble your host has been to.

Recommended reading to line your mind as well as your stomach

Kitchen Confidential: Adventures in the Culinary Underworld by Anthony Bourdain (Harper Perennial, 2001). On why you should never have fish on a Monday.

Cooking for Kings: The Life of Antonin Carême, by Ian Kelly (Walker & Company, 2005). The first celebrity chef, don't you know.

Toast by Nigel Slater (Gotham, 2005). One man's life through food.

Any Fanny Craddock cookbook for terrifying pictures of delicacies such as pigeon wings (with feathers in place) and purple mashed potato.

How to make the perfect tea and sympathy

A woman is like a teabag. You never know how strong she is until she gets into hot water.
—*Nancy Reagan*

As well as being a good talker, the life and soul of the party, it is as important, if not more so, to be a good listener. When someone dear has had a setback you should be the first person they turn to for tea and sympathy. If your advice sounds weak, even to your own ears, let the session take a more educational bent, and let the brew work its magic.

A brief history

The British have been drinking tea for over 350 years, and like to think it can solve all problems. But tea has actually been around for 4,500 years. According to Chinese mythology, in 2737 BC the Chinese Emperor Shen Nung, a scholar and herbalist, was sitting under a tree drinking hot water, and a leaf fell from the tree, into his cup. As luck would have it, the leaf had fallen from a wild tea tree. The emperor sipped the brew, and the taste for tea was born. The word "tea" comes from the Chinese words to describe the drink – *tchai, cha,* and *tay* (cuppa *cha,* anyone?).

From China it traveled to Arabia, and in turn it was introduced to Europe. When the English entered trade with the East Indies in the mid-seventeenth century they claimed tea drinking as their own national pastime.

Anna, the seventh Duchess of Bedford, is reputed to have been the orig-inator of afternoon tea in the early 1800s. She conceived the idea of having "tea" around four or five in the afternoon as a genteel way of having a light snack that would stop the ladies' stomachs from gurgling, and fill the gap between lunch and dinner. It combined beautifully with the Earl of Sandwich's idea of putting a filling between two slices of bread, and soon these habits became a good reason for social gatherings, and a quintessential part of British life.

The selection

Light your best candles, plump the cushions on the sofa, and arrange your friend comfortably, curled up with tissues, biscuits, and tea, and give them your undivided attention.

As the tea brews – listen. As you pour the tea, ask them what you can do to ease their suffering. Finally, as they drink the elixir, offer your comfort and advice.

Which tea you serve should depend on the crisis at hand.

Darjeeling
Cures homesickness and missing England when abroad; a comforting workman's classic.

English Breakfast
Good for work crises and money worries. Wake up and take on the world.

Earl Grey
Perfect for when you don't know what to wear/he left you/you have no idea how to make him fall in love with you.

Lapsang Souchong
This is for artistic and creative problems, or for when you're trying to travel in your imagination to worlds far, far away.

Silver Needles
For really, really special occasions as this is made from tea leaves that can only be gathered two days a year, in the dew at dusk. It's a fabulous limited-edition tea. This is for confiding your deepest hopes and fears, and can be the only thing for a desolate and wounded-beyond-repair heart. Serving this makes you feel like you're at Claridges, which is the only place that actually serves it, so you probably are . . .

Peppermint
Detox, destress, and demystify.

Chamomile
For relief from anxiety and insomnia.

Fruity

The hippy herbal spiritual option. Caffeine-free, but can be an acquired sweet taste.

Green Tea

Cleansing, either the palate or mind.

Echinacea and Raspberry

Cuts down on oral hygienist bills as there's no caffeine, no stain.

Lemon Tea

For tea with lemon, serve with lemon slices, not wedges, and if you are doing it properly you should also provide a lemon fork. Never add tea with lemon to a cup that has had milk in it, as the citric acid will cause the milk to curdle.

The brew

When serving tea, you should pour the tea in first and then add milk to taste. This protocol dates back to the eighteenth century, when aristocrats wished to differentiate between those possessing bone china, and those with ordinary china. Ordinary china is liable to crack when receiving hot water, whereas bone china does not. Ladies liked to check that they were drinking from suitably refined cups. The teacup and saucer, ideally in porcelain, is the ultimate for High Tea, and posh relatives. Mugs are for cosy nights in, comforting, and gossip.

Of course it's always good to have a plate of cookies on hand to accompany.

Recycling

When you've fished the teabags out of the mugs, pop them in the fridge. When properly chilled they are the perfect way to calm tired, puffy eyes. Just don't accumulate too many, and obviously only use once.

For further reading and tea-drinking tips and etiquette, go to *www.teatimeworldwide.com*, *www.theteatable.com* or *www.tea.co.uk* or try these books:

The Ritz London Book of Afternoon Tea by H. Simpson (Morrow Cook Books 1986). A real collector's item.

Tea & Etiquette: Taking Tea for Business and Pleasure by Dorothea Johnson (Captial Books, 1998).

The Tea Council's Guide to the Best Tea in England (Little Bookroom, 2002)

Or sign up for Tamera Bastiaan's newsletter, tea club, etiquette, and advice at *www.oldfashionedliving.com/teatime.htm*.

How to poach an egg,
in the style of Azzedine Alaïa, fashion designer

Egg poaching is a delicate art, just like fashion and pattern cutting. This technique is an *homage* to the great Azzedine Alaïa, who swirls and drapes fabric 'round a torso just the way it should. (Think of Robert Palmer's "Addicted to Love" video; those clingy numbers on heels were Alaïa.) Plus the egg is a relatively healthy option so no excessive weight-gain worry, a plus when reaching for one of his tight, clinging numbers.

Take a deep frying pan and fill it with cold water.

Sprinkle on salt.

Gently bring water to a boil, with heat on half, not full; this is a delicate process like cutting lace. It may take longer, but requires accuracy.

Crack egg into a glass, and have ready by saucepan.

When water starts to bubble, take a piece of white satin, six-by-six inches, and place shiny side up in pan. Gently swirl fabric so that it starts to twist 'round and 'round and 'round.

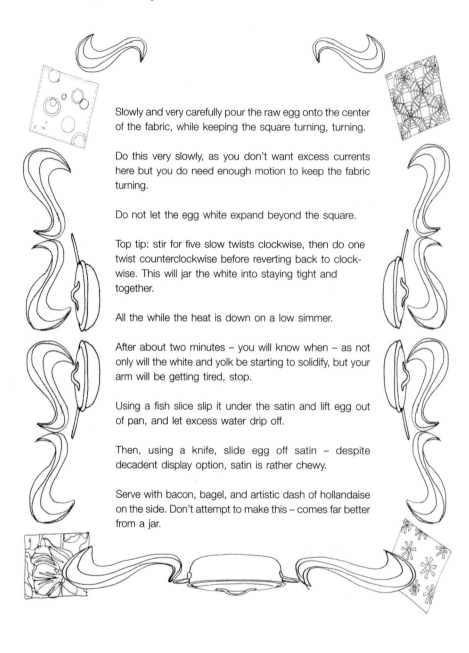

Slowly and very carefully pour the raw egg onto the center of the fabric, while keeping the square turning, turning.

Do this very slowly, as you don't want excess currents here but you do need enough motion to keep the fabric turning.

Do not let the egg white expand beyond the square.

Top tip: stir for five slow twists clockwise, then do one twist counterclockwise before reverting back to clockwise. This will jar the white into staying tight and together.

All the while the heat is down on a low simmer.

After about two minutes – you will know when – as not only will the white and yolk be starting to solidify, but your arm will be getting tired, stop.

Using a fish slice slip it under the satin and lift egg out of pan, and let excess water drip off.

Then, using a knife, slide egg off satin – despite decadent display option, satin is rather chewy.

Serve with bacon, bagel, and artistic dash of hollandaise on the side. Don't attempt to make this – comes far better from a jar.

How to blow an egg

For those moments when you want to be creative in the kitchen, knowing how to blow an egg is a lot of fun. There is nothing more dreary than someone who uses a kitchen only for cooking; be sure not to be one of those types.

Take a sharp metal skewer – a steel kebab stick will work like a charm – or a really big needle.

Jab with a quick but firm wrist action into the bottom end of egg.

Be careful not to smash the egg. If this happens, and it is bound to once or twice, clear up the mess, get a new egg, and try again.

If the shell is still intact, pierce the top end.

If the egg is still whole, apart from these two holes, it's a miracle.

Take egg and BLOW, being careful not to crack and break egg, and even more careful not to suck. This would mean you were drinking raw egg, which might result in you getting salmonella.

Keep blowing until, with a gentle shake, you are satisfied that the egg is hollow.

Leave egg to recover from the stress, bin the raw egg goo, and get out your paintbrush.

How to
Have Good
Table Manners

The hardest job kids face today is learning good manners without ever seeing any.
—*Fred Astaire*

How to decorate a table, the seasonal looks

There are many ways to jazz up a table, be it with seasonal or theme-inspired decorations, but, as with high heels and computers, there is no point running before you can walk. First things first: make sure the implements are in the right place. When presented with an entire drawer of cutlery at either side of your plate, working from the outside in is usually the route to success. But also employ some logic. If you are served soup you will not be requiring that fork; likewise watch your neighbor and see how they tackle the situation.

The table should look exciting and inviting. It's a great way to distract attention from the food, which, let's face it, may not be your forte.

Look for old china: the patterns don't have to match, but should complement each other; for example you could have lots of different flower patterns. Have a common theme but never have chipped china.

Do not underestimate the joy and color-coordinating pluses of a tablecloth. Remnant fabrics are good for this. Napkins are a must. Be they paper or posh, it is far better to supply them than let people a) wipe their fingers on your tablecloth and furniture, or b) ask for something as nonchic as a paper towel.

In spring go for a fresh innocent feel. Choose yellows, blues, and lilacs, and flowers such as daffodils and snowdrops, and scatter buds over the table.

Ideally the table will be outdoors in the summer. But if the weather is too unreliable or too hot, create the atmosphere inside. Why not cover your table in plastic sheeting, being careful to tape it down to the table, cover the table with sand, and build sandcastles for your buffet to nestle in between? Okay, the sand getting in the food thing is disgusting, but you have to have ideas that go outside the box. If the prospect of clearing this up makes you go cold, how about draping big palm leaves across the table, or huge expanses of white muslin, styling à la Lawrence of Arabia?

In the autumn colors should get richer. Try dried red rose petals strewn across the tablecloth. Or dried leaves, chestnuts, and pinecones.

In the winter you have dark nights and Christmas as two great themes to play on. Use evergreens, such as holly and ivy, and perhaps a few sprigs of mistletoe.

You can do color-themed "baby shower" dinners, in pinks or blues, or go kitsch and do a "kiddies" party with hats, jelly, and the whole works. Just make sure the table suits the dress code, the cuisine, and the personality of the guests you are expecting.

No dinner-party table is complete without some candles, fresh flowers, or plants of some sort, and the right background music. Empty wine bottles can make excellent tavern-style candle holders, and Vivaldi's *Four Seasons* and Mozart's "Eine Kleine Nacht Musik" are two perfect choices for background music.

It is bad luck to put heels on the table.

For formal table info, go to *www.mannersinternational.com*. Click on the formal table settings for an easy-to-use printout version. For more extra etiquette, read *The Rituals of Dinner* by Margaret Visser (published by Viking Penguin, 1992).

How to use a knife, fork, and spoon

First thing to remember is that these are to be used solely to maneuver food from plate to mouth. They are not weapons. The "flatware" should be held delicately and balanced horizontally on the prescribed fingers. Always cut small dainty pieces; too much in your mouth at one time is barbaric and makes talking very hard. Peas are impossible. Either spear with your fork, scoop with a spoon, or squish into another edible object. Never try to flick them with a knife as they may not land where you intended.

Halftime

Okay, so assuming all is going well and the meal is midway, don't let your guard down – you still have a few rules to observe.

Once the flatware has been used you may not place it on the table. If you wish to pause, to make some witty repartee or so on, lay it on your plate.

For a brief moment there is no rule as to location, but for longer pauses, where perhaps you need to captivate people with arm gestures, too, you are meant to place the fork on the left and the knife on the right and let them cross in the center. If you are a greedy guts and are getting seconds, you should place them delicately together to one side of the plate. And finally, when you are all finished and done and simply couldn't eat another mouthful, place knife and fork together, in parallel horizontal position in the center of the plate; but surely your mother taught you that already?

A brief history

In sophisticated, modern society it is polite, and expected, to eat using utensils. It comes about from centuries of experimentation.

The first knife dates back to Saxon England in the fifth century, and bronze knives have been dug up to prove it.

In the Middle Ages most food was eaten with hands, and served on slices of four-day-old bread – so there was no washing up to be done. Only the wealthy used utensils, because they didn't do the washing up.

Jump to the eleventh century and the Venetian Doge Domenico Selvo married a Greek princess who, along with her dowry, brings the practice of using forks.

In 1364–80 forks are listed in the inventory of Charles V's palace. But they are "only to be used when eating foods that might stain the fingers."

Another year – 1533 – another marriage, and another fork. Catherine de Médici, of Italy, brings the fork to Henry II of France.

By 1630 Governor Winthrop of the Massachusetts Bay Colony is the proud owner of what is said to be the first and only fork in colonial America, the fork fad not having caught on here yet, despite their knives being imported from Europe.

In 1669 Louis XIV bans pointed knives at the table to reduce dinnertime violence.

By the early eighteenth century the four-tined fork has become the rule in Germany. In England, however, they were still struggling with only two tines, and knives were practically spoon-shaped, flat, and rounded at the tip. But by the mid-eighteenth century, thankfully, forks had evolved to the curved four tines we know today.

During the Victorian era everything gets terribly proper and, by heavens, does the cutlery drawer expand. Tomato servers, sardine forks, jelly knives, and cheese scoops are among the popular innovations of the day.

And by the 1920s stainless steel is invented so people can stop polishing their silver. Cutlery is widespread and not just for Sunday best.

How to use chopsticks

Chinese food – you do not sew with a fork, and I see no reason why you should eat with knitting needles.
—*Miss Piggy*

This section is not a reference to the first tune any pianist will learn, "Chopsticks" (original name "The Celebrated Chop Waltz"), written in 1887, and now a very popular mobile phone ringtone. No, not at all. In this context it refers to the eating implements of the Orient, invented back in 3 BC.

The tricky sticks keep you slim; don't think it's the food, it's the lack of sustenance that reaches your mouth. You thought peas with a fork were hard, try rice with chopsticks. Serious social skill required.

Think of the chopsticks as a pair of prongs, or tweezers, that have broken. Chopsticks are operated only with your dominant hand. Put your middle and ring finger, three and four, on your thumb and you have a finger-shadow puppet of a dog's head. This is the general idea with operating chopsticks: finger shadows and sticks.

One stick you keep stationary, the other you wiggle about to secure the food. To begin with it can feel like the arcade game where you try in vain to grab the teddy bear.

1. Take one stick first and hold it in your right hand, the way you would normally hold a pencil. If the stick has a thick and a thin end, or decorated and nondecorated, hold it so that the thick/takeout logo end is on top.

2. Keeping the fingers in position, turn your hand inward until the stick is horizontal to the table, parallel to your body, and hovering above the food.

3. Your thumb and forefinger should be clamping the stick at about its midpoint. The thumb should not be bent nor rigidly straight, while all your fingers should be curved slightly inwards.

4. Now, take the other stick with your opposite hand and rest it on the protruding part of the ring finger of the hand that holds the first stick. Slide the stick towards the right, touching the tip of the middle finger and passing under the thumb until the thick end rests at the base joint of your forefinger. This is the stationary position of this stick, and it should be roughly parallel to the first stick.

5. If this makes no sense, take the second stick, lie it just below the index finger, and use this to wiggle it. Keep the lower stick steady and the upper stick looser to pivot and pick. You hardly need any grip until you have caught whatever morsel you intend to eat.

The chopstick is a multitasker; it serves as fork, knife, and spoon. It can even be used to eat soup and cut food into small morsels – which is just plain silly.

If all else fails, use your fingers and use the chopsticks as hair accessories, sushi-free, of course.

How to eat with your fingers with style

Despair not if you cannot use cutlery or chopsticks; you will not starve. There are foods that are best eaten by hand. It can also be very seductive. Just ensure that you don't accidentally swallow a diamond. Loose jewelry should be removed and safely stored, ideally in handbag or pocket. Almost everything at cocktail parties or at premeal nibbles is "finger food," proof that even the truly posh can make finger-licking appearances.

The best finger foods include:

Artichokes, asparagus (providing it is not drenched in sauce), (crispy) bacon, bananas, biscuits, bread/baguettes, canapés, cherries, chocolates, corn on the cob, chips, crudités, fast food, French fries, hors d'oeuvres, olives, oysters, seafoods, small berries, sushi, sweets, and popcorn.

How to use a napkin

As well as being the perfect white flag for foes to surrender with, napkins can be very handy come dinnertime.

The napkin is a gentle and delicate accessory associated with the formalities and more refined art of dining. Therefore it is almost certain you will be using one. Regularly.

To begin

Remove the napkin from your place setting, unfold the origami creation, and lay it on your lap. In a very posh restaurant the waiter may dash over and do this for you. Don't be too alarmed, he is not coming to throw you out or smother you.

To end

Dab your lips and place napkin loosely next to your plate. It should not be folded, as you are not trying to save your hosts a wash bill, nor should it be too crumpled and twisted – you don't want to imply that you are a nervous wreck. Also, caution: do not leave it on your seat. Superstition says that "a diner who leaves a napkin on his chair will never sit at that table again." And you know how hard it is to get a good table at the Ivy.

How to appreciate wine

Promise me one thing: don't take me home until I'm very drunk – very drunk indeed.
—*Holly Golightly (Audrey Hepburn)*, in *Breakfast at Tiffany's*

Wine is a fermented alcoholic grape juice. The perfect party and socializing accessory, available in white, red, or rosé. It is also an investment and, like a leather jacket, it really does get better with age. This is why bottles can become collectors' items and vintage vineyards are *tout le rage.*

Ordering wine is one thing, *appreciating* wine is an art form, but once you've got the knack of it you will think nothing of adding 40 percent to your dinner tab for the purchase of the beverage.

Some basic rules:

NEVER drink on an empty stomach. If you do, it suggests that your date has not bought you dinner and considers you a cheap date, or only worthy of being one, which is definitely not a good sign, but this is a whole other section.

NEVER mix and match. You wouldn't mix styles and certain labels, and the same rule must apply with drink. Choose beer, spirit, wine – red or white. Make a decision and stick with it.

NEVER go beyond the dizzy, light-headed phase. At the vomiting and passing-out phase you cease to look even remotely attractive, and the hangover will counteract any pleasure.

DON'T try to match a man drink for drink. A woman's tolerance is lower.
Don't enter into drinking competitions, unless it is your intention either
to pass out or be carried home.

Wine tasting

Wine tasting, sniffing, and spitting may strike you as pretentious but,
before you scoff, there is method in the madness.

A wine-tasting session is like going to a shoe store, with lots of different
styles and brands on offer. You need to try a few to work out what best suits
you, your taste, and your mood. That said, the spitting bit should be skipped
in restaurants, bars, and any non-wine-tasting events.

Take the open bottle and pour a small "taste" into the glass.

Lift the glass to your lips. Close your eyes. Slowly move the glass under your
nose and inhale deeply. Let your mind take you on a journey to that smell: to
the rich terracotta of the parched landscape, the rolling hills, the women with
their shirtsleeves pushed up, and their skirts trailing along the dirt path . . .
Wine tells a story, you have to listen and indulge it to experience it at its best.

A really exceptional bottle can transport your taste buds and mind. This
is why it is so intoxicating and addictive, and so potentially expensive.

How to open a bottle

If you are at home and you do not have a dashing bartender, you will need
to open the bottle, pour, and serve yourself. This is much simpler than
initially feared, but do practice, lots . . .

Firmly hold the bottle of wine by the neck. The main body can be
clamped between your knees if it is wriggling about, but not if you have
an audience. Remove all excess wrapping – reduce the layers you have to
get through – and insert corkscrew into exposed cork at the top.

Twist bottle one way, and corkscrew another. The steel ringlet will sink, piercing farther into the cork. Best to do this at an angle, particularly if it's red you're opening. Point it away from yourself in case of explosions or spillage – wine is a notoriously tough stain to shift.

When corkscrew feels firmly embedded in cork, you've got to go into reverse, so start to ease it out. Ideally go for a corkscrew with "arms" that, when ready to be pulled, looks like a lady with hairy armpits trapped in quicksand, arms raised above her head. The idea here is to push her arms back down, to reveal what look like frilly shoulder pads; much more pleasing to the eye.

Don't panic, take it nice and slow.

Hey, presto, wine should be open and ready to pour.

For Champagne you need a different knack as it is a fizzy drink, and therefore you have the buildup of bubbles to deal with. Think of all those images of Champagne bottles exploding and showering people. If you want to do that, shake the bottle. If not, execute operation with a steady hand. Pull off the wrapping, which in the past was lead-lined foil to keep the mice from nibbling it off and getting drunk in cellars on the sweet elixir. Under this you should find a wirelike garter.

Unscrew the wire cage, and keep your thumb on top of the cork so that it does not pop out until you are ready. The wire cage will have kept the cork in place, but once you loosen this safety net you have to be prepared.

Once the wire cage is off hold the cork in one hand and the bottle in the other. You will notice that these corks are slightly domed so you cannot use a corkscrew on sparkling wines, you have to use a firm grip. Turn the bottle, not the cork; ease the cork off slowly, rather than tug and experience an explosion.

Once the cork pops out it will expand, and will not return to stop the bottle, so you'd better pour for as many friends as you can find.

How to tell if it's corked

"Corked" is wine lingo, and the polite way of saying the wine has turned, and is off. Yuk. This usually happens when air has gotten into the bottle, or it has been badly stored. There is usually a slight "ting" to the smell, which should be an initial warning, but if it tastes like soggy corrugated cardboard, crusty socks, or furry mushrooms, it's definitely corked, so you have to send it back. Don't be shy.

Red wine

Reds are fruity, rich, juicy, with berry taste and deep color. They are best served with red meats, casseroles, smelly cheeses, and strong rich flavors on cold winter evenings, with candlelight.

They should be served in big glasses so that the wine can breathe and swirl around unrestricted.

Red wine is sultry, sexy, sophisticated, and brunette. Think Sophia Loren, Jayne Mansfield combined with Coco Chanel. Consequently it is best served wearing: pencil skirts, tight cashmere sweaters, red lipstick, pearls, fishnets, and stilettos. Or large sweaters, soft subtle makeup, curled up in a log cabin on a sheepskin rug in front of a roaring fire.

Reds worth name-dropping as well as pouring include:

Cabernet Sauvignon
The best vines are grown on well-drained, low-fertile soils. The wine is made from small black-blue grapes with thick skins, which produce deeply colored, full-bodied wines with notable tannins. Its spiritual home is the Bordeaux regions Médoc and Graves, which have piercing blackcurrant fruits that develop complex, smoky cedarwood nuances when fully mature. The vines that produce this wine are also grown in California, and create a rich mixture of cassis, mint, eucalyptus, and vanilla oak. They are also planted across Australia, with particular success in Coonawara, where they

are suited to the famed terra rossa soil, and in Italy, where they are a key component in Super Tuscans. Like all great reds it is rich, yet has a fruity, plummy taste, with blackcurrant, berry, and even peppery notes to confuse the taste buds. There are the collectors' items as well as the downright cheap and nasty variety, so a wine to suit all budgets and boyfriends.

Merlot

The Merlot grape is adaptable to most soils and is relatively simple to cultivate. It requires savage pruning – overcropped Merlot-based wines are diluted and bland. It is also vital to pick at just the right time as Merlot can quickly lose its key characteristics if it is harvested overripe. The best wines are found in St.-Emilion and Pomerol, where they withstand the moist, clay-rich soils far better than Cabernet grapes. At its best it produces opulently rich, plummy clarets with succulent fruitcakelike nuances. Le Pin, Pétrus, and Clinet are examples of hedonistically rich Merlot wines at their very best. Merlot is now grown in virtually all wine-growing countries and is particularly successful in California, Chile, and northern Italy.

Pinot Noir

Pinot Noir has been described as "probably the most frustrating, and at times infuriating, wine grape in the world." Makes you love it before you've taken a sip. However, when it is successful, it can produce some of the best wines known to man. A thin-skinned grape that grows in small, tight bunches, it performs best on well-drained, deepish, limestone-based subsoils, like the ones found on Burgundy's Côte d'Or. This wine is lighter in color, body, and tannins. However, the best wines have grip, complexity, and an intensity of fruit seldom found in wine from other grapes. Young Pinot Noir can smell almost sweet, redolent with freshly crushed raspberries, cherries, and redcurrants. When mature, the best wines develop a sensuous, silky-mouth feel with the fruit flavors deepening and gamey, *sous-bois* nuances emerging. The best examples are still found in Burgundy, although the Pinot Noir's grape also plays a key role in Champagne. It should be remembered that it is grown throughout the world, with notable success in the Carneros and Russian River Valley districts of California, and the Martin borough and Central Otago regions of New Zealand.

White wines

Whites are light and flirty, ripe and fruity, more
acidic than red, with creamy vanilla base notes. Best
served in tall, thin, and icy glasses. Ideal with salmon, roast
chicken, and creamy pasta.

White wine is blonde, Nordic, light, and flirty. It is Marilyn Monroe, Gwen
Stefani, Gwyneth Paltrow. It is Ralph Lauren or Calvin Klein shift evening
dresses, Jil Sander white shirts, or bias-cut Galliano. It is mink fur stoles and
diamond earrings, well-groomed luxury. Think cream cashmere polo necks,
Chanel's Allure perfume, and crocodile slingbacks. Alternatively, works well
with your Juicy Couture tracksuit, a face pack, and a brat-pack movie night
in with the girls.

White wines worth pouring and praising include:

Chardonnay

This is a variety of grape, as well as the name of a basic wine. The
name Chardonnay has been so overused it is easy to get confused and
conned into purchasing something not up to standard. There are
different levels of wine, from expensive and specialist Chardonnays to
the more user-friendly Chablis, that use the Chardonnay grape.

Chardonnay is one of the most widely planted wine-bearing vines
in the world. The Chardonnay grapevine is suited to a variety of soils,
though it excels where there is a high limestone content, as found in
Champagne, Chablis, and the Côte d'Or. Burgundy is Chardonnay's
spiritual home and the best white Burgundies are dry, rich, honeyed
wines with poise, elegance, and balance; unquestionably the finest dry
white wines in the world. The Chardonnay grape is the mainstay of
white wine production in California and Australia, and is widely planted
in Chile, South Africa, and New Zealand. In warm climates Chardonnay
has a tendency to develop very high sugar levels during the final stages
of ripening and this can occur at the expense of acidity.

Top Chardonnays include Meursault, Puligny-Montrachet, Chassagne-Montrachet.

Sauvignon Blanc

This is an important white grape in Bordeaux and the Loire Valley that has now found fame and success in New Zealand and Chile. It thrives on the gravelly soils of Bordeaux and is blended with Sémillon to produce fresh, dry, crisp AC Bordeaux Blancs, as well as the more prestigious Cru Classé White Graves. When blended with Sémillon, though in lower proportions, it produces the great sweet wines of Sauternes. It performs particularly well on the chalky soils found in Sancerre and Pouilly-Fumé, where it produces bone-dry, highly aromatic, racy wines, with grassy and sometimes smoky, gunflintlike nuances. In the 1980s Cloudy Bay, New Zealand, began producing stunning Sauvignon Blanc wines with intense nettly, gooseberry, and even asparagus notes, that put Marlborough's Cloudy Bay firmly on the world wine map.

Pinot Gris

A first-class grape variety grown in Alsace, where it is known as Tokay Pinot Gris, and in Italy, where it is called Pinot Grigio, so it is possible to get confused. In Alsace it is best suited to the deep, clay-rich soils found in the north of the region where it produces honeyed, dry whites. It ages very well, developing buttery characteristics. In northern Italy Pinot Grigio is widely planted, producing many thin, undistinguished dry whites. However, it comes into its own in Friuli where leading producers such as Alvaro Pecorari produce marvelously rounded examples.

Whites from southern France, Australia, and California are also worth perusing.

Rosé wine

Rosé is, as its name implies, blushing pink, and it is best saved for champagnes. Try the Billecart Brut Rosé Salmon for the ultimate pink fizz.

Rosé is basically when red grapes are fed through a crusher and straight into a vat, complete with their skins, before the wine is run off to ferment. It is the skins that produce the pinky-hued color. Rosé is usually dry as it is allowed to complete fermentation naturally.

Mateus Rosé and Casal Mendes Rosé, from Portugal, Lacheteau Rosé d'Anjou, and Domaine de Pellehaut Rosé are four of the best bottles to try, but don't always go for the clichéd option.

As with all wines ask your waiter what they recommend, what the house special is, and what the best is.

How to love Champagne

I only drink champagne when I'm happy, and when I'm sad. Sometimes I drink it when I'm alone. When I have company I consider it obligatory. I trifle with it if I am not hungry and drink it when I am. Otherwise I never touch it – unless I am thirsty.
—*Lily Bollinger*, on being born into the right family

Drink with diamonds, furs, and above all high heels and glamour. Best served in elegant, long, chilled, crystal glass flutes. The perfect accompaniment to strawberries and marriage proposals.

Champagne is a place in France. Only Champagne from Champagne is Champagne. The rest are fakes. The three principal regions in the Champagne area are the Montagne de Reims, the Côte des Blancs, and the Vallée de la Marne.

Champagne is made from a blend of three possible grape varieties. Black grapes Pinot Noir for richness, and Pinot Meunier for a fruity hint of spice, and Chardonnay, a white grape, for the delicate fresh quality.

The legend is that there was a blind French monk, called Dom Pierre Pérignon, who stumbled onto a cask, and when he tasted the bubbly exclaimed, "I am drinking the stars." It is not said how much he had drunk when this statement was made, but suffice it to say he loved the stuff.

As with wine there's a lot of variety and you need to decide which is best suited to your palate. Do you like a soft bubble, something fruity, something light, or whatever is offered?

WARNING: wine with bubbles goes to the head faster. Studies show that the carbon dioxide in the bubbles speeds the alcohol through the stomach wall and into your bloodstream that little bit faster. So if you're in a hurry into oblivion, order some bubbly.

The best Champagne houses

Bollinger

Founded in 1829 and still in the family. Think Edina and Patsy in *Ab Fab* swigging from the bottle.

Delbeck

Founded in 1832. Motto: Go forward one step at a time. For a classy Savile Row-wearing, connoisseur drinker.

Dom Pérignon

Part of the Moët et Chandon Champagne house. Named after a famous monk who was the most important early influence in turning Champagne into the sparkling wine we know today. Hallelujah. Now served up at Ascot and society bashes.

Krug

Founded in 1843 by Jean-Joseph Krug, this house has always put quality first and so attracts a very high-quality customer. This is for the Cartier watch-wearing, polo-playing gang.

Lanson

Founded in 1760 and one of the oldest Champagne houses. The Black Label brand is one of the bestsellers in the UK and is ideal for baby showers and bar mitzvahs.

Laurent Perrier

Founded in 1812, and the largest independent, family-owned Grande Marque house in Champagne. This is for toasting when your boat comes in or when you win at the races.

Louis Roederer

Renowned for high quality, this is the maker of great Cristal Champagne, which was first made for the tsar of Russia and his court. For swooning under the chandeliers and being very Merchant Ivory and period drama decadent with. Think *Gosford Park* chic.

Mercier

Founded in 1858, now part of the giant LVMH* group. Their Champagnes have a reputation for good value, so ideal for eighteenth and twenty-first birthday parties.

Moët et Chandon

Founded in 1743 and based in Epernay. Napoleon favored Moët and visited their cellars. This is the largest Champagne house and is owned by the LVMH group. This is drunk at fashion shows and flashy events, usually by very thin models.

Mumm

Founded in 1827, a large house whose flagship brand is Cordon Rouge. This is the best stuff for weddings and bathing in.

Salon

Made famous in the 1920s for supplying Maxim's in Paris and is still the choice *du jour* for flappers and gangsters' molls.

Veuve Clicquot

Founded in 1772 and responsible for building this brand into one of the Grandes Marques; now owned by LVMH. This is the bubbly for political and high-brow occasions.

*LVMH

(Moët Hennessy Louis Vuitton) is the French luxury-goods group, owned by Bernard Arnault, that is made up of over fifty brands, including fashion brands Louis Vuitton, Marc Jacobs, Givenchy, Dior, and Fendi and also has considerable clout in the wine and spirit industry. They own the following wine and spirit brands: Moët et Chandon, Dom Pérignon, Veuve Clicquot, Krug, Mercier, Ruinart, Château d'Yquem, Chandon Estates, Hennessy, Cloudy Bay, Cape Mentelle, Newton, MountAdam.

How to taste wine like a professional

Of all the gin joints in all the towns in all the world, she walks into mine.

—*Rick Blaine (Humphrey Bogart), in* Casablanca

Drinking is easy – tasting is different. Tasting involves and engages all your senses so you can detect every subtlety within the wine.

Sight

Does it look clear or dull? Any murk and it's got to go back.

White wine should sparkle, it should be white – lemon – gold. White wine gets more golden and deeper with age.

Red wines should be purple ruby or "tawny." With red wines the more purple they are the younger they are, the more orange/browny the older they are.

Smell

Does it smell clean or unclean? Sounds ridiculous, but usually this is the way you can tell if it's corked, musty, or off before torturing your taste buds. The smell can also give you a hint of the taste, if it's sugary, fruity, nutty, spicy, savory, and so on.

Taste

Swirl a small sip around the mouth to give every taste bud a chance. Do you taste sweetness at the tip of the tongue? Is it dry, medium, or sweet?

If it tastes like lemons, it's acidic. White wines are more acidic than reds.

Do you taste the tannin? This is the skin of the grape that's coating your teeth, and tends to dry the mouth out; acid makes your mouth water. The alcohol should be sensed at the back of the throat as a warm fuzzy sensation.

Taste will tell you about its quality, maturity (reds get spicy, whites more honeyed as they get on), origin, and grape variety.

The best way to try out wine is to travel. Always try to drink the wines that are a speciality of the local region. Unlike at home, the house white or red abroad is generally the best wine in the house.

France and Italy are the main – and are generally regarded as the leading – wine-producing countries. That said, you should not dismiss what else is on offer. Branch out and give the following a toast, in reverse order: Portugal, Argentina, South Africa, Chile, New Zealand, Hungary, Australia, California USA, Spain, and Germany.

Generally speaking, Bordeaux are the best French wines and Barolos are known as the best Italian ("the Bordeaux of Italy"). When in Spain you should opt for something from Rioja. In Germany it would be rude not to open a bottle from the Riesling or the Rhine. And America is one of the fastest expanding areas in the world for wine production. California is the nation's richest wine-producing state, with wines to rival the French equivalent. The best way to work out what you like is to try as many varieties as you have lipsticks.

Then there are the "don't even go there's"

While some may mock the English vineyards, others look alarmed at the offerings from abroad. It's a question of changing fashion as much as personal preference. However, it is fairly universally agreed that a cheap Bordeaux is as distasteful as the remnants at a car trunk sale. Also avoid cheap Champers and basic Beaujolais. Not saying you have to spend a king's ransom, but the phrase "you pay peanuts and you get monkeys" does apply here. Bette Davis, as Margo Channing in *All About Eve*, said: "I admit I may have seen better days, but I'm still not to be had for the price of a cocktail, like a salted peanut." Use this line.

To get rid of a wine stain

If you spill red wine, pour salt or white wine on top. Salt is better for carpets, white wine for outfits, but generally both are best to avoid.

Alcohol trivia to wow with

"Gif me a viskey, ginger ale on the side, and don't be stingy, baby," said Anna Christie (Greta Garbo) in 1930. It was one of the first drinks ordered in a talking picture.

Absinthe, said to cause blindness, insanity, and even death, was Picasso's, Hemingway's, and Van Gogh's favorite creative tool.

Meanwhile with Guinness the bubbles go down instead of up, because the bubbles in Guinness are mainly nitrogen. They rise like an erupting volcano and, unlike other bubbles, once they reach the top, they are too hyperactive to wait, so they fight all the way against the current to go down the glass. And then they do it all over again.

You do not become better looking when drinking, nor is your eyesight affected, but your brain fuzzes. That is why drinking and dating is bad news.

How to cure a hangover

Get out of those wet clothes and into a dry martini.
—*Mae West*

Overindulgence can lead to a mind-numbing headache, nausea, and all kinds of agony. Before you reach for two painkillers, a warm bath, and go back to sleep, try these.

Tomato juice, aspirin, and a long, hot shower.
Water, water, and more water.
Water and vitamin C (also water and calcium).
Water and vitamin B complex.
Vitamin E.
Buttermilk.
A greasy fry-up.
Fried canaries – popular with the Romans.
Munching a cabbage – relief for the Ancient Greeks.

Black Velvet – equal parts Champagne and flat Guinness; you'd need to be desperate.

A black peppercorn up the nose: it's like an anesthetic, but can cause nosebleeds.

Dark shades and sympathy.

Red-Eye – whiskey, coffee, Tabasco sauce, a raw egg, pepper, and orange juice blended together. Eugh.

If things are really desperate, lurid-pink Pepto-Bismol and water or Diorylte, the diarrhea cure. Not glamorous but certainly rehydrates you fast.

Lots of icy-cold Coca-Cola (not Diet Coke, real sugar).

Marmite on toast.

Throwing up and getting it all out.

Vowing never to drink again.

Campaigning for prohibition to return.

Preventatives should also be noted, such as coating your stomach before drinking, with milk and/or bread and butter. Do avoid caffeine, and short-term fixes; it may work in the movies, but it's unlikely those actors are really drunk. Everything is case-dependent; sometimes it's best just to curl up and die.

Hair of the dog

If you wake up and all around is debris and carnage, sometimes it's a case of better the devil you know. This is a short-term solution (before you crawl home for those two painkillers, warm bath, and sleep), but it's a good one.

Take 1.4 oz. of Scotch whiskey, 1.7 oz. of single cream, and 3 teaspoons of honey. Pour all ingredients into cocktail shaker, fill with cracked ice. Shake, and pour into a martini glass. There, isn't that better? Play it again, Sam . . .

The Bloody Mary

Of all revivers the Bloody Mary is the most versatile and glamorous, even though you take Mary's name in vain. It is said to have been first mixed in the early 1920s in Harry's New York bar, in Paris.

You need 1.7 oz. of vodka, tomato juice, spice mix, a slice of lemon, celery stick, and ice (optional).

For the spice mix: take two large dashes each of Tabasco and Worcestershire sauce to taste. Pinch of celery salt. Pinch of black pepper. Dash of lemon juice, fresh. Teaspoon of horseradish sauce.

Blend ingredients for spice mix together in mixing glass. Pour vodka into a highball glass filled with ice, add tomato juice and spice mix.

Stir as vigorously as you can manage.

Serve with lemon slice, celery stick, and steady hand.

How to look fresh after a bender

If you really, *really* can't have a lie-in after a crazed and hectic night, sometimes you need a miracle. Think of Grace Kelly and her hangover in *High Society* or Kim Basinger going off the rails in *Blind Date*. As they say, work hard, play harder, and still crawl into the office the next day; show them who's boss . .

There are two obvious essentials:

1. *Sunglasses* Big black Jackie Kennedy Onassis/Audrey Hepburn wrap frames. Choose Dior, Chanel, or YSL. Big impact. Big glamour. Think movie star. Keep the shades on, at least till after midday, have a long lunch, and then slip off to do "research" early afternoon.

2. *YSL Touche Éclat* Apply liberally 'round the eyes, and especially under eyes. Dab white eye shadow on lids. Finish with a flash of rouge, mascara, and gloss to maintain standards.

The key factor to remember here is you need to drink and drink (water) to rehydrate yourself. Evian, Perrier, Badoit, whatever your poison – make it mineral water.

Tackling Your Technophobia

Be nice to nerds. Chances are you'll end up working for one.
—*Bill Gates*

How to
Love Your
Computer

Man is still the most extraordinary computer of all.
—*John F. Kennedy*

How to understand the enemy

This section has been written in ENGLISH and will attempt to restore your pulse, demystify and answer some of the simpler, yet still utterly baffling FAQs (Frequently Asked Questions) about the monsters.

Try to remember that computers are harmless, inanimate objects. They cannot bite. As long as there is an on/off button you will always have the upper hand. Do not let them intimidate you.

Technology is constantly being updated. Vintage or old is not good in this world. To keep up, you need to have the newest and jazziest, latest version of the gadget *du jour*.

If computer books all appear to be a big zzzzzzzzzzzzzzzzz and the technical section of the bookstore terrifies you, don't worry; you are not alone. Despite the shelves being full of unhelpful self-help books, many people suffer, in varying forms of acuteness, from technophobia. This is a curable illness brought on by VRML (Virtual Reality Modeling Language), HTML (Hypertext Mark-up Language) and WWW (world wide web). Computers, e-mail, the Internet, the world wide web, downloading, and iPods are all here to stay, and will expand. You need to master the basics sooner rather than later, be it in the office or high-tech at home. Computer rage and techno stress are now the most common forms of complaint in the office; people take second place. IT departments are the most overused and abused departments in the company.

First of all it's worth explaining what we're dealing with, in the simplest, nontechnobabble way. Even Bill Gates admits, "Often you just have to rely on your intuition."

A computer is a tool that processes data in the form of code. Its memory program is written in ones and zeros (binary code). The computer processes masses of this data at incredibly fast speeds, and carries out the actions that are written in the data. The code/data then goes into English/a language that the mere mortal can understand, and while we press simple buttons, the hidden data sends rapid messages telling the computer how to operate your typed Word documents, play music, display pictures, or run DVD movies, without you having to worry about what goes on behind the scenes.

The anatomy of the computer

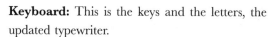

Key objects to check that you have on your desk are:

Keyboard: This is the keys and the letters, the updated typewriter.

Screen or monitor: This is what you look at, where you see text and pictures, and work on.

Mouse: Not the squeak-squeak variety. This is a handy object, either built into the computer or an enclosed plastic-cased ball that moves a cursor arrow over the screen, wherever you direct it, and opens required windows and clicks on options for you.

Hard drive: This is the brain of the computer, where the memory and all the technical stuff that make it work are hidden.

Speakers: Are for music or any sound effects that your machine may choose to make. But rest assured there is always a mute button.

Leads and connectors: Try to keep to bare minimum, but these are the links to your phone line, power supply, and additional extras.

Additional extras include printers, scanners, and joysticks.

All the above are referred to as *hardware*, and should be located near a plug socket and a phone socket, as you are likely to need Internet access. Think about this when deciding where your desk will be positioned. Leads lurching across a floor, as well as being hazardous, are terribly unsightly.

Software is the information your computer uses to process the data after the hardware is set up to make it all work.

A brief history

"I think there is a world market for maybe five computers." So said Thomas Watson, chairman of IBM, in 1943. Well, he was accurate . . .

1500 Leonardo da Vinci invents the Mechanical Calculator.

1714 First English typewriter patent.

1829 First U.S. typewriter patent.

1837 Morse code is invented.

1847 Emily Brontë's *Wuthering Heights* is published.

1865 Lewis Carroll's *Alice's Adventures in Wonderland* is published.

1867 First commercial typewriter goes on sale.

1872 QWERTY keyboard laid out.

1943 Invention of first power-generated electric computer ENIAC.

1944–52 First stored-program computer, EDVAC, is developed.

1947 Christian Dior presents his New Look. Not STRICTLY speaking relevant, but just checking you were still awake . . .

1948–51 First commercial computer, UNIVAC, is unveiled.

1951 J. D. Salinger's *Catcher in the Rye* is published.

1953 First TV dinner is served.

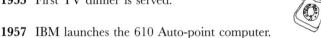

1957 IBM launches the 610 Auto-point computer.

1968 Stanley Kubrick's film *2001: A Space Odyssey*, featuring the computer HAL, premieres.

1975 Bill Gates and Paul Allen found Microsoft.

1976 Apple I and Apple II microcomputers.

1981 IBM invents the first PC.

1998 Apple launches the iMac.

2003 Apple launches iPods.

2004 Apple launches iPod photo.

2006 There are more technological developments a day than there are minutes; you can only try to keep up.

And in more detail . . .

Think of this lesson in computer history as essential; not knowing it would be like watching an episode of *Friends* without knowing any of the characters' background. You would not get nearly as much out of the show. And it's very impressive general knowledge to have at your fingertips.

The modern keyboard was invented by Christopher Latham Sholes in 1872, after he devised the first commercial typewriter. The Sholes keyboard (aka QWERTY, which is the top left-hand row of letters on your keyboard) is what we still use today. The shift key didn't appear until 1878.

The modern computer came about during the Second World War. It was invented by a German engineer called Konrad Zuse in 1941 and was named the Z3. By 1943 the Allies had developed Colossus to help them try to decode enemy messages. Next came the Mark I, in 1944, developed by American Howard Aiken, an engineer at Harvard and IBM. His computer was the size of half a football field, so not ideal for the traveler.

The first personal computer (PC) was produced by IBM in 1981. (IBM originally stood for International Business Machines.) It was then the biggest computer company in the world. In the initial computer boom IBM led the way, but was unable to keep up with demand for change and constant updating while its competitors lowered the price of their hardware.

The basic configuration of the PC uses Intel Processors and an operating system that started its life as DOS (this was the software that you needed to install to run the machine). In 1975, Bill Gates, aged twenty, along with Paul Allen, founded Microsoft. They took the cream of ideas and inventors from IBM and became an unstoppable force. Fairly quickly Microsoft came along with MSDOS, which was an improved version of DOS. While DOS could only work on DOS-compatible computers, MSDOS worked on all styles. Soon every PC had the same electronic components and the same processing system, and it made sense to go for the one that worked the best. MSDOS then gave way to Microsoft Windows, which is (basically) a ripped-off copy of Macintosh's software, an altogether chicer, more user-friendly package. This led to an ongoing court battle, like a *Dallas* storyline, except this one was played out in Silicon Valley between Apple and Microsoft. Despite all this, Bill Gates still continues to reside at the top of the rich list.

In 1981, with the arrival of the PC, people were able to start working at their desks and computers suddenly became much more efficient and much more of an essential mod con. Before PCs, computers were attached to "dumb" terminals. With PCs it became possible for people to edit their work before taking it to the main-frame, big-brain HQ – far preferable. Gradually people were able to work independently and run their own programs, then connect to the company "network" and share their information with others. It was a major breakthrough. Before, all systems had run off one shared "brain;" now they all had their own "brain," but, as with most things, they found they could put their heads together for even better results. Also on the internal network system they were able to communicate internally on a very primitive form of the e-mail system, but more on this later.

Early European computer bureaus would have call centers where the computers would access dial-up lines to open the network. Some would find cheap dial-up space as far away as the States, due to time difference advantages. It was a few years till e-mail and the Internet explosion happened.

1981 was a vintage year, as not only was there the royal wedding, and the first PC came out, in the US Adam Osborne invented the first laptop, originally called the Osborne 1. It cost $1,795 and came with $1,500 worth of programming.

Names to know

Bill Gates

Born on October 28, 1955. His success is due to his genius for working out a weakness in the system that existed and filling it with an application developed by his company, Microsoft. He is to computers what Henry Ford, and his Model T, was to cars. Bill Gates *is* software.

Steve Jobs

This is Bill's biggest rival. He founded Apple Macintosh. They launched the Apple I and II on April Fool's Day 1976, a hard-drive system invented by him and Steve Wozniak. The company has gone on to develop the iMac, iBooks, the Apple laptop, as well as the iPod.

iMacs

These are the most friendly-looking hardware, and were launched in 1998. They are the easiest to install, but don't always connect well to large systems. They are the IKEA of computer hardware – jazzy, cheap, and easy for all to understand.

Alan Sugar

He invested in the hardware system Amstrad, which was the English attempt to compete With the American domination of Silicon Valley. He now owns a real-estate company, the software firm Viglen, and a chunk of Tottenham Hotspur FC, which is where Sir Alan is most frequently spotted. He also fronted the British TV version of Donald Trump's show, *The Apprentice*.

Dell

Very successful computer hardware, but, bizarrely, it is not available in any shops. Dell sells only by mail order or online, so they don't have any sales mark-up. They mainly attract the computer whiz and big companies, making them a good option also for the home user, as they are compatible with all systems.

SONY Vaio

Sony's answer to a sexy laptop, but check that this it is compatible with your contacts before purchasing. For example, it is not compatible with Macs. Yikes!

How to buy the right computer for you

The key thing to consider when buying is why are you buying? What do you want it to do and where will you have the computer? Is it an object of desire or an object of work?

There are essentially two different types of computer: the desktop and the laptop. Desktops tend to have a bigger screen, or flat monitor, and keyboard. Laptops have a plasma screen and keyboard that can fold into one.

The computer is made up of various parts that work together to perform the data processing. Three of the most important parts are: the *processor chip* (which does all the main processing of the data), the *memory* (which stores the data for the tasks that are currently being performed by your computer), and the *hard drive* (which stores all the data files on your computer).

Various things affect the performance of your computer, but two of the most standard factors are the amount of memory and the speed of the processor chip. Logically the more memory you have available the more tasks your computer can do. If you have a faster processor chip, then your computer can process these tasks more quickly.

You need to buy a computer that matches your use, and the best way to do this is to get the right software, i.e., the memory and information *package* that will suit you. Then decide on the outer shell. The most popular types are: personal computers (known as PCs), or Apple Macintosh (Macs).

Both the software that runs on your computer, and the data referred to as *files*, are stored in *folders*. Hence the slightly antiquated phrase *desktop publishing* as it was originally designed to be – like an all-in-one desktop with electronic paper, its folders, and all the stuff you need, just tidier.

The difference between PCs and Macs

In terms of hardware PCs and Macs are very similar; where they differ is in terms of their software or *operating system*. PCs use the Windows operating system, made by Microsoft, the latest version being Windows XP. Macs use the Macintosh OS operating system, made by Apple, the latest version being OS X (operating system number 10 – in Roman numerals).

Both PCs and Macs have very similar *types* of software for word processing, browsing the Internet, listening to music, watching DVDs. However, they run differently because the operating systems are different. You can also have Mac and PC versions of the same-name software; for example a Mac version of Microsoft's Internet Explorer browser, or a PC version of Apple's iTunes Music software.

If fully charged, laptops can run without electrical leads, but desktops do need the power supply to function. Obviously the final decision depends on your usage. If you want to take it everywhere with you, note to self: think of the handbag and travel/car situation. Can you manage this? Or are you happy to have it as an ornament on your desk?

Note: laptops are usually more expensive than desktops. Also there are significantly fewer Mac users than there are PC users, despite what the advertising tells you. Check who you are going to be contacting/working with and whether your computers will be on compatible systems before purchasing.

How to make it do what you want it to do

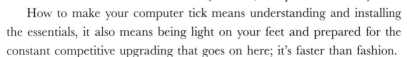

Once you have purchased your computer, plugged it in, and found the on button, you need to know what packages to select to help you proceed. A computer without its software is like a model without any clothes, except a lot less sexy.

How to make your computer tick means understanding and installing the essentials, it also means being light on your feet and prepared for the constant competitive upgrading that goes on here; it's faster than fashion.

What is Microsoft Office?

Microsoft Office is the real star of this section. It contains the programs Word, Excel, PowerPoint, and Outlook. The perfect all-in-one package. More specialist or advanced versions of Office (Microsoft Professional) contain:

Microsoft Access for databases.
Microsoft Project for project planning.
Microsoft Publishing for publishing projects.

Microsoft is now the universal software choice, so you would be crazy to get a machine without this application.

What is Windows?

This is an operating system that provides a layer between the computer hardware and the application you want to apply. In the early 1990s there was an unofficial truce and it was accepted that everyone would use Windows as the standard system. On the Mac the operating system is OS X, which is Apple's variant of Windows, but the real McCoy works, as well. With one operating system it is easier to set a standard and for everyone to be able to communicate, from programmers to the average user. What is so clever about Windows is that it lets you have more than one application open at a time. For example, in Windows you can write a document in Word, and then cut and paste it into an Excel table. You can chop and change your mind as you go along. Before Windows was invented this would have been impossible. Now you can jiggle everything together and have several items to play with.

What is Word?

Every time you type a piece of devastating prose, a high-powered memo, or a love letter, if it's done on a computer, this is most likely to be done in Word. It is basically the most common, easy-to-use system for writing. Thanks, Bill. It has different fonts, colors, layouts, and, best of all, spelling and grammar checks. It can cut and paste and wiggle stuff about on the screen to make sense of your scribbles.

Word Perfect was a package that tried to compete, but Word tweaked itself and, as yet, has failed to be toppled. Not using the Word package would be like writing in Cyrillic when the rest of the world has moved on to the Roman alphabet. Basically you would not be understood.

Turning on your computer

Check you don't have to put the plug in and turn on the mains first. If you do, have you?

Press the on button – this is usually easily identified as a large circular button with a symbol of a nearly closed circle and a vertical line cutting through it. Best way to remember this is to look for the key that is usually slightly isolated, and has what could be a cheap-looking graphic of a diamond ring.

Got it? Phew. Press it and you're in action.

Using a mouse with no squeak

One of the most useful devices on a computer and nothing to do with the rodent. Either incorporated into a machine, if a laptop, or an extra plugged in as part of a desktop.

The mouse was invented by Douglas Engelbart in 1964, and it changed the use of computers forever. It was the first user-friendly, nonscary addition to the hardware. It originally had a wooden shell and two metal wheels, and was nicknamed "mouse" as it had a "tail" that came out of the end. Engelbart also came up with an early version of Windows, but he didn't patent this so he couldn't cash in. Doh.

Mac mice respond with one click, and only have one button. But holding down the CNTL button and clicking the mouse is the equivalent to a right click on a PC mouse. The rest of the mice in the hardware industry have two clicks, left and right buttons, to action a command.

Moving the mouse around you can wiggle and twist your arrow or cursor to any part of the screen – a bit like a sparkler – and click on the option you require. Left click is to select and right click will offer you extra/refined choices within that group.

Move files with a touch of a button

In Windows it is more than simple to move a file. Using your mouse you can drag the file to its new location; or you can click and highlight desired section and then let it go, not forgetting to save the file in its new position. To drag, you place the pointer (arrow) over the item you want to move, click down, and hold down the left button. Then you move the pointer to the new position. When you release the button the item will be moved to this place. Easy.

PowerPoint

This was another of Bill Gates's brilliant ideas. It is the software for presentations. Gone are the days of clumsy slide shows and overhead projectors, now people opt for the Microsoft package PowerPoint to do their work justice.

You can download and compile text, images, and add graphs. These can then be presented using portable projectors, or printed, on acetate for projections, onto paper to bind into booklets, or e-mailed directly to the client.

PowerPoint is useful because it is compatible with other Windows packages so even the relative novice can insert pictures and text and compile professional-looking pitches, without having to hold hands with IT for the duration.

Some people also use the application DRAW, which is a basic, caveman computer-drawing package that allows you to put basic diagrams into PowerPoint, Excel, and Word with which you can build your online collage.

Use the printer

Well, you don't want to be sitting staring at a screen all day long, you'll end up with a crashing headache and feeling very cross-eyed.

The best thing to do is to print off your powerful prose and documents. To use a colored pen or highlighter is as effective and speedy as it is to edit on screen, if not more so.

First you need to purchase the appropriate printer. Make sure that you get one that is compatible with your computer; your dealer will be able to recommend what model to go for. Ink-jet printers are best for the home as they are nice and compact, while laser jets tend to be favored for the office.

Plug in the printer and then attach it to your computer using a USB lead. You may need to load driver instructions onto your PC with a CD or some software, but, just like building a Lego castle, the instructions should be fairly self-explanatory.

Once your printer is up and running, make sure that you keep the head clean and that your printer has a full color and a full black cartridge. You also want to get a good wad of paper that is the correct size and insert it into the feeder tray.

Do not ram too much paper into the machine; it will cause the printer to freak out and freeze on you. Also, do not click on too many jobs for it to do at one point; showing its human side, it will go into information overload and have a meltdown.

Instead calmly select the required document you want printed, check paper and cartridges and all connections. Click print.

You can print words and pictures, in color and black and white, depending on your printer's capability. Many new models also have the option to scan and photocopy, so keep your eye on new models on the market.

Scan a picture

My, how we have embraced the age of technology if you have gotten this far. Scanners are affordable, easy enough to operate, and now are compact enough that you can have them in your home.

Like a printer, a scanner is usually a separate piece of equipment that you plug into your computer. It can indeed be combined with your printer, but let's not complicate things too much initially.

First, ensure scanner is plugged in at the mains and connected to the computer. Place the image to be scanned facedown. It's similar to photocopying, but with this method you don't get a printout, you get the image straight on the screen of the computer.

Click on run and the scanner will start to make a grinding noise as it scans a copy of said paper. You need to stick with 2-D paper images – it will have trouble reading solid objects. So no sitting on the scanner.

Once your image is scanned, you have an option to view and an option to save.

If it is an image you want you should save it first as a jpeg. That way your computer will be able to recognize it as an image file. The jpeg can be saved into your hard-drive memory and be ready for you to access or send.

Scanners can read color as well as black and white, but black and white images use up less memory. In addition to creating jpegs or tiff image files, scanners are handy for transferring documents and signatures on to the screen.

Open a jpeg

Compressing the data into a jpeg basically reduces the number of megabytes (i.e. file size), making it easier to send and easier to download. Jpegs are the best form of sending a picture. The bit map will display on the screen what has been sent, using a simple application to decipher the digital information and translate what colors go where over the fine matrix mesh.

File extensions, which tell you what software data they are for, are only three letters long – so remember JPG, like Jean Paul Gaultier, is for images.

RGB (red green blue) are the three colors that the computer can understand and mix to form any shade or tone required.

A screen is approximately 1,000 by 800 points. The jpeg goes to your computer, via the Internet, compressing 2.5 Mbytes (1,000 x 800 x 3 points) – crikey – that can then explode onto the screen when you open it. It's a bit like cramming far too much stuff into a suitcase, getting it through customs, and when you open it up at the other end, after all the creases have fallen out, you have double what your companion managed to fit in theirs. Result.

Zip files on PCs are similar to the jpeg suitcase theory. These compress files, mainly text and PowerPoint files, into more manageable sending sizes. You simply drag the file and drop it into the zip file icon; it's a bit like all the ingredients condensed into one of Willy Wonka's Everlasting Gobstoppers. Macs use Stuffit, a rather disgusting name, so for that we try not to use it.

To attach a jpeg to an e-mail, simply click on the Add Attachment icon, open the appropriate folder and scroll down to the images/jpeg option, select, and send.

As jpegs compress images, MP3 compresses music so you can download or e-mail it, but more of this later.

Another little beaut is Adobe Acrobat

This is something you will stumble on fairly quickly. You can be sent attachments that are ".pdf." Acrobat's main characteristic is it can be used to send attachments you cannot modify, making it popular for government documents or legal databases. You can't tamper with the file, you can only view it. PDF is great for documents that you want people to read, view layout, and not fiddle with. To view Adobe attachments, download Adobe Acrobat Reader, which comes free on the Internet. The only way you can modify the files is if you purchase the Adobe Acrobat software for yourself. Shrewd.

How to survive a crash

Oh my God! You didn't! You forgot! Try not to panic. Most files can be recovered; in crashes and moments of catastrophe the work should be saved somewhere on the hard drive. Computers have a built-in autosave, so even if you don't save, they should do it for you every so often. The only problem is you will only find out after a crash how efficient and effective the software and its autosave is. Hmm, pull the plug and pray.

Due to fabulous technical advances crashes and bombs should happen less and less. But just as you are most likely to snag your tights or find your car breaks down when you are late, of course they still happen.

Generally speaking:

Bombs are due to software failure, malfunction, or error.
Crashes are more likely to be a fault in the hardware.

Both are a drag, not a drama.

If you don't have access to an IT department, or a computer whiz, the safest thing to do is to turn the machine off.

With a desktop you do this by turning off the power supply, so try pressing the on button off, but don't worry if this isn't having much effect – in addition you can turn off the power at the mains. Ha!

If you have a laptop you need to unplug it. You may also need to take the battery out of the computer. Even if you do this for only a few seconds, you will cut the power supply and stop the freeze flow before returning the battery and its energy source again.

Count to thirty – ten is not enough for the technical beast – and turn it on again.

As you won't have been able to shut the computer down in the correct way, closing all the files and so forth, the computer will have a bit of a moan at you, and then will run its own recovery/check-up and correct any faults. It's like it's giving itself a quick maintenance and tweaking any of the damaged parts so it is all ship-shape again. If only all inanimate objects, and others, could do this. Once it has gone through the tests, it is back to where you were, almost.

Save everything

This may seem obvious, but leave nothing to chance. Why lose a masterpiece?

The way to quick save is to press the Control button and the S key whilst midflow, but it's far safer, and more effective, to save it properly.

To do this use the mouse to click and open File (top left-hand of your tool bar), scroll mouse down to Save As, then you can name the file, check it is in the right location, and then confirm the save. It's a bit like checking your credit card tab before you sign.

Safe mode

Sometimes Windows does its start-up in "safe mode." What this means is that if your machine has crashed it should have preserved what you were working on and you will be able, once the machine has been rebooted, to carry on. You may have limited access in safe mode because while it's repairing itself, access to external components such as printer, CD, and other modems is restricted. In safe mode it doesn't allow any "foreign" invasion, such as a computer virus, until it feels the core is stable again.

How to find and delete viruses

Unlike the human variety, these are taken *very* seriously. They are more than a case of computer sniffles. A virus can disable a computer, wipe out its memory, and then infect all of your address book and spread the nightmare to them – and how mortifying would that be? There are preventative measures that you can take.

You must install an antivirus program *immediately*. A computer without one is like a house with no front door. You are asking for uninvited visitors. If you don't Scotch-guard suede, a puddle is the inevitable next step. An antivirus application is like installing a miniarmy of microtroops to patrol your cyber post box.

The most effective antivirus program on the market is by Norton. Norton sends you weekly updates of new viruses, so your antivirus program can recognize them, a bit like the penicillin method. It is easy to install and will zap any trouble on sight.

Most common viruses are sent via e-mail. Hotmail and most of the e-mail servers offer virus protection, but sometimes the rascals are just too clever for these.

Viruses in your hard drive or software are rare nowadays; if you get infected it usually comes from an outside source.

Viruses are less common in Macs, but you still have to be très careful.

E-mail inboxes are the most vulnerable point as e-mails are received from all kinds of servers and addresses, so it is here you need to be most on your guard.

If you get an e-mail from an address you don't know, ring Alarm Bell One. If there is an attachment on such an e-mail above Alarm Bell Two should be ringing. Delete it. NOW. Opening the attachment could unleash the virus. Look at it this way; if it is clean and important they can call you or send again.

Even so, you will find your inbox increasingly clogged up with spam (cyber term for junk e-mails). Best policy is: if in doubt, delete. And don't forget to empty your trashcan/recycle bin frequently. Be as hygienic as you are in the home.

How to understand the World Wide Web

When I took office, only high-energy physicists had heard of what is called the worldwide web. Now even my cat has its own page.
—*Bill Clinton*

The story goes that a group of academics wanted to discuss ideas and theories and so they started to compile a database. As it spread they asked more people for their ideas and the database grew and grew. Essentially the world wide web is a result of the world's largest chain letter.

Not only did it slash encyclopedia sales and end the tyrannical reign of librarians, it made access to all subjects available to anyone with Internet access. Search engines such as *www.google.com* or *www.answers.com* are good starting points for any questions, and *www.build-your-own-computer-tips.com* is good for techno worries.

You can also use the Internet for video-conferencing, downloading music, and researching images, but try not to get too ahead of yourself too soon. Remember: Rome wasn't built in a day.

Who invented the Web?

"My dear Christian! You've made the world look new!" gushed *Bazaar* editor-in-chief Carmel Snow after Dior's 1947 New Look presentation. Things are a little less fluffy in techno.

You can't credit the invention of the web to one person. Key to its success are names such as Vint Cerf and Bob Khan, who defined Internet Protocol (IP). The advent of the domain name service is also worth noting and this was standardized by Paul Mockapetris.

The World Wide Web (or W3) itself was invented by Tim Berners Lee, an Englishman based in America. Apparently other names he was considering were Mine of Information (MOI) or The Information Mine (TIM), but thought both were too egocentric.

How to download from the 'Net

Er, what?

This is the process of translating a file from one computer or server to your computer.

As with most things, practice makes perfect. The first few times you rode your bike you probably fell off; at least with the 'Net all you should lose is time and researched information. No physical damage.

There are lots of ways to download from the web and, a bit like a child in a candy store, once you get the taste for it you will be back for more, eager to try different sites. If a site has a file to download, it will normally be indicated by the underlined word "download," often written in blue. Click on this (you should see a pointy hand leading you to do this anyway) and the computer will either download and save the file, or download and run the file itself.

Cut and paste is the old faithful chewy toffee way to send information you have downloaded. PDF is another way (Portable Document Format). A flashy designer fizzer. Adobe is a flying saucer, i.e., great for images and color. MP3 is the licorice allsorts for music downloading.

Downloading can include manuals and instructions, as well as images, graphs and statistics, games, and "wallpapers" (screensavers and jazzy backdrops). You can, if you are clever, download music, video clips, and art. But be careful as they usually make you download a whole host of ads to confuse you and you'll be online for hours.

Sometimes, to access video clips or music, you are prompted to download an application that will make this possible. Follow the instructions and it should be straightforward. If you have Windows most things should download with ease and play in format, but other times you will need applications such as Quick Time or Real Player. If it gets too laborious, ask yourself if you really need to have the new Miss Piggy dance routine, or whatever it is, downloaded.

How to create bookmarks

Once you have found a good Web site you will want to come back to it again and again. Rather than having to type in the full address and faff about finding it, you can create "bookmarks" on the Web, to which you add your favorite. You do this by selecting your chosen website and adding it to the Favorites option, which is found in the toolbar along the top of the screen. You click on Favorites and the option Add to Favorites will appear. Bookmarking means that each time you log onto the Internet, it will throw up a few old faithfuls rather than making you trawl through the entire World Wide Web. If only it was that easy getting dressed.

If you are a creature of habit, or like regular updates, get a site or newsletter mailed to you. This is like a subscription, but because it's the Internet it's likely to be free. Find the website you wish to get regular updates from, be it shopping, house hunting, or the latest news headlines. Usually they offer a mailing service if you simply follow instructions and insert your own details.

How to have fun on the Web

The web isn't all technical technical – there is shopping and fashion, too!

Best sites include:

www.amazon.com: for books
www.eluxury.com: for designer clothing

www.ebay.com: for an online vintage bidding fest (see below)
www.fashionweekdaily.com: for a daily dose of fashion news
www.google.com: for any burning unanswered question
www.bluefly.com: for the latest fashions and exclusive online must-haves
www.style.com or *www.vogue.com*: for the best reviews and runway shots.

Then there are all the design houses, for example, *www.dior.com,* and magazines online. Hours of fun and no need to dress up, unless the online dating gets serious. . . . For further technical or DIY tips, try *www.howstuffworks.com.* And for the ultimate in luxury and whimsical indulgence, why not join the chic online concierge service to the stars, *www.quintessentially.com.*

 # *How to eBay*

The worldwide flea market where you can scour the globe and every stall and not leave your home, eBay is the fastest-growing way to buy and sell what you thought no one but you would ever want, which is especially helpful after Christmas. As well as uncovering treasure, there is a lot of rubbish to trawl through, but the site is seriously addictive.

Before you can even browse you have to register your name, e-mail, as well as mailing address. If you are using a hotmail or a free e-mail address, you will have to give your credit card details at this time too. This is not to say that they do not welcome window shoppers, they just don't humor time wasters. Do not lie about any of your information; what is the point? If you order anything it won't ever reach you. If you are searching for shoes you will find it has thousands for you to view, so try to refine what you are looking for, from high heels and designer shoes, to Manolo Blahniks, and see what it comes back with.

If you see a pair you like, they look good in the photo, and they are the right size, click on User Feedback. This is where you can look at the seller's history as all eBayers get rated. If they have lots of positive comments and happy customers, great – place a bid. If, however, they have never delivered, lied about what they are sending, or been a general headache, move on to another product; you don't need the hassle.

eBay is the leading online auction site as it is regulated and all users are monitored, so you cannot rig auctions or bump up prices.

The thing about eBay that is slightly frustrating is that when you see something you have to bid, and risk either not getting it, or getting so competitive you bid over the odds. But don't worry, you do not have to stay glued to the machine to monitor any rival bids – you can opt to vote by proxy, which means you log in the maximum you will pay and the clever old computer will up your bid to try to help you be the winner. And likewise, if you are the seller, there are ways to protect yourself. You register, photograph, and add a description of your product and you can place a reserve price, so you will not sell if you get less than the minimum you think it is worth.

Like gambling and other bets, there are, of course, more complex options and competitive bids, such as Dutch auctions, where you can bid on multiple quantities. But start off with one pair of shoes, calculate delivery and postage, see if the product arrives, it fits, and you are happy before going crazy.

How to use e-mail

You use a telephone network, Internet or broadband, and your computer will send written messages to different systems. Providing you have the correct e-mail protocol (in English: e-mail service) you can send e-mail instantaneously anywhere in the world, for the cost of a normal boy-length telephone call (and you know how brief and cheap those are). Internet cafés have become a sight as common as Starbucks. They have sprung up all over the world, allowing gap-year travelers and roaming wanderers to keep in touch with those of us stuck at home, and tell us what a fabulous time they are having.

The first e-mail was sent in 1971 by Ray Tomlinson. Before this you could only send messages to users sharing the same machine, so Post-it notes would have been more appropriate. His e-mail was a breakthrough worthy of a full-choir chorus of Handel's *Messiah*'s "Hallelujah!" He worked out how to send messages to other machines on the Internet using the @ sign to identify who the receiver was. E-mails are the computer's answer to the text message, and the most exciting invention since Alexander Graham Bell's first ring (he was the guy who invented the telephone in 1876).

We've come a long way since then. Now broadband is a popular option when using e-mail or the Internet as you can be on the telephone and able to send and receive e-mails without the whole put-the-phone-down-dial-up-Internet-connect drama. It uses the same dial-up network, but it allows you greater speed and memory capacity. Telephone lines break down the message into signals and intonation, and send at 50K images per second. Without sounding too much like an ad, broadband is able to send them at 1 million per second – that is twenty times as fast as the dial-up method! The faster it's sent, the more, surely, you can receive!

What happens when you send an e-mail is a message travels down the phone line. It is sent into space and is delivered to the cyber address of the recipient. You can send an e-mail to anyone in the world, providing you have the correct address for them. And unlike posted mail and parcels, each e-mail can be sent to anyone, anywhere in the world, same price, and arrive at the same second.

This is what the address format looks like: *name@address.location*

In the example *jane@fashion.co.uk* the e-mail is going to Jane, who is at Fashion, a company in the UK (@ is read as "at").

You can often decipher and decode where the mail has come from:

.com usually is an American-based company/address

.it is Italy

.fr is France

.jp is Japan

.nl is Holland

.de is Germany

.org is a nonprofit-making organization/charity in the U.S.

.gov is a government department or agency in the U.S.

.net originally means that this is connected to a large internal network

.tv was an attempt to indicate sites suitable only for broadband (lots of large content, movies, images, and music), but it hasn't caught on massively yet.

Getting an e-mail account

Nowadays there are many ways to get an e-mail account. The general way is to go to the website of your chosen service provider, select the option to "set up an e-mail account," and follow the instructions. Service providers can be of the specific communications provider type (TimeWarner, AT&T, MCI, etc.) or the more general Hotmail/Yahoo/Lycos kind, which you access via Internet Explorer.

Send and receive an e-mail

Sonnets and scribbled love letters seem to have become a thing of the past. But not to worry, you can still be wooed; and now that you can get e-mails instantaneously from all the corners of the globe, you can have a suitor in every city. Make HOTmail live up to its name. Imagine how it would have improved Romeo and Juliet's chance of a long-distance thing.

Have a package or application so you can connect to the server and send your message. If you don't have broadband you will need to have a modem that will connect your computer to the phone line so that your message can get posted onto the "server" – the cyber-space postal system – sorted and delivered to the relevant party.

There are two ways to send your e-mail. One is using the Internet browser, which is accessed via the website, e.g., Hotmail, Yahoo, AOL. The other option is to use an e-mail application such as Outlook Express, where you write your e-mails, then log on – dial up – to send the mail and receive any posts.

To send and receive you simply have to locate the icon of an envelope on your computer screen and click on it. This will open Outlook Express, or whatever your mail access is. On Macs, Quick Mail can be identified by a circled Q, or by a symbol resembling a paper airplane.

Click on Send and Receive box and, as the name implies, you will send and receive your mail.

The most important requirement to send or receive an e-mail is that you know the address you wish to contact. Well that, and also to have your own e-mail account and address from which you can send and receive.

Set up group e-mail

Okay, so you know how to send a one-on-one e-mail, but sometimes you want to send the same e-mail to more than one person. This can be either business, and you cover yourself by sending it to all and sundry, or when you are hosting celebrations and have a lot of people to invite.

First, write the main message, a snappy subject line, and add attachment, if desired.

Click on the To button.

Write in first e-mail address. Even better, you may have saved this in your address book. (This is an easy and sensible thing to do with friends and regulars in your inbox. If you have a name added to your address book you only need enter the first letter of the name and the computer will suggest possible saved e-mail addresses. You can then click on appropriate name and send.)

For a second name/recipient, click once again on the To line of your e-mail, and another line should appear below. You can now continue the entire process until you have included all the required readers/recipients.

If you need regularly to e-mail the same group of people, e.g. friends or work colleagues, you can save the group of names and title it. That way, when you click on To you can select Friends and all their e-mail addresses should pop into the To box. Voilà!

CC: This is the place you put an e-mail address when you want someone to see the e-mail, but it is just for their information, and not addressed to them. You also want your recipient to see that you have included them. So it's a good idea to CC your boss when you are getting into hot water and you want to keep yourself in the clear.

BCC (Blind CC): This is where you place the address of someone you want to see the e-mail, but not let the recipient see that you have included them in the e-mail. Cunning. BCC does not show up in the recipient's inbox. Well, it shouldn't – but don't take any chances by saying anything too inflammatory.

Have you got gmail or iChat?

From the search engine *www.google.com* comes gmail, their free webmail service to compete with hotmail.com. In addition to your normal inbox, outbox, and sent box, gmail will add a bit of thought and help. When you click on Reply all your previous e-mails attached to this "conversation" will be shown, so you can have all the information at hand. It also offers to scan your e-mails and display sidebars with relevant links to web pages on subjects you are discussing, or will send you alerts when there is news from your favorite writer or pop star.

If you own a Mac, you will have iChat. This enables your instant messaging, similar to e-mails or MSN, but in addition to the text popping up on the screen you can go audio or visual (providing you have a camera or the inclination to use isight). This is a free way of using the Web to chat face-to-face with friends. But fear not if you don't have this option, as you can also register for Skype. Simply give your details to *www.skype.com* and it will enable you to talk through your computer and save the burning hole in your pocket that is your phone bill.

How to send an attachment

Write your e-mail as normal, "Dear Ethel, blah, blah, blah . . ." and in your cover letter mention there is an attachment with your e-mail (this way the receiver will know to look out for one, and will be able to contact you if none arrives, or they can't open it). A paperclip symbol on the e-mail means that you have successfully attached your document.

When sending attachments consider the recipient, and how long it will take to download. If it's over 1MB divide it into more manageable chunks – otherwise the receiver will be trying to fit the equivalent of a grand piano through a letterbox.

Click on the Add Attachment or Insert File box and your recently used files should open. Select relevant file(s) and select Choose, click, and then send mail as normal.

The technique for opening attachments varies on each set-up, but you can easily identify them on your e-mail as they are normally represented by a paperclip symbol.

An e-mail is basically nothing more than a cover letter, so the attachment is the main document. In document form you can control the font and the layout of the text, whereas in an e-mail it can get jumbled into a standard nonfancy format.

Attachments allow you to send pictures, spreadsheets, and text that are not corrupted by the system.

Word is fairly universal and successful as an attachment format, but some computers cannot translate certain files. What a computer will do is look at the type of file it is receiving and identify it by the letters appearing after the full stop. It will then automatically apply what it understands to be the correct decoder, for example: .doc – text file, .jpg – image file. (For more about jpegs, see earlier.)

Many computers can manage without all file extensions to open most attachments. They "ad lib" just like we would, but in a technical way. One file Macs do not recognize, however, and never will is .exe, which is a Windows application, so avoid that one.

If you are sent an unrecognized file to a Mac, ask for it either to be e-mailed to someone you know who has a PC, or sent as Cut and Paste.

Love Cut and Paste

This is great for when, however many times you click on the Attachment symbol, it will not "open sesame." Never mind. It may be either a hoax or a virus, so delete, or if you really do want to read the text, play the game, or see the photo of your friend's latest conquest, call them and ask them to send it again, either in a different format or as a Cut and Paste.

To perform your own Cut and Paste, simply click on Edit in the file you want to send, scroll down your options, and choose to Select All. The text should now all be highlighted. Click on Copy, and then move the pointer into an e-mail for the intended. Here you select "Paste" (in the e-mail software, not the original one). The entire content will be then "pasted" into the body of the e-mail – some of your clever layout may be lost, but at least it will be readable.

How to have netiquette

This is e-mail etiquette.

When writing your e-mails always think of how your e-mail will read, how your voice will sound, and how your words come across.

E-mails are most often written in a very colloquial, informal way, but this does not mean you should forget to punctuate, or neglect good grammar and spelling.

Think of your intonation and your key points, and try not to waffle. Anyway, your wrists will get tired and achy if you type too much.

CAPITALS MEANS THAT YOU ARE SHOUTING!

Swear words and expletives can get stopped by scans and company firewalls so are worth avoiding, especially in the e-mail title. Think of other ways to express your rage.

it may be trendy to ignore capitals and write everything in lower case, but – Pah! Show them you have had a proper education. Similarly slang, such as "C U 2morrow," is as unbearable as fingernails on a blackboard. All "emoticons" (e-mail text abbreviations) should be banned.

CAPITALS and crappy punctuation not only make things harder to read, but could make it harder for you to be taken seriously.

You have a space key, so use it. Edit your choice of words. There is no space restriction so lay things out nicely.

Always use the spell check. It is one of the greatest and most unappreciated inventions ever. (But also always check that your spell check uses the same language as the one that you have written in . . . American English and English English are different.)

Finally, think twice before you hit Send and Receive. Re-read your mail.

Never send poison mails, they will come back to haunt you. Never, ever, join in on a chain e-mail; you will never win millions, and you may have just opened Pandora's box to viruses and all sorts of trouble.

Send e-mails safely

No. E-mails are not dangerous. Mostly you will only receive e-mails addressed to you, from names you know; junk mail and other nuisances are easy to delete. Chat rooms on the Internet require you to be careful. The age of chivalry is not totally extinct, but close. As the Internet and e-mail get ever more popular there are increasing horror stories of people assuming fake names in chat rooms, or sending viruses. Rule of thumb:

if an e-mail is from a name you don't recognize, or expect, don't open the attachment as this could be a virus. Likewise, if you meet someone in a chat room, err *slightly* on the cautious side. Don't agree to elope to Timbuktu, or give them access to your life savings, until you have at least met (in public place first time) and checked they are who they say they are.

Is Big Brother watching you?

Before you go into extraordinary details of a hot affair, how you deal with internal politics, or exactly how you got your promotion by demonstrating a few pole-dancing techniques, a word to the wise: office e-mails can be monitored and tapped into by internal systems and God only knows who. If you want to keep your private life PRIVATE, try code, Hotmail or discretion. Politicians have crumbled, marriages have hit the rocks, and faces have gone more than a healthy shade of red when secrets have been spilled.

How to sit in front of your screen

Posture, posture, posture.

Don't sit slouched over your computer all day; you will either end up looking like Quasimodo or have dreadful neck/shoulder/back problems.

Make sure that your screen is at eye level and the keyboard is around waist height. A curse of the laptop is that it causes either slouching shoulders or eye strain. Another tip to remember with a laptop if using it for more than thirty minutes, is to invest in wristbands because it does get scaldingly hot to the touch; and never balance it on your lap for same reason.

Back to the positioning: elbows should be tight to the body, shoulders back, and wrists resting lightly on the keyboard. Ideally you should have your feet flat on the floor or on a small footstool, to ensure your back can remain in a straight upright position. Some people place cushions behind their lower back for additional support. Another good idea is to make sure that you have a supportive and comfortable chair, at the correct height.

Health and safety logic suggests that desktops are better than laptops for greater use as you stoop less to use these. Whatever you use, never sit for too long at a computer without stretching or taking small breaks; however drastic the deadline, you will be crippled, and that really isn't chic.

Deskercises

Once the computer is set up you can avoid locking your shoulders, and visits to the chiropractor, by doing these simple exercises.

Shoulder shrug: Help relieve neck and shoulder tension build-up. Sitting straight on your chair, roll your shoulders back, pulling the shoulder blades together and puffing your chest out. Roll shoulders in clockwise motion then repeat in a counterclockwise motion.

Head turns: Tilt head from side to side, left to right, ear to shoulder. You can also roll your head, tilting head right back to relieve any developing neck tightness.

Don't forget your fingers! : Stretch your hands out to their fullest span. Every now and then imagine you are playing a quick couple of piano scales, albeit in midair, to relax fingers right through to their tips.

If anyone in the office looks friendly you can ask if they want to give you a shoulder massage.

Culture

Books about computers (that are genuinely interesting to read):

Microserfs by Douglas Coupland (HarperCollins/Regan Books, 1996).
Eerily accurate view of Silicon Valley – and it name-checks Microsoft. Guess Bill Gates was just too busy to sue. It is now being made into a film by Universal.

Artemis Fowl by Eoin Colfer (Miramax, 2002).
Artemis Fowl is to computers and codes what Harry Potter is to wizardry, but he is using his technopowers for evil, world domination, and fights against fairies. He's only twelve when the saga of his ingenious decoding and criminal career starts. This is also being given the Hollywood treatment by Miramax and Robert De Niro's company, Tribeca.

Truly crap computer-inspired movies

Weird Science: downloading perfect woman from Internet.

You've Got Mail: Meg Ryan and Tom Hanks cheese.

The Net: Sandra Bullock in bikini using laptop; she must have burned her legs.

Truly great computer-inspired movies

2001: A Space Odyssey: HAL set the world's expectations for computers.

The Matrix: think about it. The Matrix is the Internet of the future.

AI: or are computers with emotion one step too far?

How to Climb the Career Ladder

Mr. Smithers picked me for my motivational skills.
Everyone always says they have to work twice as hard when
I'm around.

—*Homer Simpson, (Dan Castellaneta) in* The Simpsons

How to deal with office dramas

Now you know how to deal with the equipment, you will be eminently more employable than you were before. The office is not only a way to make your mark on the world, to fulfill your ambitions and shine, it can be sociable and fun – on good days. An office can be somewhere you go to, or can be at home; that depends on the job. But if you are working from home, try to keep all your work in one part of the home and discipline yourself to work designated time slots, just like you would do in an office. "Conquer the career in the day, and be the life and soul of the party at night" is an even more important rule for those working from home; you must not forget to stop. You do not have to work extra hours just because you are doing it from home, but likewise you have to be your own boss and make sure you get the work done. If starting on the career ladder try to learn in an office environment.

They say never mix business with pleasure, but that all depends on you; it can certainly help encourage you to get to work on time if there's a chance of a message in your inbox, or a frisson to enjoy in the elevator. If you work in a très specialized area, such as brain surgery or mushrooms, most likely you will have interests in common with your colleagues. But as with all things, a note of caution: don't let a passionate love affair eclipse glittering career opportunities. Nor should you ever succumb to sexual harassment in the workplace. Behave professionally to others and in a way that you wish to be treated yourself.

How to get a job

To fund the lifestyle of an independent woman you need to hold down a job, unless you've been born into royalty. It may be nice to be born with a big silver spoon, but there are few things as satisfying as earning your own keep, knowing the value of money, and achieving your own goals. Honestly.

To choose what job you would be able to excel at, first you have to write your résumé/CV. This will list all your achievements, education, and awards. Then think of what you enjoy, what you are good at, and where you see yourself working. Is it in an office or in a field? Target what it is that you are looking for and tailor your CV to fit.

You should aim to make your CV as impressive and as economic with the truth as possible. This is not to say lie, no, a CV is the paper version of an advertisement, and you have one side of A4 to sell sell sell yourself.

If first impressions count then this is what you have to concentrate on making irresistible. List previous jobs and responsibilities. Employers like to see that you have stayed in a position for a certain length of time, so do not list all the baby-sitting jobs that you have ever done. Likewise, even if you did work in Starbucks for three years every Thursday evening, think: will this be relevant to getting onto a law conversion course?

A successful CV will lead to an interview, and for this you have to wear your most sensible and executive outfit, have a knowledge of current affairs, know why their company is perfect for you, and be able to sell yourself – rather than sell your soul/body. Go to interviews pressed, punctual, and prepared. Ask as many questions as you have fired at you. Size up the competition as much as the company and scope for promotion.

Once the job is yours, and you have secured the regular pay packet, the climb on the career ladder can begin. When you have been hired you can start to put all your great ideas into play, inspire teams, and develop leadership skills, as well as listen and learn. Nothing can beat firsthand experience.

How to be very busy doing nothing

Obviously you want to come across as very hardworking, very keen, and very efficient, and very often you are. But we all have days when we need to go slow, or have other things on our mind, so do not overdo it in your enthusiasm to impress. Look too capable and you will never have any you time. Don't get yourself lumbered with so many tasks you have to move your pillow and sleeping bag under your desk. A job is to fund a lifestyle, not eclipse it. Work to the best of your ability, get the job done, even take work home, but do not let it consume you.

Keep your desk very tidy, and constantly keep papers sorted, Post-it notes updated, pens with lids on, and stationery drawer full. Chaos is time-wasting and stressful. File papers into "to do" and relevant subject piles. Being organized now saves time in later panics.

To keep noisy people away from your desk, so you have enough time to paint your nails properly, try tutting as you shuffle paper. Mutter under your breath (audibly) one-liner clues such as "Oh, I've got so much to do," "Phhh, won't be able to take any time for lunch today – might have to order in, snowed under." They should take the hint and leave you alone. But if you think they haven't been witnessing the Oscar-winning performance of the "stress" you are under, you can *always* resort to an "emergency call."

"Hi, you know I hate making personal calls from work [*ting*, first gold star], but listen, I have no time [*ting*], I am swamped. I am sorry I can't see you tonight [*ting*]. I have to put my work first [*ting*]." That is a four-star perform-ance, top marks. Not only is it a great way to dump someone, but it will raise impressed eyebrows in the office. So what if you left this message on your answering machine at home? Dress for the job you want, and act like it's already yours. Use Melanie Griffith in *Working Girl* as your inspiration.

How to surf the Web unnoticed in the office

Now the office is aware that they need to leave you to get on with your heavy workload, you can get back to surfing the 'Net for your ideal minibreak or miniskirt. Well, why shouldn't you? Being a computer whiz you e-mailed in over the weekend, and spent Sunday doing research; call it time in lieu.

But just in case anyone decides to come snooping 'round your side of the office, have a few documents open onscreen – thank God you mastered Windows – that you are genuinely meant to be working on. Also locate a very dry, official-looking Web page; that way, if anyone wanders just a little bit too close, you can click on the scary "hardworking page" and shoot them a look of utter contempt that they thought you would be doing anything other than the task at hand. *They* might have time for tea breaks, but you most certainly do not.

As with e-mails (see *Send and receive an e-mail*, page 228), be slightly careful how much of your soul you unburden on the 'Net as big corporate companies tend to have hard drives on backup. If you are plotting to spit in your boss's tea, perhaps plan it via Hotmail, which cannot be detected on the company scan system. Perhaps any shopping should be delivered to your home, unless you need to do a try-on session and get second opinions. Argue that at least you will be in the office, able to answer questions and continue empire building, as well as model. Brains as well as beauty.

How to work on two hours' sleep

Presuming that this is a self-inflicted problem and you cannot pull a sickie, you will have to don the shades and stagger into the office, especially if you threw the party or are the boss. It is likely that all the best gossip will occur on the one day you are off, and you wouldn't want to miss this, particularly if people are going to be talking about you. If you are planning a crazy evening, a Friday is the best night – as you can then languish in a semicomatosed state for the rest of the weekend and not lose any pay. If this is *not* how things turn out, then you have to suffer the consequences.

As soon as you arrive, state that you had the most dreadful food poisoning last night, and that you have only staggered in because you are a conscientious worker, but you need everyone to be very, *very* quiet and someone to get you a coffee – fast.

If you have only just landed that morning from an international jet-set mission, albeit a holiday, and are cruelly expected into the office, go via your home to freshen up first. There are always delays at airports, so that should buy you a few hours; just remember not to turn your mobile on and give the game away. By the time you get into the office, have got your coffee, gone through your mail, voicemails, and e-mails it should be at least lunchtime and you'll be able to coast through the afternoon without biting too many heads off.

Do not book meetings for days such as these; you might physically be there, but being able to make a decision is unlikely. If you know you have a hellish week coming up, try to get an early night.

Note: you have no excuse not to come in the morning after the Christmas party, everyone will know that you were the one who ended up singing karaoke on the desk and went home wearing only a sprig of mistletoe. Christmas is a time to forgive, forget, and be photographed . . .

How to create a filing system

When you start at an office you should be shown around, and as well as working out where the photocopier is, and who sits where, you should find out what sort of filing system they use, whatever your position. With the world domination of computers, filing is becoming more and more obsolete – hooray! – but filing systems are still very useful, and sorting papers is a great way to fill whole days when you don't want to think, and occupy interns without them causing too much damage. It is always handy to keep hard copies of crucial information to hand.

First, decide what needs to be filed. Does this need to happen daily, weekly, or monthly? Then how you will divide it – alphabetically by surname or first name, by company, by job number, by case, by what? Select what you need to put in each file. Find a filing cabinet and categorize all the files, then start to sort. In the first file, put a "how to use" guide to your filing system, even add a contents list of where stuff is sorted, so if someone else is searching they have a slight chance of locating the information they need.

The more efficiently things are stored the easier they are to find, and the more time you get to spend on the more fun and creative things. Similarly, try to organize files on your computer, and divide into easily accessible sections, so that you can find letters, documents, and so forth, however cryptic the file name.

How to use the office equipment

If you are working in an office try not to put yourself in the position of Little Miss I Know How to Use All the Office Tools. Executives don't, they delegate. This is what you should aspire to; you are not aiming to be general dogsbody, but future president – but keep that to yourself. Ambition can scare some people. While being shown how to do the faxing, or admin, just you watch how a great boss will glaze over so that they are never asked to perform this task again, but will find someone else to do it. Bingo. Learn from them.

Treat every time you approach the photocopier as if it is your first time. There is no point learning and trying to remember how to use these machines because just as you have cracked it, it will do something temperamental, break down, or they will upgrade to a new model just as you have sussed where the on/off button is. IT departments were invented for a reason. Similarly, color and complex enlargements or scanning jobs mean a visit to an expert, and could coincide nicely with an extended lunch break.

You can have a casual relationship with the photocopier – press green and it goes, select paper size, how to enlarge, and how to do more than one copy – but anything else, you want to do slowly and manually. Don't attempt to photocopy a million pages on double-sided, do it one at a time and feed it through. If they need a million done double-sided surely you can be utilized more effectively? Give this to someone else to do for you, unless you want a nice little errand outside to get some fresh air.

Another worthwhile fact to absorb is that tights, fabrics, and nonpaper objects melt and burn if fed through the photocopier. Only experiment to see what works and what does not when your boss is not about, or more to the point when no one will see it's you who's jammed the machine again.

Changing cartridges on printers (and worse still, opening the photocopier) should be avoided at all costs; you could not only break the machine, but have inks explode all over your smart office look. Try to do something else to keep you busy and avoid being the one to have to change the cartridge. You can always be the one to volunteer to call IT and then swiftly get on with something else.

Send a fax

Now that there is e-mail, this is a fairly outmoded form of communication, but you just never know. It is still favored when signatures are needed to be sent through in a hurry, or you want to decorate your note with hand-illustrated hearts and kisses. Get the number and correct dialing code, write a cover note with clear name and number of pages they should expect. The trick here is to know what way up the paper should be – facedown or up? Check the machine for directions. Dial the number and press send. Wait for it to chug out the other end, print a confirmation, and all is done and dusted.

The joys of headed paper

When you are printing letters that you need to coordinate landing on your headed paper, make sure that all the room knows this and no one else selfishly hits print when you are about to go, or they will end up with your headed paper and you will have done a misfire.

If you are in a rush and are not sure which way up paper should go, put the paper in facedown, logo at the top, underneath facedown logo at bottom, underneath faceup logo at top, underneath faceup logo at bottom, and hit print four times. One is bound to work. But just try to work out what the correct way is when in less of a hurry as it causes masses of recycling.

As for typing on envelopes, this is fine if you have a typewriter – but using a computer and printer requires extraordinary levels of brilliance. Instead why not use envelopes with windows and line up the letter so that you print the address on the letter? Or you can opt to print the addresses on sticky labels and attach while you make a few calls. But never forget that a hand-written envelope still has a lot of charm and character.

How to meet a deadline

When you are asked to do something, write a brief, do a job, always ask when the deadline is. Forward planning. You have to know what the date is that you are working to. Do you have ages, or do you have a day? And if you have ages, does this mean you are expected to do lots of research? Do not leave things till the last minute; the only one who will suffer will be you.

Draw up lists and timetables and, just like when you were studying for exams, set yourself realistic goals of when you can get things done by. If you need to interview people or go places, allow extra time. Don't talk about how much work you have to do, get on and organized about it. Get yourself a year planner and stick it above your desk: that should scare you into reality and action, if nothing else. Do not arrange to go out the night before something is due, as inevitably you will have had a week of constant interruptions and you will need every remaining minute you can get your hands on.

How to get a pay raise without sleeping with the boss

If you feel that you are working far too hard, and they are getting more from you than you are from them, assess how realistic it would be to get a pay raise.

First, consider your boss. Are they friendly or psychotic? Are they always in a good mood, or do they sit with a black thundercloud above their head? Do they have any weaknesses? If they have always had a soft spot for you, now would be the time to be teacher's pet. But if they hate every pore in your body and are jealous of your youth, beauty, and talent, then you don't need a raise, you need a new job.

Prepare your argument. Assess your position and contribution to the company. Are you being challenged or has your degree only gotten you as far as the kettle? Be assertive. Know your worth. Ask to speak to them, alone. Do it either first thing or at the end of the day, but choose a moment when you are not all frantically busy. Present your case in such a way that they cannot say no. If they do say no and they plan to continue exploiting you, then you are laboring under false pretenses. You should realize that you will never get promoted or treated well here. It is time to start looking elsewhere and preparing your letter of resignation.

How to resign

Ideally, resign with another job already lined up; this way you can be smug, vitriolic, and free all at the same time. If, however, life has become too unbearable, leap out of the frying pan anyway; there is always something better around the corner. Think long term, and about yourself and your career rather than staying loyal to something that is stifling your talent. Get a new job and let the past become a distant memory. When you break free, you will wish you had done it months ago. What are you gaining from the torture? After moments of agony it will be over, and once again the world will be your oyster.

Remind yourself a job is not for life, it is for money, to live life, to learn and be challenged. Once your quality of life has degenerated to you being a gibbering wreck, curled up in bed all weekend dreading Monday, it is time to consider your options. Check how many days' notice your contract requires you to serve, if you have one, or can you take any owing holidays?

A letter of resignation can be in many formats. Check out *www.google.com* and ask them for some harsh resignation letters, if you lack inspiration. But it is probably best just to think of writing these, rather than sending total fireballs. The best kind are the short, polite, to-the-point versions. After all, you may still need the company to provide a reference.

How to fire someone

If you find yourself in a position where work is unbearable but you cannot leave – it's your company/department – you have to locate the source of the pain. Sadly, if there is a bad apple, you've got to get rid of it before it rots the others and causes mutiny in the ranks. Take the troublesome person aside in your office or, better still, out for coffee on neutral territory. Discuss the matter privately with them. Tell them how unhappy you are with them, reason with them, talk about their work/their attitude, and see whether they think they are working well, and try to work out *what* is the cause of the problem. Go with examples of their horrible behavior, and a few past events. Then if they have run out of chances, give them a month's notice, or pause and give them the opportunity to beg or resign themselves. Go on, be nice, let them save face slightly.

But if they have committed a crime, theft, or a serious offense, then you do not need to do them any favors. Get them out. Sack them immediately.

Note: never mix business with pleasure, as it fuzzes the lines and could turn them into a stalker if you fire them when the relationship comes to an end.

How to Juggle Gadgets and Gizmos

Never send a human to do a machine's job.
—*Agent Smith* (*Hugo Weaving*)
in The Matrix

How to get cellophane off CD covers

It is a fact not mentioned when you are trying to become a music aficionado that you need a degree in plastic wrappers to be able to get the top cover itself off. Why they do not go into business with Weight Watchers and start putting their suction-packed cellophane on chocolate boxes is a mystery.

You need to take a sharp object – such as a knitting needle, nail file, key, or pen – and stab the plastic at one corner of the CD. You want to be careful not to scratch the cover or break the CD inside.

Score around the edge and hopefully the plastic should start to peel off. Do not be tricked into thinking that your fingernails are strong enough to take this task on. They are not. You want to get under the first layer of plastic and then tear around the cover. If any alarms or plastic security tags have been left on, you may want to go back to the store because these are hard to remove and will raise the probability of you completely destroying the CD that nestles underneath.

How to burn a CD

This is how those in the know refer to making a copy of a CD. No matches are involved. When you create a CD you etch a pattern onto the Perspex platter of the CD, which is then read by laser beam. This etching is called "burning."

Most modern computers have readers and recorders, so they can play as well as make copies. When you record a CD it allows you to create your own unique compilation, just as one used to do in the olden days on cassette tapes. Or you can simply copy your favorite CD for your friends, but this is considered piracy – so caution, shipmates, punishment can be more costly than walking the plank.

To burn a CD you need to have the relevant application. Windows Media Player is a good package to choose as it is Microsoft and will therefore be compatible with your other computer software. Apple offers you the snappily titled package Toast, as in burned bread – get it? The icon for you to click on to burn your music is the appropriately named Apparatus, or a slice of bread.

Then you have to decide whether you are making an audio or a data CD. (A data CD can be seen as a large-capacity floppy disk and is not just used for music.)

If you want to make your own CD copies, you will need to get Windows Media Player and then follow these easy steps.

1. Open Windows Media Player on your computer.

2. Click the Open option for the music on the CD that you have inserted in the CD drive.

3. On the vertical toolbar, on the left-hand side, click on Copy from CD icon.

4. If connected to the Internet, track title, artist/composer name, and album name will all be included. If you are not online it will have less info, so you will get "track 1" and so on.

5. Having chosen which songs you want recorded, click on the Copy Music icon, which you will find in the top right-hand corner of the screen.

6. This process will then save all these particular songs to your personal Media Library, which is part of Windows Media Player.

7. Select Copy to CD or Device from the vertical toolbar. You can now look through your media library and select all the songs you want burned onto the CD.

8. Having selected the songs, click on Copy. The selected songs will be burned to the blank CD in the CD drive.

9. Pour yourself a gin and tonic. By jingo, you've done it.

Note: for copying onto CDs, you need to copy to a *CDR* or a *CDRW*. This is good lingo to learn, so listen up. CDR means "CD recordable" and may only be copied onto once. This CD cannot be erased and no further music can be added. CDRW can be erased and revised as many times as desired, as this is called CD rewriteable. How straightforward is that!

Once you have mastered the art of burning data you can move onto burning images, creating a disc worth of pictures (jpegs), and producing a slide show. You can also download and burn copies of DVDs, but for this you need to have a special DVD recorder.

How to find music on the Internet

First there was the LP, then there was the cassette, which in turn was replaced with the CD. LPs will remain "cool," thanks to DJs and limited-edition vinyls, but you are going to be *so* behind the times if you don't know how to download from the Internet.

The key thing to find out when looking for music on the Internet is whether the music is downloadable or live-streaming audio. Most artists' and radio websites have live-streaming audio, which means you can listen to the music, but you can't save it or make a copy of it for your hard drive.

Quite often, recording only works with broadband rather than the standard dial-up connection services because listening to, and downloading, music requires a hefty connection and that tends to be beyond the humble dial-up. There are, of course, ways to record live streams, but this requires two PCs, a lot of extra wires, and a lot of patience.

Now where you find the music all depends on your taste, one man's meat being another man's poison, so to speak. Good "general" places to log on are:

www.napster.com
www.emusic.com
www.iclasssics.com
and of course *www.apple.com/itunes*

The number one download site, thanks to the success of the iPod, is *www.itunes.com/www.apple.com/itunes* from Apple. You have to download the software first of all, but this is free, then you can download and burn it all in one session. They have more tunes than many other sites, and are amateur user-friendly. It has the largest download catalogue on the web and can automatically sync it up with your iPod. As the market gets ever more competitive, it is continually updating itself. Models (and we're not talking waify runway girls here) are going past their sell-by date as fast as milk. And yes, before you worry – although iTunes is Apple, it works just as well on Windows PC as on Mac.

Download the tracks from your favorite artists, or compile your own selection. Listen to radio stations online and see what is new; go to online stores and get the CDs sent to you directly. Alternatively go to a search engine, such as *www.google.com*, type in the name of your favorite group or genre of music, and see what they throw up. There is no limit to how much you can download, though different iPods have different limits. You do have to keep in mind you can listen to samples live for free, but downloading has a cost, usually under a dollar, but it all adds up, so keep on eye on your enthusiam.

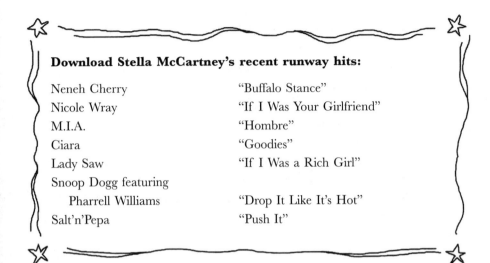

Download Stella McCartney's recent runway hits:

Neneh Cherry	"Buffalo Stance"
Nicole Wray	"If I Was Your Girlfriend"
M.I.A.	"Hombre"
Ciara	"Goodies"
Lady Saw	"If I Was a Rich Girl"
Snoop Dogg featuring Pharrell Williams	"Drop It Like It's Hot"
Salt'n'Pepa	"Push It"

To download music from the Internet you need to go to the web page or site where the music you desire is. There you will find the step-by-step process of how to download the track, telling you what to press and when to click. You need to do a right click on your mouse, select Save Target As, and choose the required destination. You can either simply listen online, if it's live stream, or you can save to your hard drive and then burn onto a CD to listen to at your leisure, both of which you now know how to do.

There are three ways that you can download. Two are legal and one verges on the illegal.

Record companies make music available on the Internet and charge you to listen and download it. This is usually done as a monthly subscription, with a minimum rate for a number of tracks. This helps the labels recover some of the money they have lost since the advent of downloading. As there are no overheads, the prices are lower than in the shops.

Many groups have tracks that you can download from their websites. These are often live tracks or unreleased studio exclusives. So that ends the careers of the bootleggers. Whatever tracks are available is fully at the artist's/label's discretion. But there is often a little exclusive for the devotee.

Napster is a file-sharing format developed to trade massive amounts of music files over the Internet. Lawsuits forced the original version to be shut down, but the Napster technology is re-emerging on a subscription-based service. It provides a forum for people to share music, like a chat room, and was, in its purest sense, meant to be an arena for unsigned talent to show their material, and for enthusiasts to share their finds. The idea was that you could donate copyright-free music and swap it with other people. But it got invaded fairly quickly by greedy, cunning people, who used it to download free copies of popular releases, which in turn led to a dramatic fall in CD sales. It had a crippling effect on the music industry and many artists were very "anti" it, as ultimately they lost out on their royalties. Now sites are carefully monitored and charge subscription fees.

The heavy-metal group Metallica showed they weren't as "anti" the system as all that "wild men of rock" behavior would have you believe. They have been the most vocal opponents of Napster. Admittedly, being very popular, and with a massive back catalogue, it meant they stood to lose a lot. But how many eyeliners does a man need?

The hip-hop industry, although they are unlikely to admit it, supported the idea of Napster. The rebel site led to their music being heard by people who would not normally listen to it, and Napster is a main contributing factor behind the rise of hip-hop culture, and the popularity of R'n'B.

When Napster got closed down, hip-hop group Public Enemy showed their support for downloading music by making their new album available only if you downloaded it. This was successful, but, boringly, a CD of the same album was released to the shops some six months later for the full retail sting, so the exclusivity lasted only a short while.

Since the demise of the original Napster, more file-sharing programs have appeared, such as Kazaa. The key difference being that this is more search engine than website. At the time of this writing, record labels have come up with a plan to stop these newer file-sharing programs. There

could be some interesting cases in the future as
music conglomerates try to take ten-year-olds to
court for downloading the latest boy-wonder hits.

Know what an MP3 is

To get a decent quality, CDs use 44,000 samples per second. Notes and
instruments can vary, but the sound quality can't. An MP3 can replicate
the same quality, if not higher, of a CD, hence the popularity of downloading from the web.

An MP3 is a way of getting music from your computer to a more
user-friendly format, such as a CD. And yes, the advent of the iPod has
institutionalized it. It is, in fact, a much easier way to collect a whole
library of sounds. It does this by putting the music into a data compressor
so that it is all condensed, and you can get more music and more downloads
faster and easier.

A full CD will occupy 650 Mbytes while an MP3 can compress it to 65
Mbytes. A super zip file is for sound. You then need to get devices that can
play your MP3 files and translate the data into music. This device is an
MP3 Discman (its brand name), but it is a bit out of date now as everyone
is opting for an iPod.

How to be cool enough to own and use an iPod

An iPod is a player for the MP3 files and is a mini-minicomputer that is
able to read the files and convert them to music without bothering you with
all the technical wizardry. Music lovers will never want to listen to anything
else after sampling this sound quality, and, best of all, it's as small as a pack
of cards, and equally addictive.

Because of their huge memory capacity and the speed with which they can read and download tunes, iPods have taken over the marketplace. In their mini or full size they are hoping to knock CD players off the top spot. And they are cute. They come in pink, gold, green, and blue, as well as white, silver, and black so are always in fashion.

An iPod is the chic way of playing music, and is more compact than previous portables plus a lot less fragile. Its huge RAM memory means it is able to store thousands upon thousands of tracks, say 15,000 on a full size and slightly less on a mini. Can you even think of that many tunes? You can load all your saved or downloaded MP3s onto your PC, and then send or "import" them to your iPod, usually using iTunes. In other words, an iPod can hold a pretty inexhaustible library of music, maybe not a whole mega-store, but more than you will ever be able to listen to, so no longer do you need to lug around your entire CD library. Just don't put too many tunes on or else you will never be able to decide what to listen to. Download your existing CDs, from the web or iTunes, and compile your own personal sound-track. A tune for every outfit, a wardrobe of choice the size of your hand.

With the success of the iPod, and all the accessories that now go with it, speaker stations, arm bands, iTripping, and so on, it can be hard to keep up. In the past two years it has already changed faster than imaginable; first it played songs, then stored your photos, podcasts, and now it will even let you download and play your favorite videos. Microsoft is now in talks with Sony to invent a rival as they have been totally cut out of the loop at the moment with iPods, iShuffles, and the iPod Nano all now as slim as a pencil and light as a feather, yet able to contain as many songs and videos as a whole day on MTV could show you. The consumer can only win in the price wars, and it is nice to have a bit of knowledge of current techno affairs to have to drop into conversation on some occasions.

Loading it up

Once you have selected the color and the size and you have taken your purchase home, it is only a matter of time before you can be dancing to your trendy tracks in your living room. Set aside an evening to load up your favorite tunes and get the little thing up and running. The iPod works with iTunes music software, but don't worry: a CD of all this comes in the box with your groovy gadget.

iPods, despite being an Apple product, do work with both Macs and PCs. All you need to check is that you have a machine that you are able to plug in to the iPod's USB port and that the lead is connected from iPod to computer. But before you get to this dizzying height, don't skip the basics: plug in and charge the iPod as there is no battery here. If this is your first time, insert the CD into your computer and install the software. Luckily, as this is an Apple product, the instructions are kept, thankfully, simple and concise. Once you have clicked and agreed to all their questions, you can start compiling your own soundtrack. It's that easy.

Importing music from a CD

If you already own a CD you can transfer (download) any or all of the songs into your iTunes library. Insert your chosen CD into your computer, and once you are online and the iPod and computer are connected, the CD will automatically be selected and taken to the iTunes option. Then the CD's listing and track names will appear on the screen. You can select which tunes you want by clicking the check boxes or unselecting as you desire, then it will chug away and before you know it your iPod will have a copy of those songs.

Buying music online

The easiest, and therefore most sensible, way to do this is to go to *www.apple.com/iTunes* and click on the Music Store option. If you are hunting down something more obscure you can ask this site to try to locate it for you, or you can google more specialized, off-the-beaten-track sites. But if you do see a tune that you like, first open an account, which is done by clicking on the Account icon, and logging the details that they ask for.

Once this is done you are able to roam the music store, like a child in a candy store, only this time it won't add weight but a wiggle to your hips.

Pick and mix to your heart's content, and it will do all the importing for you. All you have to do is have good taste and keep a vague eye on how many tunes you are clocking up as it might really add up in your excitement.

Be careful, though: with both of these options you must not disconnect your iPod and go offline until your iPod displays "OK to disconnect." If you disconnect too soon you risk losing all that you have spent hours selecting, and with an option of 15,000 songs, that would be more than a tragedy.

Once you are loaded, you are ready to go. Style with stilettos and shades for the ultimate cool. You can hook your iPod to your computer, with its special wire, select Random, or Shuffle, et voilà, with the assistance of the computer's built-in speakers you have your own minidisco/radio station. Tracks you've chosen, sans all the irritating chatter. So much more compact bijoux than a stereo system.

But is music enough? Well, not to worry, you can flick through your photos, or even watch a video, so your trip to town or the office will become so much more entertainment-filled. (For the photos, you simply transfer and download a jpeg; for videos, it is the same process as downloading music, only the egg timer symbol will take slightly longer to complete this task.) Some things are too clever for their own good. But which technology you choose depends on how long you take to jog around the park or how much house-cleaning aerobics require background music. Just be careful when listening to it in the bath; at the time of writing, there were no models that were yet waterproof . . . that'll be next week.

How to compile your own soundtrack
by Jade Jagger, jewelry designer

My day is definitely full of music. I get up by playing a record, or turning on MTV. It's the easiest way to open my eyes. Music has always been a huge part of my life; my childhood was spent visiting recording studios, seeing my dad on tour, even now I get a strange twinge of pride when I hear him on the stereo.

I am always traveling. I split my time between London, Ibiza, all over, but even in my day-to-day life I always have music with me. I bought three CDs today, and I can't go out of the house without my CD Walkman, big earphones, and at least ten CDs or a fully loaded iPod. I don't listen to just one type of music – but most of all when I listen to it, I listen to it LOUD! I get my friend Darren to mix the music for the Garrard stores and I like to have it up to date and really loud, so it blows away the cobwebs.

It's hard to pick my favorites, there are different periods, different memories. Lately I have been listening to pop music – but that's because it's better to agree with my children on a CD than all try to outblast each other. At the moment hard hip-hop has been replaced by Britney Spears, but that's part of life's rich tapestry, I guess.

If I was to do a compilation soundtrack of my life, I would include:

Bob Dylan	"Isis"
A Tribe Called Quest	"Benita Applebaum"
Shinehead	"Billy Jean"
The Rolling Stones	"Hotstuff"
Nina Simone	"Wild Like the Wind"
Madonna	"Lucky Star"
Michael Jackson	"Wanna Be Starting Something"
Snoop Dogg featuring Pharrell Williams	"Drop It Like It's Hot"
Louis Armstrong	"Making Whoopee"
John Coltrane	"A Love Supreme"
Jay-Z	"I Just Wanna Love You"
Bob Marley	"Don't Worry"

Each tune says and means something different to me, reminding me of a moment, a place, or person in my life.

How to understand the difference between a palm tree and Palm Pilot

A palm tree is usually found on white sand and sun-drenched beaches, and is a picturesque location to drink your cocktail under. This is VERY different from a Palm Pilot.

A Palm Pilot is the popular version of the PDA (Personal Digital Assistant). It is for those who need something to organize their lives, or are control freaks and need to be in charge and in contact at all times. This little gadget is their life; their diary, contacts, everything all accessible in the palm of their hand.

Just as Pinocchio had Jiminy Cricket, you can have your own guardian angel to remind you about meetings at 9:00, and lunches that you tried to forget.

The most popular applications to use are the diary and the address book. These are more useful than a Filofax as you can download and synchronize your diary not only with what is on your computer but also, if you are really clever, with the whole office, so everyone can see how hard you are working and what you are up to. Although sometimes this is not a good thing.

You can also use your Palm Pilot to store recent e-mails and some files. You can even get newspaper headlines downloaded, to keep you in touch.

To download and swap files you have to rest your Palm Pilot in a cradle, which will simultaneously charge it. The gadget will sit on a little "hammock" and can then be connected to your main computer via a USB lead that is attached to the computer. Why they give it this strange name I don't know, but put simply, any lead that is connected to your computer will be able to send messages, files, and memory via a USB port, which is a special high-speed port. It is this lead that lets you download the latest information.

But read on, because mobiles didn't like to see these Palms taking their trade so have come back into the competition fairly quickly with their answer to the PDA.

How to benefit from pagers, Palms, and BlackBerrys

These are all, essentially, pocket computers and once you have one you'll be hooked. They are a Palm and mobile in one. They have smaller and therefore simpler memories than computers do, but that's really all you need as they are more like a pocket prompt until you are reunited with your full office, computer, telephone, assistant, coffee machine, and executive chair.

A pager just flashes up a text message when you are needed, ideal for glamorous ER-style characters. They let you know to phone home. Immediately. A Palm is the hand-held assistant, as described above, that is a combination of Letraset and a minicomputer. The BlackBerry is a nonedible computer that is a wide phone, which can retrieve corporate and personal POP/IMAP e-mails, and make them easy to download. E-mailing isn't its only trick, as it's also a fully functioning Tri-band mobile phone, which means your phone will work on both sides of the pond and you can keep your social life going anywhere across the globe. It can handle GPRS (General Packet Radio Service – i.e., faster Internet connection dial-up), SMS (Short Message Service – i.e., texts), WAP (Wireless Application Protocol – i.e., how to get on the Internet when not at a computer), HTML (we've done this – Hypertext Mark-up Language), Internet browsing, Java games, and has a PC-synchronizable calendar, tasks and contacts, blah blah blah. Most importantly of all, it fits into your handbag, which is a big phew. Resist a BlackBerry for as long as you can – once you've clicked on, it's a hard habit to quit . . .

How to keep time and timepieces

In an age when we are obsessed with time management and effective time use, we are surrounded by timepieces, but the watch is becoming increasingly obsolete. That is not to say we are now telling the time by the sun and the stars, but a watch is now a luxury accessory, like earrings. Time is kept on your mobile, on your computer, in the dashboard of your car. People now only bother to wear a watch if they're making a statement, or it's a designer number, a limited edition, or has particular sentimental value. With that in mind, the designs of timepieces are on the up as time is the ultimate in luxury – so you should be one of the glamorous ones who can afford to indulge by wearing it. Also, watches are great to help you adjust to new time zones.

How to get the most from your mobile

There is NO excuse for people not to call and not to be able to get hold of you, not since the invention of the mobile phone. If they say they are going to call you, they'd better – most mobiles have caller ID and report missed calls, even if the caller didn't leave a message.

A mobile is the most essential accessory for keeping you in contact with the world, and therefore it is essential that you know how to use it and get the most out of it.

As with getting dressed in the morning, know when and for what you want to use your mobile. They can text, take photos, browse the Internet, store names, addresses, and birthdays, makes notes, do calculations. They also ring, can act as an alarm clock, and have made the humble wristwatch fall from favor in the timekeeping department.

Mobiles can come in a variety of shapes, sizes, and colors, and, depending on you, can do pretty much anything. It's up to you to choose your model, network, and ringtone and keep your hotline fully charged.

A brief history

Can you believe that fifteen years ago mobiles were a rarity? A mere fantasy? Now can you even imagine life without one? When was the last time you used a pay phone, or, when in England, have you stood in a red telephone box (not that many are in fact red, but you see how times are changing?)?

A cellphone/mobile is basically just like a radio. It picks up signals from towers and transmits through these, which is why you have better signals in some areas and why it doesn't work underground (yet).

It all started in the 1870s with Alexander Graham Bell and an analytical chemist called Michael Faraday who began research into whether space could conduct electricity. His discoveries were crucial to the development of the cellular phone.

In 1946, on June 17 in St. Louis, AT&T and Southwestern Bell introduced the first American commercial mobile radio-telephone.

There was a lot of tinkering and experimenting with transmissions and transmitters, and by 1973 Dr. Martin Cooper made the first call on a portable cellular phone. The former general manager of Motorola is considered to be the inventor of the first portable handset.

In 1977 mobile phones went public. Public cellphone testing began, the first trials being in Chicago with two thousand customers, then spreading to Washington, D.C. and Baltimore. Japan began testing in 1979.

1988 was another key year in cellphone history, with the development of the Cellular Technology Industry Association (CTIA). Despite demand it took over thirty-seven years for the cellphone to become commercially accessible in America. It is now an industry that grosses over $30 billion per year. Make sure your contribution counts.

Phones have developed and changed with fashion, going from the bricks carried by Melanie Griffith in *Working Girl* to the micromini phones that are being consistently updated, and shrinking by the minute.

Get a good ringtone

Just as with rings, ringtones matter. Is your engagement ring from Tiffany's and have you downloaded the latest chart track or some achingly cool melody as your ringtone?

To download a ringtone you usually press 0 on your mobile. This should connect you to the mobile's Web browser, the WAP; if it doesn't, you are very unlucky and you will have to ask your operator what to press. Then you scroll down through the options and it will offer you a variety of the latest ringtones. The phone networks do charge for this service, so choose your tone with care – you don't want to be changing it every day. And "Hello Barbie Let's Go Party" may make you smile, but how will it go down in a board meeting? Keep up with the times and trends, and besides, if you leave your phone on silent you may never find it.

Use a mobile and text

First charge your mobile and turn it on.

With a Nokia, the simplest and most widely used mobile, you should check that you have all the bars on the left-hand side of the screen showing, as this indicates 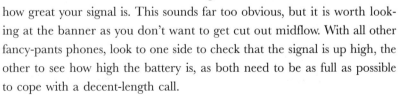 how great your signal is. This sounds far too obvious, but it is worth looking at the banner as you don't want to get cut out midflow. With all other fancy-pants phones, look to one side to check that the signal is up high, the other to see how high the battery is, as both need to be as full as possible to cope with a decent-length call.

Dial the number that you wish to ring, or scroll through your address book, and select name to find number.

Then hit the logo of a phone handset lifted up, as in "in use," as in ringing.

You should now hear a ringing tone, and hopefully fairly soon a voice at the other end will answer your call.

When your call has finished you hang up by pressing the handset graphic; this will end your call.

Mobiles work in a similar way to normal telephones, the main difference being that you can have one number that will work anywhere and, providing you have the correct type of phone (you want either tri-band or quad-band), it will let you make and receive calls anywhere in the world.

The main techniques to master are ringing and texting. Competence with any other gizmo is an added bonus.

The joy of sms

"Standard Messaging Service," or texts to you and me.

You have an inbox, an outbox, and a write/create message box.

Similar to e-mails, yet much more primitive, text messages are sent between mobiles and arrive in your inbox from other people, can be written in your write message box and can be saved in your outbox.

Text messaging is a way of instant contact, without the chat.

Despite what others may send to you, do not give in to peer pressure and resort to nauseating abbreviations. Always use the Queen's English, and try to punctuate where possible. If you find yourself on the receiving end of some of these truncated horrors, the following should help you to translate.

Emoticons and codes

C U 2morrow? Not likely if you send a message like this. A strange new dictionary of phrases that, being part of the modern world, you will need to translate:

A

AML All my love * AWHFY Are we having fun yet * AKA (Also known as) and ASAP (As soon as possible) are permissible abbreviations

B

B4 Before * BF Boyfriend * BBFN Bye-bye for now

C

CUL8r See you later * Cm Call me

D

Dur? Do you remember?

E

EOD End of discussion

F

F2T Free to talk * FYI For your information – this is also acceptable

G

Gr8 Great

H

H8 Hate * H&K Hugs and kisses * H2CUS Hope to see you soon

I

I2I Eye to eye * IOU I owe you – this is fine, predates text illiteracy

J

JFK Just for kicks (sure the late president would be thrilled)

K

KHUF Know how you feel

L

LOL means "lots of love" to the Europeans – "laugh out loud" in the U.S. (so careful who you send it to) * L8r Later

M

MYOB Mind your own business

N

NE1 Anyone (I mean HOW are you going to guess that?) * NC No comment

O

O4U Only for you

P

PCM Please call me

Q

QT Cutie

R

R Are

S

SOL Sooner or later * SME1 Someone

T

T+ Think positive * T2ul Talk to you later

U

U You * UR You are

V

VRI Very

W

W4u Waiting for you

X

X Kiss (finally a phrase you will be familiar with)

Y

YBS You'll be sorry

Z

Zzzz (you guessed it)

Smileys are said to express mood. But if you want to express mood, and not cause a bad mood, call the person. This is just the tip of the emoticon iceberg:

:)   smiley happy face

;)   smiling winking face

: (sad face

Send concise messages rather than codes that will baffle and irritate the receiver.

Predictive text has also become a feature on most mobiles, and this will anticipate, sometimes with bizarre results, what letters they think you are going to need. As long as you read what you have written before you send, this is another tool to ensure full and healthy sentences.

Another bonus is that text messages do not expire, but they can be incriminating evidence; it depends if you are giving or receiving, in or out of love.

Think before you send.

Also save any really good text messages as long as you have space, as they can perk up your inbox on a really crap day.

And God created voice-mails

To quote Stevie Wonder, "I just called to say I love you."

If you cannot reach the person you are trying to talk to, the mobile will normally offer you the option of leaving a message. This is great, but try not to waffle and keep the message concise, to the point and informative:

State your name: there are a lot of "just me's" about.

Your reason for calling: can't meet you later, etc. Wanted to talk to you is obvious – you called.

Leave a number you are available on for them to call back, or say that you will call them again.

When leaving numbers, in particular, speak SLOWLY, or say it twice. There is nothing more frustrating than having to root around to find a pen and paper only to have to listen to the message nine times before you can catch the number spat onto the machine at high speed.

Never break up with someone via a voice-mail/text.

Never pour your heart out or ramble on for too long: bear in mind that they can play your message, perhaps even on speaker phone, to an entire gaggle of friends before it expires.

If you have left more than three voice-mails and still had no reply KNOW WHEN TO GIVE UP!

Send picture messages

Away on holiday? Lying on a beach? Or in a store and having a complete "does my bum look big in this?" crisis and need a second opinion? Well, thank the Lord for picture texting.

   Now most mobiles incorporate the option to take photographs with a mini built-in camera. This can be very useful, but you need to have a friend who is able to receive photos. This is crucial as to whether or not you need to learn how to do this.

   A basic digital camera allows you to direct a teeny-tiny lens at said situation, click, and photograph. This is then saved as a jpeg on the mobile and, providing your recipient understands their photo-messaging service, you can share the image. Jpegs are to pictures what MP3 is to music. Remember: a problem shared is a problem halved, and it is a fact that all mirrors in changing rooms have some kind of optical illusion going on. Mobiles can also send text pictures to e-mail, once the correct setting is installed.

Send a videotext

Really fancy new phones can even send moving images – videotexts. Get to grips with texts and photo messaging before graduating to moving images. Networks now can show you movie trailers, or minivideo conferences, which is great if you are a budding Hollywood director or don't mind enormous bills. If not, truth be told they zap a lot of energy from your phone that could be better spent discussing last night or your eventful bus journey over a coffee face-to-face.

How to use a camera

Aim camera at subject, look through viewfinder, check the lens cap is off. Ensure you have tops of heads and all the body parts in the frame you wish to see. Point and shoot.

Modern cameras deal with the shutter release, aperture control, focus, and so on.

To take pictures most cameras have auto-exposure and focus so all you really need to do is to get the right speed of film. Get a fast-speed film, as you don't want the exposure so slow it doesn't take the photo until your arm's gone numb. And remember that for darker situations you need even faster film so that the shutter opens and closes quickly and has more chance to grab the image.

Fanatics can buy cameras that they have to focus and decide on correct settings for, and so forth. But better to take time composing a good image rather than waste hours, and miss the moment, tweaking the technical knobs.

Once you have gotten to the end of the film, be it twenty-four, thirty-six, or forty exposures, it should automatically rewind and then you need to take it to be developed.

Many pharmacies, as well as specialist photo booths, can do a variety of services for results in anything over an hour. They can also now offer a service to put the images onto a CD.

With the growing popularity of digital cameras, photo-developing labs now offer a service whereby you can take the memory card in and they will download all the images and print them out for you. This will probably end up costing you less than the inks and the paper if you were to do it yourself.

As the memory card is reusable it can be argued that you would never need to get negative film developed again, simply doing it digitally. But people should still take pride in filling their photo albums, and get photos printed up to fill them. Think of Christmas with the relatives, and, indeed, of your future grandchildren in the years to come... heavens.

A brief history

The camera was invented in 1841 by Joseph Nicephore Niepce, when he used his camera obscura to take pictures of the nearby rooftops. But don't forget the contributions that came from Aristotle (384–322 BC), Roger Bacon, and Leonardo da Vinci. In 1884, George Eastman invented flexible, paper-based photographic film, making it far more accessible to the general masses, and by 1888 Eastman had patented the Kodak roll-film camera.

Everyone wanted to have their photo taken, or to shoot photos, be it for business or pleasure, so the race was on to make pictures better and equipment easier to use.

There are two types of still (photographs) and moving (movie or camcorder) cameras. They use either film or digital memory cards to capture an image, in black and white or color, and freeze that split second in time forever. All brands and cameras can either do as much, or as little, as you want, depending on whether you are Mario Testino or Joe Public.

Loading film

This obviously depends on the type of camera you have. Digital doesn't have film – it has memory cards that you insert, but you probably need to do this only once and then you can download and save the images onto your computer, wipe the card clean, and reuse.

Polaroids are an all-in-one gadget, and although not the sharpest of image they do give you instant gratification. Negative film in cameras you can use only once. You can choose between classic film with negative, or an APS, which has the film enclosed in a hard plastic canister, which is never exposed.

APS films are easier to load, as you simply open, insert film into casing, and snap away. More traditional films involve opening the back of a camera, pulling an exposed piece of film across and tucking it into the other side so that the film can roll from one side of the camera to the other as it gets more and more exposed, i.e., as more pictures are taken.

Check that the battery is not flat and react accordingly; camera will not work with sluggy battery. With a digital camera, rechargeable batteries work better, but check these are all pumped up.

How to take a decent picture
by Alexi Lubomirski, fashion photographer

Use the flash sparingly, assess the situation – if the lighting is already great don't charge in with auto-flash and bleach out the atmosphere.

Consider the whole frame; try and put the head near the top of the photo, and fill the whole shot. A head in the center of the picture could lead to images with large expanses of ceiling.

Just before you press the shutter take your head away from the camera and make eye contact with who you are photographing. Humanize the interaction, it is hard for people to relate to a little metal box.

Try and have a fun, relaxed atmosphere when taking a picture, even if you are nervous; make them feel like there's nothing to panic about, leave that for your camera to do. Keep a stream of banter going; light chitchat will lighten the mood, and if you are the fool they should feel more in control.

When taking someone's photo always take a couple in each pose; if you take a few you should at least have one good one. With digital or Polaroids you can see straight away if you have got it. And, if the first one is great, people will feel good when you tell them you got it in one – they are a natural!

Take a camera everywhere; if you only pull the camera out at Christmas or to capture a view from your window you will never have an exciting variety of shots. Always have a camera close to hand to capture a moment. It will not only improve your skills, but it will help nervous photophobes to get used to having their picture taken and help them find their best angle.

A good place to start when finding someone's best angle is to have the person facing you, then turn their body 10 degrees to one side so that you have a slight tilt in the body. Head should tip down ever so slightly; it is a myth that if you turn your head up it makes you taller, it actually gives you double chins. Aim to shoot head to shoulders, or below, but tell the person how much of the body you are getting in. Don't go too close, you do not need to see every pore.

Be careful of hands and feet, fold them in delicately, especially on women – as due to perspective anything nearest the camera will be largest.

Don't forget to take a photo of yourself! A photographer is often the one person who is not photographed. Try and angle the camera so you compose the shot and then, holding the camera in same spot, twist 'round and stretch your arm out in front of you, holding the camera so that you are in the shot, too. Not only is this a great distance from which to take the photo, you will be at a three-quarter angle, which is the most flattering.

Above all try and make it fun. You want to capture a great moment, not a frown!

How to look good in a photo
by Gisele Bundchen, supermodel

What should you do? Other than try and get an option on some super-trendy photographer?

Whether it's work or fun, the most crucial thing is lighting. If you get bad lighting, you are screwed. Know where the light is. You don't want it below you or above you, you want it to shine directly at you.

The key thing is no shadow. If you are being shot outside, do it in the morning, or wait till the two o'clock shadow has passed. And also don't let pictures in magazines stress you out – all the pictures are taken by great photographers, and all the faces have had pimples taken out by computer. Come on!

Tip your head and learn what angles work with your face; everyone is different so you have to learn what suits you. You can practice in passport photo booths for as long as it is your turn, to learn what angles suit your face. Tip your neck to elongate it, make eye contact with the camera. No one can look bad if they smile.

For long legs, point one leg into the center of the frame and get the photographer to shoot looking up your body.

For just leg shots, lie upside down and raise legs in the air for the best angle, it thins ankles and shapes calves.

Keep shoulders back.

Always have mouth slightly open, enough to put a penny between your lips, as this will make your lips look fuller.

Tilt eyes down and look up just as shutter is clicked for full eyes.

Delete any evidence of a less-than-perfect photogenic moment, everyone has off days.

How to use camcorders with class

The home movie has gone from horror to kitsch must-try. Be a star, albeit in your own living room.

Aim at intended and press On. Don't forget there is most likely a built-in microphone so do keep the commentary flattering.

Take a camcorder with you everywhere, but try not to annoy your subject by putting it too much in their face or intruding when not wanted. Reality TV is overrated, explore more creative avenues. Remember that not everyone is photogenic or has a wish to be famous, so respect their privacy. Never let an enthusiastic relative/first-timer film your wedding or special event. You wouldn't let them install the electrics in your house, would you? So hire a professional. False economy is for fools.

As with cameras, you need to have enough light and your subjects should be engaged in an interesting activity. With a moving image it is preferable for your subject to be leaping around, dancing, and so forth. Try to get them to talk to the camera and not be too contrived. Remember that all great filmmakers had to start somewhere.

A camcorder can record either onto videotape or onto DVD. These can then be played directly onto your TV screens. DVD is quickly becoming the best option as it is digital and therefore better quality, and the machines are smaller and easier to operate.

Do exercise some restraint when showing home videos. See whether your audience is still conscious after three hours of your holiday footage before sharing the remaining seven hours.

A great *edit* makes a great film. You can do this on your computer, with a program you can download, called Windows Movie Maker, from Microsoft, of course.

Inspiring home video moments to reference include: *The Blair Witch Project, The Wonder Years,* and certain classic scenes from *America's Funniest Home Videos*.

How to
Set Off Your
Square Eyes

If there is no TV in the room, what
is all the furniture going to look at?
—*Joey* (*Matt LeBlanc*), *on* Friends

How to have television feng shui

"Television is for appearing on, not looking at," said Noël Coward, but unless you're an actress you'll know to ignore him.

If there is no TV, what on earth can you do while having a TV dinner? Books are very tricky to hold while eating. TVs are as essential to a room as the sofa, light fittings, and so on. TVs can bring the outside world in, so have it in a suitable place of worship. Try to position opposite a comfortable chair/sofa, with a footstool and coffee table in situ for the ultimate pleasure and relaxation. TVs should be in either the sitting/living room or the bedroom. You do not need a TV in the bathroom, kitchen, study, or a portable in the car. Try to limit the number of TVs to the number of people in the house.

Flat screens can be hung on the wall, while larger models can sit proudly in a corner. What type you get is up to you, as with desktop versus laptop computer. It is an aesthetic issue. What size, what width screen, what number of channels, is all personal choice. The resolution now is as good on a two-inch plasma screen as it is on a more bulky, more standard fifteen-inch. Just, whatever you do, don't have your TV next to your computer or else it will be very confusing knowing what screen to look at.

How to tune a TV and VCR in sync

Well, the easiest and most sensible solution is to make sure you purchase one that does it automatically. VCRs are a dying breed so prices are very competitive. Sling your old model out and replace with a more up-to-the-minute automatic model, which can convert the signal, read what frequency and time to set itself to, and tunes without you doing anything.

If, for some unfathomable reason, you are deeply attached to your old video recorder and still think you might want the option of recording, connect your VCR through the aerial and tune a specific TV channel to the video signal, making this the designated VCR channel. Before you reach for the smelling salts, this is not as complex as you may fear. Put in a video, press Play and then flick the TV channels until the film you are expecting to see leaps into action on the screen.

Stop the video you've had playing.

Press the Options button on the remote while the video is still in place and a menu of choices should appear on your screen. You then need to scroll the arrows down until you select Channel Tuning, and then you need to follow the simple instructions, clicking OK, until it is done.

If you want to connect the VCR to the TV and you have cable, your initial thought might well be, Damn it, I only have one coaxial cable – this is likely to have been preceded by wailing Ooohhh, it's just so complicated, but stay calm. Most televisions have two holes on the back. One, as explained before, goes to the TV. Then you can insert a coaxial cable into the second that can connect directly from the decoder to the VCR. When you decide you want to stop watching cable and record a video it will automatically cut directly to show you what you want. Pretty clever, these cables.

If your cable is connected to the VCR you will always be able to record, as cable can pick up terrestrial as well as the other options and doesn't need tuning. You just need to ensure you are on the right cable channel. You leave your VCR setting tuned to AV. This requires no aerials and accesses all channels.

How to be friends with your remote control

Sofa to TV set can be a very long way, especially if you have curled yourself up with a cup of tea, the best cushions, and have strategically positioned your cat/rug/boyfriend so that your feet are toasty warm.

Act immediately before you get too comfy. Locate and claim the remote.

Always know where the remote is; if it's not in your hand, you need to know where it is hidden. Great places include tucked under the cushion on favorite viewing seat, and under the base of the sofa, so that only you can find it.

There is absolutely no way that you want to be forced to watch anything that isn't exactly what you fancy. This is why you need to be not friends, but BEST friends with the TV remote.

In addition to the on/off button you should have channel numbers and volume. There are also a lot of fancy buttons that it is unlikely you will need, but never say never. Mute is a key button which lets the action continue, soundlessly. Unfortunately this has not been invented in real life, so it's good to exercise this power as much as possible with big onscreen names.

Also be aware of the friendly AV source button. Huh? This is the button that switches the TV to your VCR/DVD (that is if you connect via a scart lead).

How to load a DVD player

A DVD player is very similar to a CD player – so the chances are, if you can operate one of those then this shouldn't be too much of a trauma. Press Open and put the DVD into the player, pattern side up, shiny side down. (The label is so that you can have a last-minute check you are about to watch the film you are expecting.)

With the television on, select the audiovisual channel. Press Power On to turn on the DVD player. If you are not on the right channel, flick through all the channels to see which channel displays the DVD option when you flick past it. Ah, there it is! A slow but flawless technique.

DVDs are fast outstripping the VCR and soon they will have taken over, which is no bad thing as the DVD players are so much more streamlined and will look far better in your designer pad. When not playing, DVDs can double up as topical coasters, whereas VHSs aren't even that effective as doorstops, not that a stylish girl would consider anything other than a Vivienne Westwood patent platform heel for this job.

Getting it to play

Okay, so there is no point knowing that DVDs are the way forward, and that they can now record from the TV, as well as play, if you don't know how to do any of this. So get ready to enjoy superior digital image quality.

Providing you are on the right channel, the TV should flash up a welcome, letting you know that you are tuned in to watch a DVD-style page.

Press Play on your DVD player. It will then display a screen saver related to the movie, scroll using the arrows on your remote, select Play Movie, and you are off. This stage is crucial, unless you want to be looking at a screen saver all night.

You can also, as with CDs, jump to your favorite scenes with much more zippiness than a VCR. If you're feeling pushed for time, with a DVD you can summarize a movie by watching just the best bits, you can leap from scene to scene with more accuracy than fast-forwarding. A DVD player is not as complicated as you may think. You essentially need only five buttons to operate them: these buttons are Play, Fast-forward, Rewind, Record, Stop/Eject.

Extra feature buttons worth locating include:

Subtitles button

Press this button for subtitles. Good for the hard of hearing, but also makes understanding obscure art-house foreign flicks possible.

Audio button

This can give you special extras, like the director's commentary explaining extra scenes. Great for the die-hard enthusiast.

Angle button

This is really clever, so don't be too scared to find it and to press it. With this button you are in the driving seat. Say you are watching a concert, with this button you can choose whether you watch the lead singer, the drummer, from the wings, or view the audience – can you see yourself? Cool!

How to curl up with something stylish

Once you have selected your DVD and dimmed the lights, if you are alone you can softly slip off the stilettos and sink your toes into a shagpile rug or curl them up under you. If you are entertaining, perhaps start in a negligee and a pair of sexy satin-and-marabou heeled slippers. Think Monroe, Bardot, or indeed Agent Provocateur. Heeled mules are ideal to wear for DVD nights as you can easily slip them on and off. Complex buckles and bows are cumbersome on this occasion, as the lights will be low and you will not be able to see clearly how to slip them off. Think style and grace, rather than tripping into the mantelpiece as you fight with a shoe horn.

Shoe designer Olivia Morris's favorite movies to watch in her marabou slingbacks include:

Single White Female (especially the scene with the stiletto)
Faster Pussycat Kill Kill
Breakfast at Tiffany's (diamonds are a girl's best friend)
Grease (check out Sandy dancing in mules)
Some Like It Hot (watch her move)
The Wizard of Oz (the ruby slippers are reason enough)
Walt Disney's Cinderella, the box set of *Sex and the City*, and a good selection of brat-pack movies are also essential when building a DVD collection

How to preset the VCR/DVD player to record

Note: not all DVD players record yet. For this you need a DVD recorder. Check what type of machine you have.

It is absolutely inevitable that the one evening you get asked out on a really hot date, there is an unmissable program on the telly.

Don't for a moment consider canceling; get smart with the Preset button. Record the program and you can watch it later. Dates cannot be replayed, however hard you try.

Both VCRs and DVD players have the ability to record a program and save or store it so that you can watch it later at your leisure. They are the TV's baby-sitter, and they are there for your convenience, so make use of them.

Select the correct AV channel and then you will be asked what time you want to start recording, on what channel, and what time you want to finish recording (be generous with the finish time, as there is nothing more annoying than missing the crucial last moment of a film). Press Select, leave the player on standby, and you're all set; the machine will be able to turn itself on when the program is due to come on.

If you have cable, make sure you don't have anyone tampering or flicking with the decoder once you have set it to Record. The machine can recognize the instruction to record from the cable channel, but while recording you cannot flick around different channels on the system; this will make it completely confused, and most likely you will record the wrong channel – unless you leave it locked on the one you want.

Put in your video/DVD. Click onto the timer. Check the decoder is on the right channel.

Go paint the town red.

How to enjoy your DVR

You're all cabled up and happily watching your DVDs, so how ridiculous is it that you still have to program your VCR to record your favorite shows (or more likely, you forget to program it, or find that for some bizarre reason it just didn't record – infuriating – didn't it know you wanted to see that show?). Not to worry, you don't have to decline all dinner party invitations, there is help at hand to get you back onto the social circuit. Indeed, once you've seen the joys of the DVR, there's just no going back. There's TiVo, of course, which is a DVR that you must purchase and subscribe to, but many cable companies now offer DVR systems as a regular upgrade. DVR stands for Digital Video Recorder, and it's a hard drive that replaces your cable box. Now when you want to record not just this week's episode of *The Sopranos*, but the entire season (repeats and all); well, you are an all or nothing girl), all you need do is go to the menu and press "record entire series." And when you want to watch, it's just in there, that simple. (Just make sure you watch it relatively soon, or use the "permanently save" option as the system isn't a mind reader and might accidentally delete it, leaving you back at square no show one). Genius. So now you won't miss a trick – on the box and on the town.

How to book a pay-per-view film

Even for those who have cable there are still some evenings when, despite having a trillion channels, you can't find anything you want to watch.

Before leaving the sofa and heading out to the rental store, see what's on offer for subscribers of pay-per-view movie specials. These films are usually slightly in advance of video/DVD rental release.

All systems vary slightly, but the general way is to go to the channel that advertises what movies you can pay to view and watch the options.

If any of these appeal, you now go to the checkout, so to speak. You have to phone and make your selection or, if you have an interactive TV (through cable), you can do this by clicking select buttons. Once you select the movie it should either start immediately or at the stated time. You can sit back and enjoy, just don't scrimp on the popcorn.

How to make popcorn

Before you curl up in front of your favorite film, it is important that all the right props surround you, and the most important of all is popcorn. You can usually purchase this at the same time as you rent your film, but if you are having a night in and you don't want to take the slippers and face pack off to leave the house, you need to know how to make your own.

For sweet popcorn you will need the following ingredients

3 tablespoons of butter
2 tablespoons of oil
$\frac{1}{3}$ cup of popcorn kernels
$\frac{1}{3}$ cup of sugar
$\frac{1}{4}$ teaspoon of salt

When you are next aisle gliding, pick up a packet of kernels in the supermarket, the rest you should have in the cupboard.

Method

1. Melt the butter in oil, stirring in a saucepan on a medium stovetop.

2. Gently stir in a few popcorn kernels at a time. They won't do anything too exciting straight away, but make sure that you have the lid close to hand.

3.   Spread the kernels out so that they are lying in a single layer over the bottom of the pan.

4.   By now the popcorn will be starting to pop. Stir carefully so it doesn't leap out of the pan.

5.   When the kernels are popping away merrily, pour in the sugar and slam the lid on tightly and quickly.

6.   Turn up the heat to full and shake back and forth over the heat. You will now be listening to the popcorn equivalent of "The Charge of the Light Brigade," as the firing and popping will be in full chorus now.

7.   Turn down the heat and shake with the sugar, and then after a minute or two remove from the heat altogether.

8.   Stir in an extra knob of melted butter and the salt, pour into a bowl, dim the lights, and press Play.

Homes & Gardens

Click your heels three times and say, "There's no place like home."
Dorothy (Judy Garland), The Wizard of Oz

How to Buy a House

Zsa Zsa Gabor is an expert housekeeper.
Every time she gets divorced, she keeps the house.
—*Henny Youngman*

How to understand the home-buying process at a glance

Buying your little nest will be one of the most important and stressful things you will do in your life. Regardless of your taste in shoes, fashion, or fine art, buying a house is simply the most expensive thing you will ever do. But before you move into your dream home and start drawing up the fantasy soirée invite lists, there are a few bridges to cross.

Take a deep breath and prepare to get onto the property ladder. Not only is this very grown-up, it is far more sensible to pay off something that is yours for keeps than line the pockets of a landlord. Also, if it's your own Aladdin's cave, you can really let rip with the creative juices.

Before you charge into the property game and order the change of address cards, know what you are letting yourself in for.

1.   Work out your price range. This will depend on your (or joint) income, your outgoings (and what you can cut down on), and finally the size of the deposit you can afford to make. You can now borrow between three to five times your salary, depending on how convincing a performance you give.

2.   Decide what type of mortgage you want. This is a bit boring, but at the same time quite important, as you need to get the right one for you, so get someone to explain the current benefits of fixed versus variable and so on, because you'll be stuck paying it off for the foreseeable future.

3.   Before you start searching for that dream home, you need to talk to the bank and Mr./Mrs. Mortgage and get an "agreement in principle." This means that when you make an offer, you have already worked out with the bank how much you are able to borrow, how much you can put down, and have had a satisfactory credit check. This saves time and hassle when you want to slam down the best offer quickly.

4. Now the good bit. Go shopping!!! Or, as the
bank would put it, "start house hunting." Look
around and find what suits you and your budget best.

5. Now it's time to reach for the smelling salts. Make an offer.
Only put *one* offer in on *one* property at a time, or else you will get in a horrid
muddle – a bit like making two marriage proposals to two different people
on the same day, only this is trickier to get out of. Get in quick, slap your
offer down on the table, then, if you are accepted, find a lawyer. Your lawyer
will then get in touch with the seller's lawyer and begin the whole legal
process of transferring ownership over to you. Now all you do is basically
chase the lawyer, sign huge checks, and take deep breaths. Pray you don't
get gazumped . . . you're not home and dry until you exchange.

6. Fill in your mortgage application form. This is a really dull yet necessary
bit, so have a strong coffee and good nail varnish to hand. You can do this
face-to-face and they'll talk you through filling in the form, in which case
skip the nail varnish. Alternatively, do it over the phone – the call will be
long enough to do a thorough and non-joggly home French manicure and
let it dry on both hands. If you are confident, you can also apply for your
mortgage online. Hold your head up high as things move from hypothetical
and start getting scarily real. Say how much you want to borrow, give them
all the details of the property, your details, credit history, and so on. This
is also a good time to think about insurance, so why not kill two birds with
one stone? Absorb and agree to this while painting a topcoat.

7. Valuation and survey. The people supplying your mortgage will arrange
these through your lawyer, all you do is pay for them. They are vital to
check that the property is held together with more than a bit of Elmer's
glue and that you have found something worth buying. The survey is actually for the lender, not you, and is based more on structural info rather than
letting you know if you have got a good deal. You need to find that out, as
a separate option, for an additional fee, with a thorough home inspection
by a trained structural engineer.

8. Finally, finally you can exchange contracts. (Well, that is if the mortgage is agreed and your lawyer is happy that all paperwork seems legit.) When you exchange, your lawyer usually sets up a completion date for two to four weeks later, which is when it is officially yours and you can move in. Once you exchange there is no backing out, so you have to be sure or else it could cost you in hideous legal fees.

9. Completion doesn't have to take a long time, it just depends on how faffy the lawyers are being. It can be days or weeks. But don't worry about this; there are so many things to be getting on with, so this is the least of your worries.

While you hemorrhage cash, you could:

Get quotes from moving companies/truck rentals, or ask Daddy very nicely.

Contact gas, electricity, cable, water, and telephone companies to get connected at the new and canceled at your old.

Send out change of address postcards, weeding out those you no longer wish to be in touch with, and giving people an address to send housewarming gifts to.

Arrange to collect the keys. Go to Tiffany's to buy a key ring for them.

Book some time off from work and get a massage, as this is all **VERY** stressful.

When you *really* complete, it's time to cough up. You have to pay the lawyer (a certain percent of the purchase price), FedEx fees, and your first mortgage payment. So maybe skip booking a holiday to recover, at the moment.

10. Move in, choose the color schemes, and work out if the spare bedroom is big enough for your wardrobe.

How to get started in the search

There are several steps to this house-buying/home-owning lark, as well as lots of new people you will have to make friends with.

1.   Decide on the area that you want to live in, and make a list of why.

2.   Decide on the area that you can afford to live in. This may differ from the first.

3.   Decide on your budget. And no, you should not decide on your budget and look accordingly; shop for inspiration, then juggle to fit. Do not start with a compromise.

Drive to the area that you are interested in and see what it is like. Maybe drag a trusted friend along and have dinner there, suss out "the locals." It is best to pick an area that will suit you, and your lifestyle, as well as your budget. Know what you need:

Public transportation, if applicable to your lifestyle.
Library and good local facilities and essential stores, i.e., grocery
     store, post office.
Good park or garden.
Nearby doctor/beauty salon/massage/therapist.
Dry-cleaners and cobbler.

Where is the nearest branch of your bank? Favorite bookshop, clothes store? Nearest decent coffee shop? Where is the local police station? Is the area rife with crime? Any other horrors you should be aware of? Try to pick up a local newspaper, or look it up online.

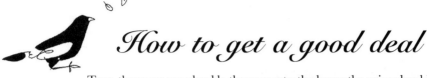

How to get a good deal

True, the more ramshackle the property, the lower the price should be. But here you should employ the same logic as buying vintage: can you fix it and is it worth the hassle? Becoming a property developer is a full-time job, as only a few hours of daytime television demonstrates. What is the construction like? When was it built? As much as you love it, if there are major structural problems, it is often better to pass, unless you have lots of funds and time, or you and your extended family are professional builders.

Before making any decisions you need to view the property and see it in the flesh. If you have read the details, it's in the right place, right price range, or you have a feeling in your stomach, now is the time to view it. This applies if you are looking to rent or to buy. You cannot know if you can live somewhere unless you go and get a feel for the place. Statistics say you will know within three seconds of entering a property if you can live there, so you won't waste too much time. If you view a property and think it is "the one," don't tarry. Stake your claim, as this is where you could be happy for the rest of your life.

When you make an appointment, try to group several viewings together in one trip, then you can compare and contrast. Appearances can be deceptive, and this is a cutthroat process. When arranging a time, try to go when the owner is out; that way you can look critically. First impressions matter, and with homes you do sometimes need mentally to install your good taste before dismissing somewhere out of hand. Redecorate rather than reject.

How to charm and understand real-estate agents

The first mythical creature that you will encounter in this strange adventure is the real-estate agent. They are a rare breed who think everything is "marvelous" and only see things through rose-tinted glasses. Generally everything they say should be taken with a pinch of salt. Real-estate agents are actually aspiring literary geniuses. Perfectly awful places that would make a sane person reach for the Tylenol and run for the door are described as having "an exciting and creative decor." Just as when you ask a sales assistant, "Does my bum look big in these hot pants?" the answer will be "professional" (i.e., wanting the commission) rather than honest.

But once you find someone who is rooting to find the right property for you, you are onto a winner. At the initial signing-on meeting, be firm. Be clear about what you want and where you want to live. If not, you will be wasting their time as much as they will be wasting yours while you both trail around every "good value" squat in town. Talk money, location, and the fixtures and features you expect.

If you have been forced into seeing a property that looks like it is decorated in porridge oats and held together with string, either you have not explained your needs clearly, they have a sick sense of humor, or you will strike it lucky next time. If the real-estate agent is any good at reading people, they will sense this wasn't a clever move and will want to dazzle you with their next idea, or risk losing the sale – and their commission.

Note: they do not get any money until the exchange. Their fees are paid by the seller.

There is no rule saying you have to be exclusively tied to one agency. See as many properties with as many agencies as you can stomach. Viewing properties not only gives you a clearer idea of what you want, but is a great interiors-inspiration road trip.

A final word of caution: to avoid getting yourself into any sticky situations, check that the real-estate agent you are going with is a reputable one. If you are going to view a property, make sure someone knows where you are going.

As well as real-estate agents, there are Internet search engines such as *www.remax.realtor.com* and *www.realtor.com* that are great ways to search for your home from your desk.

Decoding property descriptions

Read between the lines.

Recently refurbished means it's so down at the heels that they painted it in a last-ditch effort to make it look presentable.

Rare opportunity/never seen anything like this means too weird for words.

In need of modernization means Ebenezer Scrooge still hasn't fixed the broken window, and installing electricity wouldn't be a bad idea.

Charming means it's nice for your granny.

Above commercial means above the local pizzeria, but once you get used to the fighting kids and the smell of garlic on your clothes, you will love it.

Open plan means all the walls have fallen down, so you have no privacy and need to hope you get on well with your flatmate.

In need of cosmetic attention means "needs a miracle."

How to love your real-estate lawyer

Everyone needs to have legal representation. Now before you get carried away with the thought of ferocious courtroom battles, and the exchange of razor-sharp one-liners, as the battle rages over who gets the lightbulb above the kitchen sink, press Pause. There ain't none of that going on with a property lawyer. This typical lawyer is very sedate. If lawyers were designer labels, property lawyers would be the Gap. These are the people who will hold you together, should you encounter any cowboys, and they will fight in your corner, so you always come across as the good guy/gal. And typically they charge a flat fee for the purchase, so there should be no hidden costs or concern about billable hours.

How to get a mortgage

Your own bank can quote you a mortgage, however, as with most things, it is best to shop around for the most attractive deal. The best deals are often found with mortgage brokers. Gone are the days when you need to apply for the loan in person, now all you need do is go to Google, type in "mortgage broker," et voilà. You need to know what kind of mortgage is best for you, so look at a few brokers' offerings, ask friends, and don't rely totally on the broker to guide you. Tailor things to suit you. For instance, are you planning to relocate after a few years? If so, then maybe you want to go for a low, short-term interest rate. Or, if the current interest rates are really low and you're planning to put down roots, go for the lowest interest rate you can find and lock it in for the longest possible term while you can. There are numerous online resources – and books – that can help you with every possible permutation.

How to get the offer in, and stand out from the crowd

So you have put in your offer, but don't think it's over. It's only just begun. Has the seller accepted? Is the real-estate agent for you, or are they still showing people 'round the pad? Argh! You could always stand outside with a sandwich board and pretend to be petitioning against the ladies of the night who work the street, to put the competition off your home. All's fair in love and property. If you go and view the property and there is a line around the block of other people who think that their offer has been accepted, it really is time to crank up the pressure.

Call the real-estate agent and ask them what they are playing at. Who put in the offer first? Then check that yours was the offer that was accepted. If not, how can you make sure it is? Check that you have your mortgage preapproved to the amount you need and that your down payment is fully at the ready.

Buying a home is said to be one of the most stressful things you can do in your life, well, now you can see why. Double the stress if you are doing it alone as everything is your fault, your responsibility, and your checkbook – but just think, you will have your own space and your own peace and quiet. And don't worry if the whole process brings on a nervous breakdown: you have just taken out some good health insurance.

Remember that you cannot go and splurge at the sales; home buying is made harder because retail therapy is an out-of-price-range temptation. Keep shopping out of sight, and out of mind at this time.

But back to your offer; you are so nearly there. If you are competing with another wannabe buyer, help things along.

Are there any (working) household appliances you can offer to buy? Any lighting fixtures or window treatments that you could bear to pay to stay?

Write a personal letter to the seller, expressing how this home was built for you and is the key to your future happiness.

If there is still no joy, and the offer of a couple of thousand for the ugliest curtains ever seen has not tipped the balance, pull out the trump card.

Offer to pay the real-estate agent's fees for them. Try to give them a lump sum that does not affect your main offer, without doing any dodgy cash backhanders.

Play fair – but play to win. In offering to pay the real-estate agent's fees you will be giving them approximately 10 percent of the property value, and you will ensure that all the seller has experienced from this sale is profit. And don't forget, when all is completed and you are settling in, always say thank you to the real-estate agent, and they will help you if you ever attempt this again.

How to move in with the right person

So are you going to live alone? Or are you going to find a flatmate? It can be fun to live with a friend, but are you compatible? Do you know about their tuba-playing tendencies and tarantula farm? Everyone has a few wacky habits; just check that you are living with someone who is below average with these. You do not want to move in with someone and discover you have a real-life *Single White Female* situation going on.

If you are renting you are making less of a long-term commitment, but if you are interviewing potential flatmates, try to suss out any psychotic behavior before handing over the spare keys. The same applies with moving in with your other half. If you have been dating for only a week it is too soon; likewise, if you have been living together for over eight years and there has never been any discussion or hint of a wedding ring (and this is what you are hankering for) throw him/his clothes out of the bedroom window. Do not get a mortgage with a fling or casual "distraction"; you need to know more than the surname of the person you are signing up with, and what if something better comes along? You will have double the amount of form filling and trouble.

How to install a burglar alarm

The older makes are notoriously complex to install and could often result in a police visit for an irregular opening of the fridge, but the newer models are infinitely more user-friendly. They are now wireless, and affordable, so every home can have security sensors and panic buzzers. You should always make sure your house is secure. Chains and bolts should be added to doors, as well as extra catches to windows. There is no point investing in creating your dream home if some creep is going to come in and loot it, is there? And, if you opt for a fancy model, they also send a fancy (and hopefully cute) man to set it all up for you.

How to find lost keys

Keys, glasses, and makeup are the three things, in that order, that you must never lose. Choose early on a regular resting place for your keys, and ensure that when you are not using them they are kept there, in the bowl, or on a hook. If, however, you are the type of person who is incapable of keeping keys in a sensible space: admit it.

If you know that you frequently lose your house keys, you need to take steps. Purchase key rings to help. A Tiffany's key ring will be so delicious you will never want it out of your sight, but an equally successful alternative is to get a key ring with a built-in beep. (Providing that you keep the battery topped up.) They act as a calling system, and if the keys haven't gone too far, you can clap your hands to activate the beep. You can then follow the sound till you are reunited. Just one note of caution: don't forget to turn the system off at concerts and meetings because any clapping will cause them to join in.

Hand out spare sets to reliable friends and approachable neighbors.

How to be stylish when locked out

If you find that the wind suddenly whips up and blows the door shut, leaving you on the doorstep, or you dash to work and leave them in yesterday's handbag, there are several steps to take.

First, assess the urgency: look yourself up and down. How dressed are you? Fully or nearly or not at all? This will determine the urgency with which you need to get back inside.

Next, survey the door – is it tightly shut? Give it a push. Damn it.

Do you live on the ground floor? (If you have a house this will also include you.) Have you left any windows open? Or any other way in?

If you live a few floors up, can you see any windows or balconies that look open enough to make scaling the building worthwhile? If you are only in a towel, rule that out, as speed is of the essence. Knock on a neighbor's door, regardless of how well, or not, you know them, and, covering as much of your modesty as possible, explain the predicament you are in, as if it is not perfectly obvious. You need to borrow a ladder and warn them you are not a burglar but a resident before you start climbing the walls.

Do you have a phone with you? Is there anyone close by who has a spare key? You might ask the neighbors to use their phone, or indeed to give you a cup of tea to calm your frayed nerves; see how friendly they are.

Then, if you have tried windows and possible key holders and gotten nowhere, it is time to call out a locksmith. This is expensive, so exhaust all other options first. Once safely inside, locate keys and scold them. Vow never to do that again.

How to put up a tent

Should you ever be conned into sleeping under the stars in a field, make sure that someone sensible is in charge of the sleeping arrangements. If the word "tent" is suggested, you might question whether this is the trip for you, or indeed how well these people know you. But fear not; if you march straight into your nearest outdoor outfitter you can see the latest varieties that are on offer. Forget the nightmares you remember from Girl Scout camp, it is now possible to purchase waterproof, unzippable numbers. With these you simply unzip, shake, and done. The tent will leap into life, like a pop-up, all by itself. They're like microwave meals: people might scoff at them, but why make life any more complicated than necessary? If you are with hardened campers who think this is a cop-out, bad luck – get them to put up the tent themselves. It is so last season to do it the hard way.

How to Handle Mains and Mice

The attempt and not the deed confounds us.
—*William Shakespeare*

How to find the electrical main

Every time you poke a fork into a toaster to retrieve a piece of toast, you are potentially dicing with death. Metals *conduct* electricity and you do not want to be the circuit through which it flows. Rubber, plastic, and wood are not able to transfer electrical supplies; this is why they are called "grounding" or "earthing" materials, as they conduct the electricity away from you. Leave the Russian roulette of what will conduct electricity to others, and know when to get a "man who can."

That said, things electrical are not something to shy away from totally and there are times when you do need to have some handyman competence about the house.

Every dwelling has a circuit box (main), and you need to locate where it is hidden. First place to play I-Spy is under the stairs. If you don't have any stairs, are there any likely-looking cupboards? Or any multiswitch boxes on show? NOT likely to be under the sink or near water as that is a dangerous mix. Once you've found it, you'll see the box is made up of "trip" switches that are able to bounce on and off and can cut the main supply in emergencies. If you are installing an electrical object, light fitting or switch, you have to turn the electricity off at the box while you do this. You need to remember to switch it back on when you are finished so that the power will come back on.

How to open a plug

A plug (and no, we are not talking about the bath variety here) is most commonly a black or white insulated plastic-coated device with metal pins, that fits, like Cinderella's foot into the glass slipper, into the electrical sockets. These are most likely found in the walls, around skirting board level, and they make the electrical circuit connection complete.

In the unhappy event that your appliance does *not* have a plug prefitted, or in case you venture into antique, foreign or other electrical territory, you will need to take it in to an electrician to swap out the plug.

How to change a fuse

"Did they blow a fuse?" is a phrase commonly associated with anger and a total explosion. Actually "blowing a fuse" is the opposite, as it is what prevents a total explosion (electrical only) from happening. In older homes and apartments that haven't been updated with a switch box, there is instead a fuse box. A fuse is a component of wire strips that goes within an electrical circuit to act as a buffer to excess electricity. It is also usually the crucial part that spies, heroes, and James Bonds have to fiddle with when detonating a bomb.

Electrical fuses are much less intimidating than the name implies. They are like mini macaroni-size dumbbells.

The fuse lies proudly up the right side of the inside of a plug as you look at it, and is always connected to the live/brown wire. It rests in a spring-clip compartment, the fuse snapped in at each end. Changing a fuse will be no trouble – the hardest part will be opening the plug. Taking your screwdriver, gently ease the tip of the tool under one end of the fuse (they are usually metal tipped), and flick it out of the holder with a click. It's like using a shoehorn, really. Flick fuse out. Snap in a new one. That's it!

Once the new fuse is in place, all you have to do is close the lid of the plug, and it's all over.

Changing a friendly fuse

For a "friendly" fuse you simply take your three-pin plug, lay her legs up and you should spot a small rectangle-like post box. You don't even need to unscrew the plug, darling. Slip your screwdriver in at one end of the post box and lean screwdriver to one side. The lid should now pop off and before you know it out rolls the fuse. Slip in a new fuse, snap lid shut, and pretend you did it the hard way.

Of course, if you have a switch box, then you don't need to worry about any of this. All you need to do is look carefully at the switches to see which is the one in the "off" position and just switch it back over to the "on" position.

How to change a lightbulb

This isn't always as simple as it sounds. Is the bulb a screw-in one? Or a bayonet? The bayonet is the trickier of the two and looks like Frankenstein's head with the two little nodules sticking out on either side. (References to bayonet swords and rifles may be more historically accurate, but are not helpful visual aids.)

Screw-fitting bulbs are simple; bayonets require a push in before you twist. First things first: turn off the electricity to the fixture. Then, check which fitting is required (bayonet or screw) and find a replacement. You should also note what the wattage (how bright it is going shine) is. This is normally on the bulb itself but, if not, the light fitting will be marked with the maximum wattage it can take, not only for that appliance, but for the supply of voltage in the house.

Screw in the new, step down, and look up to see if it seems secure. Then click the switch back on and "let there be light."

When purchasing light fixtures, have a look at the bulbs. Tubes and halogen bulbs, especially those sunk into the ceiling, may look nice but require more patience and Spider-Man–like skills to remove. Ask yourself if you *really* want that fitting, and then when it is installed ask the electrician to show you how you can change the bulbs, and how often this drama is likely to be necessary.

Everyone should change their own lightbulbs. Electricians treat bulb-changing calls like crank calls, so if you know you will *never* manage to change the bulb, either move house when it goes, or go with another illuminating option. Candles.

How to cope in a power outage

First things first: are you sure that it's not a case of a blown lightbulb? Is it night or day? And is it *your* fault?

If it's daytime you can ignore it – okay, you can't have a cup of tea or watch the telly, but it is a lovely moment of quiet when you can read a good book. Not too much cause for alarm, just amble over to your last electricity bill, dial the number, get put on hold. If you ever get through, tell them you are out of power. Easy.

If it's night, there is more of a knack required because not only do the kettle, telly, and so on not work, neither do the lights, and in these circumstances it could be difficult finding the bill. An organized person would have the electricity number easily to hand, programmed in their mobile (which never leaves their side). But this person would also probably be too unbearable to associate with. Too much organization is a dangerous thing.

If, as mentioned above, it's your fault – keep very quiet. If you live in a flat and you have just put a nail through the supply for the entire block, admire the newly hung picture, and keep it to yourself. For future happy neighborly relations, denial is definitely not only the best, but the ONLY policy here.

If the power outage goes on for more than a few minutes and you are not ready for bed, you have only three options left.

Light all your Diptyque candles and continue entertaining.
Go out. There must be a 24/7 something open that has illumination.
Or order takeout (thank heavens mobile phone lines are not affected

by a blackout) and by the time it arrives you will have been able to prepare a candlelit grotto.

Go to bed, and hope to goodness things have returned to normal when you arise.

How to stop a flood

When it is raining inside put up an umbrella (on occasions such as this the bad luck thing does not count), don the wellies, and turn off the electricity. Water and electricity lead to indoor lightning and danger. There is no time to do your "Singin' in the Rain" routine. Locate where the water is coming from. Fast. Is it coming from the outside in? Or from the inside and trying to get out?

If it is coming in from a storm, secure the doors and windows and hope it passes. If it is coming in from the roof, either the guttering or tiles on the roof have slipped. If you live in a flat, and there are people above, knock politely to ask if they are building an indoor swimming pool. If you live above the ground floor and are ankle deep in water, worry about the neighbors on the floors below and hope they have snorkels.

If it's you that is causing the flood, locate and eliminate, and contain it as fast as possible. Baths should not flood as they have "overflow" drains at the top, as do sinks, but they can spilleth over if you leave the taps on, plug in, and go out shopping . . . which you would never do.

How to turn off the water main

If you've got your own Niagara Falls, you need to find the stopcock, the water main tap, and turn it off as soon as possible. Water main taps are in even harder to find locations than the electrical main. Think of the silliest place to hide something and look there first. Try under the sink, under the bath, under the stairs, or even across the road. Once the water main has been turned off, call a plumber – you cannot:

a) Get someone to stand with their hand over the leak forever.

b) Even be expected to have the first clue what to do here.

How to deal with ballcock problems and plumbers

There are all kind of pumps and complex innards inside sinks, toilets, baths, and so on. But a bit like the passing knowledge you have of the bladder and kidney, you don't need to know all the graphic details, you just want it to work, flush, and so on. If there is a problem with the ballcock, this usually means that a pump or cylinder valve is not working. You can poke around and see if you can give it a nudge, but frankly, would you poke around and try to remove your own appendix? Exactly. Call the plumber.

Always say it is an emergency, because if you are calling a plumber you clearly need one. As with other service and delivery personnel, try to pin them down to a slightly less approximate time than the usual "sometime in the morning" nonsense. Be very polite, but firm, and appeal to them saying that you are a special case and you need them right now. When they arrive say you would offer to make tea, but you have had to turn off the electricity for safety and nothing can be done till they help you. Damsel in Distress – always a winner.

How to bleed a radiator

Thankfully there is no real bloodshed involved here. No, bleeding is the technical term for dealing with a radiator that's as cold as a spurned lover. Bleeding is the way to let the air bubbles out of your radiator, so that it can heat up and warm the room again. Log fires are all very cozy and mood enhancing, but a radiator involves less woodcutting and manual labor. Insert a radiator key into the little studlike hole at the end of the body of the radiator. Just like opening a bottle of fizzy drink, when you open the radiator the air can escape. Be very quiet; can you hear a gentle scream coming from the radiator, like a whistling kettle? That is air escaping. But do remember to try to shut it before the water gushes out. Likewise, if you turn the key and there is no air to set free, it will spray water on you, and most often it is brown and rusty. Have an old towel at the ready.

How to unblock drains

Unblocking drains is really yuk. This is definitely not for you, so get someone else to do this. Go out for the day and hope that the problem has been "resolved" by the time you return.

How to catch a mouse, rather than gain a pet

If confronted by a mouse, before you shriek and leap on the nearest chair, there are three things to remember:

1. They are possibly more frightened than you.

2. They are no bigger than a bar of soap.

3. Mice can't climb upwards – but *rats can*. Which is absolutely no comfort. If the thing is climbing the chair leg, run for the door and scream like hell. Rats might be considered "adaptable, successful, and clever" in the zodiac, but in real life you have to accept they are just too revolting a concept for even a truly heroic feline to deal with. Get them OUT.

Being calm is not really important at the initial meeting, it is how you react afterward that counts.

It does not matter how small and "cute" a mouse or a rat may look. Are you crazy? This is an optical illusion and no one sane should keep them. They are germ magnets. Mice, rats, and all rodents are simply not fun, which is why this problem is an emergency. You definitely do not want it as a pet. Cats, dogs, goldfish are acceptable, guinea pigs borderline. If you have room, why not get a horse or a dolphin or something exciting and exotic?

If a mouse moves in, you have to move fast, charge rent, or evict them before they start to breed. According to the Department of Health, a Mr. and Mrs. Mouse can have up to 285 babies a year, and you certainly don't want to be housing that. Remember who's the boss – you are. Who's paying the rent? Exactly. Don't give them free stay at the Penthouse Pantry with twenty-four-hour room service.

Draw up a battle plan.

1. Do you have a cat? If so, have a chat with it; any chance of it doing its job? Making you proud?

2. Do you want to get a cat or do you have any other pet that wants to tackle the situation for their beloved mistress?

3. Can you get rid of it humanely? It is still a living thing so you don't have to kill it. You will find in supermarkets, large department stores, and even pet shops ways to rid yourself of rodents that are alternatives to poison. You can buy all forms of traps that will simply keep them till you set them free. It is recommended, though, that traps are inspected at least once a day, preferably every couple of hours, to avoid stress to captured mice. They don't, however, mention anything about your stress levels in doing this.

After the culprit has been caught, assess your house from a mouse's point of view. Tidy up any tasty, easy-access foods, board up holes that make things easy for them. Clean and polish every nook and cranny, get professionals if it's too huge a task. Mice like to travel under safety of cover, so remove any chance of that. If they get a whiff of food, particularly sugar, that's it, they're hypnotized. Keep things out of harm's reach. They can squeeze through gaps as small as an apricot.

Air attacks

Use a chance "mouse in the house" visit as a warning sign to secure your home against any further attacks. Another problem is literally swooping in. Pigeons, rodents with wings, are as stupid as they are dirty, but are making a habit of flying into homes in towns, so don't give them the opportunity to view your nest.

If your windows are open, try to leave them so they are not open enough for birds or beasts to squeeze in. If you hear a scratching and flapping noise, locate the creature fast. Close the door to isolate it in one room. Gather your thoughts, dash in, and throw the nearest window open as wide as possible to facilitate a speedy exit for them. Turn off the lights, rip open the curtains, and help the stupid bird realize it's time to fly. If they flap towards you – exit. Throw a towel or something over your head, and grab a tray, or mop, to help nudge them toward the window. They need to leave before feathers and droppings are littering the room.

How to clean out a goldfish bowl

Ideally goldfish bowls should be cleaned out once a week. Goldfish are very submissive pets, they don't moan and fuss, nor do they talk (back) to you, and they only have a three-minute memory, so you have to look after them. If you have a fancy aquarium, they are usually so fancy they are self-cleaning. But if you won these fish at the fair and have them in a nice glass bubble, this is how you should keep it clean.

Using a fish net, a mini hand-held one from the pet shop, or a soup ladle, catch the fish and transfer them into a saucepan or bowl of room-temperature water. It may be kinder to put them in one that is opaque so they can pretend it is nighttime, when fish sleep.

Once the fish are moved to safety, tip all the remaining fishy contents – water, stones, et al – into a colander (for goodness sake, not your regular one), under a running tap. Wash off all the grimy buildup and residue – have your rubber gloves firmly on for this task. Try not to use washing-up liquid in excess as the suds are rather toxic for your underwater friends, and they prefer to make their own bubbles.

Rinse and clean the bowl to get rid of all the slime that has built up on the glass. Dry so it is not smeary and replace the stones and pebbles. Reposition castle and any other ornaments. Then carefully add fresh room-temperature water till half full. Add in fresh seaweed to give the fish a feel of the wild, and some privacy, then fill to three-quarters full. Let the water settle for a few minutes.

Carefully tip the fish back into the bowl, sprinkle fresh fish flakes or food on surface of water, and move back to normal home.

Note: you should not keep fish bowls in direct sunlight, on a boiler, or anywhere where a cat can get his paw in.

How to Be
Handy Ma'am

We should learn from the snail: it has devised a home
that is both exquisite and functional.
—*Frank Lloyd Wright*

How to blend in at Home Depot

No matter how horrifying a proposition a visit to the DIY store may seem, there are times when a royal visit is necessary. DIY stores may have wonderful long aisles that exceed the supermarket in aisle glide possibilities but, as much as anywhere, you have to know the dress code. If you teeter in wearing the latest trends you will be in danger of alienating the staff who could assist you. In this context, high fashion can make one appear to be merely a Barbie doll. Being thought of as a bimbo is never to be encouraged. A pair of jeans, sneakers, and a sweatshirt should suffice. You don't have to look horrid, but there is no point snagging a favorite cashmere on a shelving unit to an unappreciative audience.

Preparation in home improvements is key, and none more so than in the wardrobe you should adopt to mastermind the transformation. When working with paint or building and decorating equipment, designate a T-shirt, a pair of jeans, and shoes for the task. Shoes should be flat, comfortable, and ideally sneakers, and they must be worn at all times, as you never know where a stray nail or shard of glass may have dropped. Safety must prevail over frivolous style in these circumstances. If paint lands on your clothes or shoes, it will probably be permanent. On the upside, paint splashes on an old, battered pair of jeans can really enhance a look.

Most importantly, don't forget your hair. If it is long, tie it back. This is a safety as well as a practical tip. Whether hair is long or short, tie a scarf or bandanna over the head; this is particularly necessary when painting ceilings or tricky corners where you may inadvertently lean your locks on the wet paint. You do not want a crown of white emulsion after the money you've invested in your cut and color. A bandanna is more stylish than wearing a shower cap, which frankly will look (and feel) so dreadful you won't be able to concentrate.

How to purchase paint

First select color option paint cards. It can be worth buying a minisample pot before committing your hallway to years of pea green. Once you have come to a decision, return to purchase enough gallons to cover the walls in your chosen room. A half gallon tin of paint covers ninety-eight feet/thirty-two yards. You'll need to do at least two coats. Make sure the paint for the walls is matt, unless you are painting woodwork, when you might prefer gloss, or your bathroom, when you need gloss or semigloss paint.

How to undercoat

Undercoating is a bit like underwear: you have to get the right type. If you wore a purple bra under a cream-coloured T-shirt, it would be a disaster. The same principle applies with the undercoat. To eliminate the folly of (presumably) a previous owner, you need to undercoat with white, and depending on how dreadful and deep the offending color was, it should vanish in a couple of coats. If walls are really bad, lumpy and cracked, it might be worth using a lining paper, similar to putting up wallpaper, and then painting over this. A neutral base is essential.

How to paint the room, including skirting boards and other problem zones

The main walls and ceilings require a simple and methodical arm sweep up and down, with either a brush, a painting pad, or a roller, depending on your preference. The bigger spaces offer an all-over body workout to the painter. Matt paint can be slightly watered down to make coverage easier, and make the paint go farther, but only do this on large surface areas. Put newspaper, or an old blanket, on the floor to catch flying paint splodges. You do need to be careful; however "nondrip" the paint professes to be, it will drip. Newspaper is best as it will give you an idea of the date. If you still have the paper on the floor three weeks later, chances are the paint is going to be dry enough for you to remove them.

With picture rails, or fancy ceiling features, you cannot, unfortunately, use masking tape, as it might peel off the wall paint. You have to be very careful and have a steady hand, and do the gloss-work features first. Paint walls and then, with a fine brush and even steadier hand, touch up the gloss with a second finishing coat.

If you are painting the ceiling and walls, the woodwork deserves to be freshened up, too. You may think the woodwork and the window frames are already a more than adequate shade of white, but when you give them a wipe and look closer you will see the paint is sun faded. Sorry.

Before you even crack open the can of paint you need to wipe, sand down, and dust all the woodwork; painting over cobwebs makes for a rather lumpy finish. Sanding down allows the paint to get a better "grip" and gives a smoother finish. It is also worth doing this on the walls.

With windows the aim is *not* to get paint on the glass. The best way to avoid this is to carefully use your masking tape to mark off 'round the frame. This will not only act as a guide to you, it will catch any slips. Caution: do not leave the tape on too long – on hot sunny days the tape can bake and seal itself to the window, and this will add *hours* to your work. As with nail varnish, gingerly touch the paint with a fingertip to see if it feels hard enough to pull off the tape. It can take overnight for the gloss to be hard enough to be considered "dry."

The key to successful skirting-board painting is also in the masking tape and preparation. You will need kneepads, especially if you are crouching on wooden floorboards or, worse still, marble floors. Decide whether you will be doing the woodwork in matt or gloss paint. Rub sandpaper over the woodwork to ensure smooth surface. Using masking tape, cut strips and tape the nearest edge between skirting board and floor. This will catch all corner and detail drips that may slip past the edge of the newspaper that you will need to lay down to protect the floor from paint drips and wobbles.

How to use a spirit level

Nothing to do with your alcohol intake, spirit levels are there to get things straight. This is one of the most useful yet underrated *essential* tools of the DIY world. Nobody, unless they have had excessive plastic surgery, has a perfectly symmetrical face, just as nobody can get things perfectly straight without a little help. If you look at a spirit level, there are usually two little bubbles inside, or one larger bubble, with multitasking skills of showing horizontal and vertical. These bubbles are isolated liquid in a see-through capsule that is suspended in the bar of the inch or meter rule.

Hold the chrome/aluminium ruler up to the wall and subtly angle it until the bubble is centered. Once the bubble is in the middle, the level is perfectly straight and horizontal. It's at this point that you can make a little pencil mark, move the beast, and bang in a nail.

How to put up pictures

If it's going on the wall, really it should be framed. Posters and Blu-tac are very student and amateurish, and even if you are the first you are definitely not the latter. Do not overclutter your walls. Less is more. Think of the Summer Exhibition at London's Royal Academy: there is so much squeezed onto every available surface that you go cross-eyed. You want to avoid this. Pictures, as with mirrors, absolutely need to be hung straight. With mirrors you need to use masonry nails, or the strongest available, to prevent the potential threat of seven years' bad luck. If your walls are hard you will need to drill a hole and insert a molly, then the nail.

Hold the picture against the wall, or more sensibly get someone to do this while you stand at an artistic distance and direct. Once you are happy with the position, mark it with a tiny pencil dot at the top or a corner, to be your guide. Look behind the picture to see how it is to be hung. Is it on a string? Or does it require more skill and measuring as it has two hooks? (You may berate this now, but actually it is a foolproof way of keeping it hanging straight.) This will also determine if you bang in one nail and use your eye to wiggle the picture in place, or whether you have to measure, use the spirit level, and bang, bang, hang. Pictures are a quick room fix, and more pleasurable to put up than shelving. If you require shelving, try to buy a piece with installed fixtures or buy a nice shelving unit; it's much easier than doing a spirit level master class.

How to assemble flat-pack furniture

As much as you will hate to read this, with assembly-required, or flat-pack, furniture the best rule is to follow their instructions. You have to assume they know all the best shortcuts, even if they did skip conventional English classes. When building from a flat pack, it's like a ready-made meal – they provide all the ingredients, you should (simply) be able to mix it all together. Before you get going, count all the pieces in the set and check that this corresponds with the instruction manual list you should have. You cannot complete a twenty-five-piece jigsaw with only twenty pieces and the same applies here.

Sometimes you will need to ease things into joints, but when an ease becomes something more forceful, stop and check it is really meant to fit in there. Flat-pack furniture is supposed to be easy – even for those without woodwork, physics, and language degrees. Just as you count the pieces, check all pages of the instructions are there and written in your mother tongue, or at least have clear diagrams. If in doubt, buy antiques or ready-assembled furniture and get it delivered to your door.

How to hang wallpaper

My wallpaper and I are fighting a duel to the death. One of us has to go.
—*Oscar Wilde* (These were his last words; don't let them be yours.)

As with painting, you have to ensure that your walls are washed clean, smooth, and any cracks filled. If there is existing wallpaper, you need to sponge it really wet, which will help you to peel it off. Then you have to rub the walls down. Sometimes, to ensure a smooth finish, you need lining paper, like an undercoat, which is a good opportunity to practice your hanging-and-pasting skills.

Take your new paper and decide which way up you want to hang it – this is particularly important if it has a distinct pattern. Then go to any of the four walls and, taking your spirit level, draw, in pencil, a straight vertical line. Others may prefer to start in a corner, but the spirit level does not lie, so use this as your guide for lining up the paper. Measure the length you need. Apply paste to paper on a table and be sure to cover right to the corners as it will peel off otherwise.

Climb the ladder and you are ready to apply the paper from top to toe. Smooth the first sheet all the way down, pressing firmly into place, then come down, paste, and collect the next sheet. The next one should line up with the first; use the picture rail if you have one to guide you, and ease it in close so it is touching, but not overlapping, its neighbor.

If patterned, make sure it matches or follows on.

Above all, do not rush. Allow lots of time as once you have started you have to finish, you cannot leave a wall half-wallpapered.

How to lay tiles

Apply the grout to the back of the tile, and start from the bottom, working up. The bottom row of tiles should be resting on something, such as a shelf or bath rim, as it will need to have something to take the weight. If there is nothing to support it, add a wooden border for it to rest its heels on. When applying the tiles you need to use plastic spacers to ensure you get a uniform gap between each tile. Of course you should also judge with your eye, but the spacers keep everything in line while you focus on laying the tiles down. Leave to dry overnight, then take out the spacers, seal the grout, and be sure to test it is rock solid before allowing water to splash near it.

Ceramic tiles are the toughest to cut, but "standard" bathroom tiles are not too tricky to tackle. You can buy great purpose-made cutters that slice through these like a hot knife in butter. You can usually get crazy shapes, to go 'round taps and so forth, done at the hardware/DIY store, which will save you the bother.

How to make your home look like Versailles

If Botticelli were alive today, he'd be working for *Vogue*.
—*Peter Ustinov*

Being original, and creating the WOW factor, requires some research. *Vanity Fair* and *House and Garden* are great magazines for starters. *Architectural Digest* is also v. impressive to leave lounging on the coffee table. Travel magazines are also très inspiring, as are the glossy magazines, or even late-night "Cribs" on MTV or inside stars' homes on VH1 for a glimpse of those celebrity "at homes." Iconic films may prove helpful, such as the table settings in *The Age of Innocence*, the New York loft apartment in *Friends*, Audrey Hepburn lost in the luscious library in *Breakfast at Tiffany's* – a good collection of books is not only a great prop, it is a symbol of scholarly worth – intellect as well as style. Merchant Ivory films are always good for period dress and historical ideas, *High Society* for entertaining, *Amadeus* for decadence, and the opening scene of the original *Sabrina*, as the camera pans across the mansion and then to the young Hepburn watching the ball from her tree, can only be topped by the opening line of Alfred Hitchcock's version of Daphne du Maurier's *Rebecca*: "Last night I dreamt I went to Manderley again."

Obviously, as a jet-setting frequent traveler, your home will be decorated with pieces gathered from the far-flung places you have visited. Imagine your home is being filmed for *Lifestyles of the Rich and Famous*. You want to hint at your personality, and show glimpses of your stylish brilliance. Your home should reflect your hobbies, interests, extensive education (books are so much more than decorative), and fashion sense (style on hat stand as well as in the, ideally, walk-in wardrobe).

Above all, your home should demonstrate an eye for color. It may be chic to wear head-to-toe black, but different rules apply in the home. When decorating, a different "you" is called for. Aspire to make your home as unique as Versailles and as lavish as Buckingham Palace, yet as comfortable as a much-loved pair of slippers. A home is where you lay your hat, where you are ruler of all you survey – so whether it is a one-roomed box or a palace, it is *your* castle and proof that you don't have to be as rich as royalty to have a lovely home, you just have to care for it.

Ensure that you have good taste, good feng shui, and good house-warming soirées. Gifts are great to help you along the way. Decide on a color or a theme and spread it throughout the house; this doesn't have to be rigid, but should reflect your personality. Let the personality of the property also have a voice in the decor. Mix old with new, antiques with junk, but above all keep it original.

Ideally plan your decor before you move in, but at the very least decide what should go where before you have moving-day chaos. Decide what will be the feature of the room and enhance it. Mirrors make a room bigger, dark colors on the ceilings sink them down.

Collect pinecones, shells, old stones, and bleached wood; the "natural" art thing doesn't look like you're trying too hard and it is free as well as interesting.

Frame pictures and decide where the telly, the comfy chair, and the bed go, and fit the rest 'round this.

Buy a grandfather clock; the tick-tock sounds like a heartbeat, and, once you get used to it, it will stop annoying you and make your home feel tran-quil. Alternatively, take up the piano, or an instrument, that is neighbors and space permitting.

Moving is the time to be ruthless and have a sentimental spring clean. Get rid of old clutter. But do not forget you are not a robot, nor should you live in a sterile environment. A squishy chair you can curl up on to watch the telly is essential. Your home needs to be inviting, but not too inviting: guests who won't leave can exhaust a hostess. The balance you are striving for is: 15 percent mood; 15 percent personality; 20 percent comfort; and 50 percent style.

Make your new place tidy yet comfortable; you can look at show homes, but should never live in them.

Remember that clothes can be great as wall hangings, chiffon scarves can adorn sofas, and shoes can be doorstops. Be creative.

Feng shui basics

In Chinese *feng shui* means "wind and water." It was a technique originally used for choosing burial sites for the wealthy and plots for palaces. Nowadays it is popular as a technique of "working with nature" to make the best of the environment that you have. It advises you on how to avoid putting furniture in unlucky or inauspicious positions. Designing the layout of your home with feng shui in mind can enhance your home, while working against it can bring sorrow and misery.

The first and most important rule is, Always trust your intuition. Your inner voice is the most important tool you possess.

Remove clutter – people, furniture, and rubbish.

Regular shapes are preferable to irregular.

For every "problem" there is a "cure."

Wind chimes, crystals, and bells dispel negative energy and attract and invigorate the *chi*.

Plants and flowers: choose rounded tips, as spiky plants, cacti, and Yucca plants can create a "spiky" atmosphere.

Mirrors: position with care, as what you see doubles. Therefore opposite money pots or walls is good as it doubles your money or space. You should never have a mirror opposite the toilet, and more importantly, never opposite your bed, as this could lead to infidelity.

Put up happy family photos on the southwest wall.

Water features: fish tanks or fountains are good fortune enhancers, leaks and floods are not.

Display pairs: couples are always preferable. If you have ornaments, display in pairs to ensure relationship success.

Bed position: whatever you do, never have the bed with your feet facing the door as this is known as the "coffin" position. Move it today.

Fireplaces are best on the south wall – if on the northwest wall, experts would go as far as to suggest that you close it up. Get a compass and check you are okay.

In an office always sit with the wall behind you – sitting with your back to people can signify "back stabbing" and betrayal.

How to clean and tone, dust and burn

A woman's place *can* be in the home, given the right encouragement, and lighting. Rather than thinking of yourself as a harassed cook-cum-cleaner, visualize yourself as a cross between a French maid and a Helmut Newton dominatrix. There is much to be said for aprons and rubber gloves.

Remember: if it is *your* home, *you* have to clean up after yourself. If you share, establish a few ground rules before you move in. Coffee cups and plates do not have their own legs, nor are there any makes of crockery that are self-cleaning – they need to be carried to the kitchen and either loaded into the dishwasher, or washed.

Make a chart of what must be done, and turn "chores" into an aerobics routine. Think *Stepford Wives* meets Olivia Newton John. Musical backing optional.

Break up the load into lots of five-minute jobs rather than half a mundane morning. Allocate each task a different track on your CD or iPod. If you need to work on your body, adopt the following tasks. More Jane Fonda than Cinderella.

Hoovering floors: Great for thighs and bum toning.

Hoovering stairs: Works the legs, bum, and tummy.

Polishing: Tones upper arms, neck, and shoulders.

Loading the dishwasher/washing machine: Your abs.

Putting washing on the line: Abs and upper arms.

Dusting the skirting boards and picture rails: Abs and upper body.

Washing the floor: Thighs, buttocks, and posture.

Ironing: Abs, upper body, and posture.

Washing up: Upper body.

Gardening: Cardio and full-body workout.

Shopping: A total body workout.

If you are a really messy person consider a) hiring a cleaner, or b) moving into a hotel.

Housekeeping checklist

Make a list of rooms and corresponding jobs. If you live in anything with over three bedrooms you are entitled, if not expected, to have help: a cleaner, gardener, ironer, and so on.

Know what the tools of the trade are as they are essential for home improvement and making life easier. There are the trendy, covetable Dysons in bright-colored plastics to liven up the job, as well as more traditional vacuum cleaners to choose from. The good home should have:

Dustpan and brush and broom, the Cinderella essentials.

Wiping cloths, tea towels, feather duster, as well as all the cleaning agents and utensils they require.

Washing machine, dishwasher: essential; tumble dryer optional extra.

Once a day

Bed: Make it.

Phone: Charge it.

Laundry: Dirty – wash/launder; clean – put it away.

Windows and curtains: Open and air room.

Cushions: Plump.

Write "to do" list: Do you need to go to the grocery store, get fresh milk or tea?

Tissues, clutter, junk mail: Take to garbage or recycling, and empty.

Kitchen garbage: Empty, especially crucial if you have had a smelly takeout.

Black trash bags: Take them OUT – so unsightly.

Washing up: Load and empty dishwasher or, if not part of twenty-first century, ensure washing up is done daily, if not after each meal, to avoid build-up and growth of mold.

Wipe down: Worktops, the kitchen table, and any frequently used surfaces.

Blow out: All candles before leaving the house.

Sweep room: If time, or dustpan and brush.

Water plants: Indoors and outside, and check shelf life of cut flowers.

Once a week

Duvet covers and pillows: Change them. Note: pillowcases and duvets must always be part of a matching set.

Carpets and rugs: Vacuum.

Get your mop out and take it for a spin, particularly in the kitchen and bathroom and on any linoleum flooring.

Toilets: Disinfect. Grim, but got to be done. Put your marigolds (rubber gloves) on.

Have you left anything for the garbage men? Put black trash bags in the bins for them, and they will make them disappear (but remember to pack it up neatly so the bags don't explode over your front path). Never forget their Christmas bonus.

Washerwoman: Get your laundry up to date; essential to keep clean undies and freshly pressed jeans in constant cycle.

Grocery shopping: Make online selection for supermarket home delivery, unless you have a pair of shoes that need supermarket training.

Once a month

Wipe, dust, and polish: Your lair from top to toe. Yes, this does include windows and windowsills. For wooden furniture use beeswax polish; not only is the smell heavenly, but the furniture will repay you for your care and attention.

Vacuum or sweep: (Flooring dependent) under sofas and beds.

Fridge: Ruthlessly eliminate any foods that are past their sell-by date. Apply this to magazines and old papers; will you really want them in three years? If yes, file; if not, relegate to recycling bin.

Stove inspection: Have you used it? If so, clean it, and the same applies to your microwave: give it a wipedown inside and out.

Dance around: With a feather duster, and midroutine try to get corners and ceilings and any cobwebs that are being spun.

Feeling energetic? Flip the mattress on your bed, if at all possible. Brochures recommend once a fortnight, but you can ignore this; once a month is ample to ensure the springs stay in shape.

Go deep: Go right to the bottom of your laundry bin and check that nothing is loitering there.

Once a year

Outing: Manuals and well-groomed housewives recommend an annual trip to the cleaners for duvets, quilts, and rugs.

Curtains and blinds: Take down for an annual spring clean.

Dust: Attack the tops and bottoms of all the nooks and crannies that you neglect in a weekly or monthly blitz.

Investigate: Exactly what you have stored under the stairs.

OR – get professional cleaners to come for half a day and blitz everything with industrial strength while you go to a gallery or something.

In addition to "I'm washing my hair," reasons given for refusing a date can now include:

Filing paperwork, love letters, and bills, doing tax returns.
Cleaning cupboards, in kitchen, bathroom, or beyond.
Dusting your chandelier.
Polishing silverware and jewelry.
Sorting out underwear drawer – refold, and chuck the old and well worn.

Cleaning tips

Make a list of chores and tick off your checklist; similarly, keep a list of cleaning products and always replace before they run out.

Clean as you go – that way you minimize the horror and stay on top of things.

Vacuum upholstery and even give sofas a quick go with the hose to get rid of crumbs.

Hang cedar blocks to freshen your wardrobe and prevent moths.

Sprinkle baking soda on the carpet and leave overnight to absorb musty odors, then vacuum off in the morning.

All homes should have welcome mats, not so much for the greeting, but to encourage people to wipe the mud off their shoes before entering.

Emergency services should not stop at 911

You should have either on speed dial, memory, or in an easily accessible place numbers for: doctors, taxi service, electrician, plumber, builder, locksmith, good cleaning lady/maid service, computer technician, takeout delivery, cleaner/garment repairs, cobbler, florist, and vet – if applicable. Or simply delete all above and just dial Mom/Dad. Get someone else to deal with drains, plumbing, gutters, and dangerous situations, such as tiles falling off the roof and dodgy electrical problems.

ℋow to make a bed

The hardest part is to get out of bed, but assuming you have overcome this hurdle, it is time to make it.

First, smooth the base sheet and to and make it as flat as possible, pull it tight around the edges. Don't even bother with flat sheets, unless you are a Girl Scout leader or a nurse; fitted sheets are the answer.

Take the pillows off and give them a good shake or simply throw them on the floor; they are like the glacé cherry and are to be added as the finale.

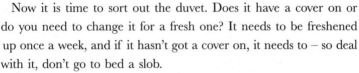 Now it is time to sort out the duvet. Does it have a cover on or do you need to change it for a fresh one? It needs to be freshened up once a week, and if it hasn't got a cover on, it needs to – so deal with it, don't go to bed a slob.

Hold one corner of the duvet, then attach a safety pin to the outside of the duvet cover on the corresponding corner. Pushing the duvet inside the cover, head for the safety-pinned corner. Check first that you know which corner you are heading for. When you reach your chosen destination, either top right-hand or top left-hand corner, rejoice. Attach the safety pin from the outside (it's not going to stay there, so don't fret about visuals) to the corner of the cover and to the corner of duvet below.

With that corner firmly anchored in place, feel your way inside along the top line between the duvet and the cover until you hit the farthest corner. Secure another safety pin to opposing side corner. Then give the duvet, and its cover, a good shake to pull down all the crumples and creases, and check that the top corners are in the right place. Lay it on the bed in a rippling wave movement. Start from the head/top end and smooth the duvet down on the bed. A particularly eccentric au pair used to iron the duvet into place, but it is actually best to iron the duvet cover first, without duvet inside, so all the fluffiness stays in. Real pros can "pinch" the corners of the cover to pull the finer creases out. Once the duvet cover is in a satisfactory position then, do up the little buttons or snaps, and tuck in, or not, as required. Don't forget to remove the safety pins.

Retrieve pillows from the floor, puff, and place them back in prime position. Then try to resist the temptation of leaping back under the covers again . . . it will only make you late.

Another, more speedy, way to put a duvet cover on is to fold the cover back so that it is three-quarters inside out, then put the duvet in the remaining quarter, lay it on the bed, and fold out the remaining section.

How to hoover the stairs

Hoovering can be one of the most glamorous and body-toning tasks about the home. This is not to say that you want to do it all the time, but it is a great opportunity to get out your heels and practice on carpet – with the vacuum cleaner as your pushable stabilizer. It's an "in house" way of checking you can walk on carpet backward and forward at varying speeds.

However, it is best to do the stairs in either flats or bare feet, and probably on your knees.

Take the hose part of the vacuum cleaner – this is often located at the rear – and unwind. With the thing all plugged in, on, and so forth, get going with the nozzle, leaving the main body of the hoover at the base of the stairs. Don't overstretch the tube; when you are finding it hard to reach an individual stair, go down, get the hoover, unplug it, and take it to the next landing, or top of the stairs, and locate a place to plug in up there. A drag but necessary, but now double caution is needed because if you overstretch or pull too hard, the whole thing could topple and land on top of you, and that would be a calamity, plus a visit to the ER.

When designing and decorating, consider a darker or user-friendly color of carpet. Beige and neutrals may be chic but require much more audience participation in general upkeep.

How to wash up

Fill the basin with hot water and enough washing-up liquid to provide a generous supply of bubbles. Take off your rings, bracelets, and watches and disregard any claims that they are waterproof – why risk it on a pudding bowl? Locate your rubber gloves, and slip them on. Despite advertisements singing the moisturizing benefits of soap suds on skin, they surely only mean the bathing type, and ladies do not want hands that feel as though they have done hard manual labor.

Roll up cashmere sleeves and cover any silk or satin tops with an apron to avoid any stray splashes.

Take plate and scrape any excess food into garbage, rinse well, before placing in bowl – you don't want salad floating about and complicating matters.

Wash smaller objects first, then big, and don't leave too many things in the bowl or else you might lose them. You can leave things to soak; for saucepans and oven dishes this is often a good idea – just don't forget that you need to come back to them. The secret to washing up is common sense, but then if you have any of this, why don't you have a dishwasher?

How to load the dishwasher

As with washing up, first you need to scrape the plates, empty glasses, and so forth. Liquids pour into the sink, food and debris into the garbage. Rinse off any sauce that seems indelibly stuck on the surface as dishwashers can clean, but they can't work miracles.

Place objects into the machine in sensible secure positions. Glasses and mugs on rails at the top, plates and larger objects on bottom shelf, and cutlery in the plastic holder. But try to turn them so the handle is down in the holder and fork prongs and heads of cutlery are sticking out and up, so they are able to get in maximum cleaning contact.

How to get the right sparkle

Square-cut or pear-shape, these rocks don't lose their shape. Diamonds are a girl's best friend.
—*Lorelei Lee (Marilyn Monroe), in* Gentlemen Prefer Blondes

A diamond is the most constant thing that you can have a relationship with. It's an investment and it sparkles. As Shirley Bassey said, "Diamonds never leave you – men do!"

It is quite a common (and sensible) complaint to have an "allergy" to "cheap" jewelry. Nickel-coated rings and fake frosting may work in your teens, or indeed from a distance, but should never be passed off for the real thing. Not only will they stain your fingers, or the skin they are in contact with, they dull with age. The real thing is not lacklustre. Some extremely fortunate girls have a real allergic reaction, where the skin can go red and blotchy if forced to wear a fake. You really don't want to risk finding out if you fall into this category.

How to clean your rocks

If you are building a collection to rival the crown jewels, or, at the very least, Liz Taylor, it is worth having a vague knowledge on how to make it sparkle. Diamonds are the ultimate symbol of love and, suitably, the symbol of high maintenance. Assuming that someone has bestowed upon you some real rocks, and the diamonds are as close to flawless as possible, follow this simple rule: if it is worth insuring, it is worth knowing how to clean it. Marilyn was right, but there are other worthwhile purchases, aka gifts, worth accepting. They include your birthstone, so make sure you know which gem you are.

Month	Stone	Color
January	Garnet	Deep red
February	Amethyst	Purple
March	Aquamarine/Bloodstone	Pale blue
April	Diamond	White/clear
May	Emerald	Green
June	Pearl/Moonstone	White/purple
July	Ruby	Red
August	Peridot/Sardonyx	Pale green
September	Sapphire	Deep blue
October	Opal/Pink Tourmaline	Multi-color/pink
November	Citrine/Yellow Topaz	Yellow
December	Blue Topaz/Turquoise	Blue

Your birthstone may not be the most flattering for your coloring, so you needn't be too literal with the interpretation; for example, if you met in July a ruby would be a nice thought.

Anniversaries and holidays should not be neglected. It is worth reminding all suitors that anything from Tiffany's is welcome any time of the year. Gifts are not solely for birthdays, they can make random days special occasions.

Back to the job at hand. Don't waste time cleaning costume jewelry or anything cheap. Just as you only dry-clean the tricky stuff, so, too, should you only clean the real gems. And if it turns out your engagement ring tarnishes or changes color from cleaning, chances are it's a fake. Why in heaven's name are you accepting?

Before you start, check that there are no wobbles or loose settings, clasps, or stones. A careful dab of superglue and a squeeze with a dainty pair of pliers may be needed here, but if it requires something more than a common-sense "tweak," take it to a jeweler's where they have all the right tools.

Use a *nonabrasive* jewelry cleaner (i.e., something that will not scratch the stone; sandpaper is not appropriate). They are available in supermarkets or jewelers, or you can ad-lib with soapy water and a cloth.

Dip cloth into solution and gently wipe and polish. Then, using another corner of the cloth, rinse and dab clean with clear water. Finally, with another corner, buff the ring or object of your affection dry.

With any cleaning agent, apply sparingly, and remove delicately yet thoroughly. With silver, the more you wear it, the less it tarnishes, so that's a good reason to aim to be adorned at all times.

How to knit one purl one, wash, and sauna

by Julien Macdonald, fashion designer

Lots of people like knitting now. If glamorous icons like Catherine Zeta-Jones are hand-making ponchos as Christmas presents, now is a very stylish time to start.

I'd choose larger needles if you're a beginner as it is easier with big stitches, and you finish sooner. If you know how to loop the wool, tuck over and under, all you need to do is select the color. Always go for something daring that stands out. If you don't know how to cast on get someone to show you, or cast on for you, and you're away.

I've been knitting ever since I was a child; when I am not doing crochet patterns I like knitting top stitch, which is a combination of plain and purl. Purl is the reverse direction of stitching to plain. They are the easiest to follow and doing these two together, alternating, gives a nice thickness to the yarn. You just loop 'round, under, and through. Knitting is a technical art form; the pieces I produce for celebrities are couture, because they are hand-made. But once you can do it, you can take it anywhere; when I am stressed I find crochet very relaxing.

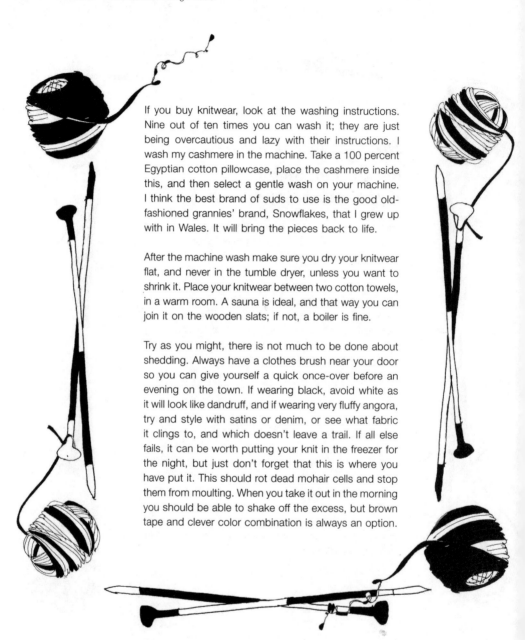

If you buy knitwear, look at the washing instructions. Nine out of ten times you can wash it; they are just being overcautious and lazy with their instructions. I wash my cashmere in the machine. Take a 100 percent Egyptian cotton pillowcase, place the cashmere inside this, and then select a gentle wash on your machine. I think the best brand of suds to use is the good old-fashioned grannies' brand, Snowflakes, that I grew up with in Wales. It will bring the pieces back to life.

After the machine wash make sure you dry your knitwear flat, and never in the tumble dryer, unless you want to shrink it. Place your knitwear between two cotton towels, in a warm room. A sauna is ideal, and that way you can join it on the wooden slats; if not, a boiler is fine.

Try as you might, there is not much to be done about shedding. Always have a clothes brush near your door so you can give yourself a quick once-over before an evening on the town. If wearing black, avoid white as it will look like dandruff, and if wearing very fluffy angora, try and style with satins or denim, or see what fabric it clings to, and which doesn't leave a trail. If all else fails, it can be worth putting your knit in the freezer for the night, but just don't forget that this is where you have put it. This should rot dead mohair cells and stop them from moulting. When you take it out in the morning you should be able to shake off the excess, but brown tape and clever color combination is always an option.

How to sew

A home should never resemble a department store at sale time, with buttonless garments. If you spy something without a button, thread a needle.

Always have a full and healthy sewing kit or box at home, including a selection of colored threads, plus your standard black and white cotton and needles. Fine to start with one of the hotel "complimentary" kits, but you will soon discover that their needles vanish or snag after one use and, inevitably, there is never quite enough thread to do much more than practice threading a needle.

Threading a needle

Cut the estimated required length of thread, not too short and not too long. Too short and you won't be able to finish the job, too long and it will knot and tangle and leave you in a horrible mess.

Lick the end of the thread. This will stick all the fibers together so when you send it through the eye of the needle it is easier to push through.

Hold the needle in your left hand, and with the right slowly push the thread through the eye of the needle (reverse if you are left-handed). Insert with the cotton pointing away from you, as if you insert the other way, things leap out of focus. For learners you can get needles with larger eyes, but remember the bigger the eye, the clumsier the needle, and the larger the holes punched in the fabric. It's best to double up the cotton. This means you have equal amounts of cotton on both sides of the needle. Knot it at the bottom, or cast on by stitching a few running stitches on top of each other. That way the needle won't escape from the job and it gives you double-strength stitching.

Before replacing a button, look at how the others are attached. What shape they are sewn in: square? Cross? Vertical or horizontal lines? Copy so your button is part of the same team.

How to turn up trousers

Put on the trousers or garment to be hemmed. Stand in front of a mirror and decide whether you need to hem something up or down.

Fold and mark place with a pin then carefully take off the garment. If you have an extra pair of hands assisting you, there is the option of pinning all the hem, or both legs of the trousers, with the garment on. But if you are alone, you can judge the rest from your strategic pinpoint. Don't pin all the way 'round with your trousers on if alone, as all the bending up and down will keep altering the length.

Pinning may seem fussy, but it is absolutely essential, especially on hems. The proverb "A stitch in time saves nine" really does apply here. Check trousers are the same length: standing permanently at an angle could be tiring.

Once the hem is pinned in place the extracautious, or first timers, should "tack" with white thread over the pins, along the hem to be stitched. Tacking is big white running stitches that keep things in place while you sew your neat stitches on.

If you feel this is just not meant to happen, take it to a dry-cleaner's as they nearly all have good alteration services. Another trick is to iron the trouser leg so you have a crisp fold to work with; it also helps cancel fabric pileups.

Finally, select and thread needle with cotton of the nearest matching shade to garment to be sewn.

Sew in the smallest, neatest stitches that your eyesight deems possible. Try the herringbone stitch, which is a cross between a running stitch and a back stitch, as the stitching practically overlaps. Blanket stitch is another option; flowers and daisy-chain stitches, though, are not ideal. Machining is not the norm for hems.

Stitch as close to the edge of the fabric as you can, trying to leave as little of the thread as possible showing on the topside. Invisibility is key here.

Iron and you are good to wear them out.

If there's not any time for all of the above, or you are running from the office, take your stapler and gingerly gun the situation back together.

DO NOT do this on silks, satins, or delicate fraying fabrics; be sure to remove before you wash, and *absolutely* before you take to the dry-cleaner's. This is not a method you should brag about, but is ideal in emergencies.

Darning socks

No one darns socks anymore, so this is a perfectly ridiculous skill to want to learn. If you find you are wearing a peep-toe pair, discard immediately. Not only could it cut off your tootsies' circulation, it is unsightly. Keep them hidden in your shoes till you get to a trash can.

For snagged tights that need to survive just a few hours longer, take a dab of clear nail varnish, or a slightly wet bar of soap, and draw a rim 'round the hole, or start of the ladder. This will seal the nylon and prevent it from running further.

How to talk to your tailor
by Stella McCartney, fashion designer

I discovered bespoke in my parents' wardrobe. My mum, as well as my dad, had suits made to measure by Tommy Nutter. They were made just for you, so they sculpted and fit like a glove, and it was this attention to detail and design that fascinated me. Yeah, it's more expensive than ready to wear, but in the end it lasts you a lifetime, so the cost is relative.

The most important thing when going to see a tailor is to know that if you are ordering bespoke you can have anything you like. You are the designer, if you like, and the suit is tailored to your mood and personality.

Do not feel intimidated, be strong-minded and tell them what you want. Traditionally tailoring was geared to men, but women should be able to have things tailor-made to fit their shapes. My mum would mix her bespoke jackets with floral printed dresses, and her style was very inspiring and individual.

Ask questions, and follow your fitting. Does it fit under the bust? Are the shoulders tight enough or too tight? Can you move your arms? What part of your silhouette do you want to enhance? And what do you want to conceal? Getting a bespoke suit made helps you understand the

shape of your body. It's a great way to hide anything you're unhappy with. The knife goes under the fabric – not you! Over the years, as your figure changes, you can bring the suit in and get it altered to fit your ever-changing shape. I want women to keep coming back and make the suit part of their wardrobe, their life. Why should men be the only ones to have suits that give them the perfect physique and have clothing that can hide a pigeon chest and so on? A tailor is your ally, he keeps your shape a closely guarded secret and, like a sculptor, will make you a new shadow.

If you aren't happy with it after three fittings, a tailor will keep going till it is perfect. You can sit in a bath in your jeans to shrink them to fit, or you can get a tailor to teach you the tricks for your size. Work with them and create the perfect curves.

The fibers in really good suits are wool, so you shouldn't dry-clean as the chemicals will strip them down; just take it back to the tailor and they can steam it with the industrial iron and revive it. A crease down the center front of a pair of trousers is the essential finishing touch. On my bespoke there is one pink buttonhole, so those in the know see just how well suited you are.

If ordering bespoke, I usually recommend that you get a single-breasted jacket with two varieties of trousers, say a low-slung hipster pant and a more classic style. This is the staple that can never fail. Women can look powerful as well as sexy in a suit; think of Bianca Jagger in her white pant suit, or Madonna. I don't let Savile Row intimidate me, you know it's not a man's world. So why let them be the only ones to wear the trousers?!

How to iron the blues away
by Bella Freud, fashion designer

Just on the cusp of adolescence, when I could already feel the stirrings of the avalanche that would be teenagehood, I got a Saturday job doing the ironing for my next-door neighbors. We lived on a splendid estate in the heart of the Ashdown Forest in what had been the Laundry, and our neighbors occupied the Coach House. They were a retired army couple, friendly, but from a different world. I wasn't sure that I knew how to iron, but I needed the money to buy . . . anything.

Joan, my employer, led me upstairs into a small room with a mountain of crumpled things. She didn't seem like the ironing type herself, but proceeded to give me one of the most useful lessons of my life. "First, take the shirt, drape it over the board back down, and iron the yoke and the back of the collar. Then do the cuffs, followed by the sleeves. Do the sides next, then go back to the back. Your final loving stroke is devoted to the collar" (maybe not her precise words). I followed her instructions to the letter and found I had a knack for it. Then I experimented a bit as I couldn't believe her sequence of applications could really make much difference – but it did! It was like the perfect child's routine: change it and everything gets muddled and

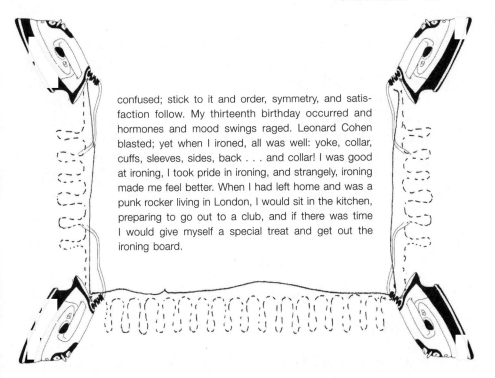

confused; stick to it and order, symmetry, and satisfaction follow. My thirteenth birthday occurred and hormones and mood swings raged. Leonard Cohen blasted; yet when I ironed, all was well: yoke, collar, cuffs, sleeves, sides, back . . . and collar! I was good at ironing, I took pride in ironing, and strangely, ironing made me feel better. When I had left home and was a punk rocker living in London, I would sit in the kitchen, preparing to go out to a club, and if there was time I would give myself a special treat and get out the ironing board.

How to make a curtain

There is drawing a curtain, draping a curtain, buying a curtain, and then, only if you have exhausted all the ready-made options, there is making a curtain.

Before measuring up, decide on the drop and what type of rail you'd like, as this will affect the width gathered, length, and so on. Then think about coverage. Usually for pulleys and rod-operated curtains you should add an extra three to four inches on each side for the operation, and say a generous six to eight inches above the frame for all the hooks, rail, etc. With this knowledge, measure the right height and width. Measure the frame, but don't forget the extras you need to add to your calculations.

Purchase or, more sensibly, borrow a sewing machine, collect swatches, and choose pattern of style to be attempted. If you're a novice, go for something simple, and remember there's a lot to be said for the benefits of bohemi-anly draped swathes of raw-cut fabric. Make sure your curtain fabric is heavy enough in weight for the style.

When you get the fabric home, and providing the washing instructions allow it, whack it into the machine to soften it up. Then carefully, following your pattern, start to cut as directed. Pin, tack, hem, and then you are ready to machine together. Don't forget to line the curtains. This makes them look far more substantial, and otherwise the object of the game will be defeated, as sunlight will still pour in. Thread through or attach hooks, attach to curtain rod above window, and let them hang.

How to decorate a Christmas tree

In the UK, in Trafalagar Square, (London), the Norwegian Christmas tree goes up on the first Thursday of December. Norway first presented this to Britain in 1947 as a thank-you for their alliance in the war, and have contin-ued to do so ever since. It towers in at around seventy feet. The tree at Rockefeller Center in New York is another global tree. Trees at home need not be as tall.

Traditionally speaking, you don't have to put the tree up until as late as twelve days before Christmas, and if it's a real tree the closer to Christmas the better to keep needle dropping to a minimum. The crucial thing is that you take your tree down by twelfth night, the Epiphany, January 6.

A bit like padded bras and fake tans, plastic trees are good, but never as good as the real thing. There is one rule you must not break: trees are green. Blue, white, or silver trees are not an option.

When buying your real fir tree, select the freshest one available. To test this, grasp a branch and give it a gentle tug toward you; very few needles, if any, should fall. If you're able to give the tree a shake or a bounce, and it leaves a pool of needles, move on. If you are not decorating straight away, store the tree in an inch of water, ideally in a garage out of the wind or sun. You should stand a tree in a corner. Keep it away from radiators, which will cause it to wither and die. Hoover or brush under tree daily to avoid needle buildup.

A naked tree is a sad sight. The first decoration should be the fairy on top, particularly as you may need to bend the tree to get her on. She is going to supervise how her tree is filled. Then the lights. These will inevitably fuse, but need to be added at this stage so you can ensure they are evenly distributed. Wind from top to bottom, toward the plug socket. Candles are cute, but go for the electrical variety, as real flames on trees are a hazard. Then start spreading over the tree your themed decorations. Do you have a color? Is it traditional or kitsch? Sparse or crammed? Is it child-friendly or just for you? If it has chocolates, be careful not to locate them too near the lights as they could melt.

How to Be a Green-fingered Goddess

Mary, Mary, quite contrary,
how does your garden grow?
With silver bells and cockleshells
and pretty maids all in a row.
—*Nursery rhyme*

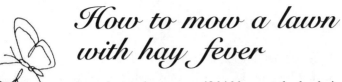

How to mow a lawn with hay fever

An unkempt lawn, even if hidden out the back, is a disaster and must be rectified regardless of the sneezes it will induce.

Sprinkle the lawn with a hose to make it damp, or, if you are an early riser, do it at early dawn with the dewdrops making the lawn moist. The damp will stop the pollen from throwing itself about while you are cutting the lawn, thus making this task possible. But if your eyes are still watering, there are acres still to cut, and the damp is not easing your hay fever, tie a handkerchief over your nose, and, a bit like peeling onions, breathe through your mouth, try not to rub your eyes, and mow fast. If tears are streaming and you are coughing and spluttering, opt out; you don't want to get puffy eyes and you have given it a good try.

In a dream world, you will have either a gardener or one of the golf buggy-looking mowers that you can cruise around the grounds with. In more normal households, however, it is more likely you will have to operate a manual mower. Plug in and turn on, get to a far corner and walk, just as you would with a heavy trolley, pushing it up and down the straight aisles. Remember that it is important to mow in as straight a line as possible. Also be very careful not to mow over the extension cord as this will give you an electric shock and, among other things, a very strange hairstyle.

Despite the very tempting Pucci wellies, you can, indeed should, wear heels. Outdoor aisle gliding is very good practice for any summer weddings or garden parties and your heels will also aerate the soil nicely as you teeter along. Obviously don't soil a really good pair – have a pair of gardening heels for this job.

How to trim a hedge

Shears, manual and hand-held, are much less dangerous than the electric hedge trimmer. Think of Edward Scissorhands and all he managed to achieve. But remember that you are not trying to create complex shapes; you are just there to tidy. As with trimming bangs or bushy eyebrows, do not take things to excess.

How to put up a fence

Fencing is a chic form of exercise, as demonstrated by Madonna in the Bond movie *Die Another Day*. But for the wooden kind, don't be silly: call a gardener. If the wretched thing has fallen in the road you can prop it up, but sinking foundations and stuff like this are to be done by a master. After all, you could get splinters, ruining a decent manicure.

How to have window box chic

This is the chic, compact, and relatively low-maintenance way to have a garden, even if you don't have a garden. There is also the added bonus that you don't have a lawn to mow, so perfect for flower lovers with allergies and busy lifestyles.

First, purchase a rectangular holder from a garden center. Check that the box has a few holes at the bottom, and also at the side, near the bottom, as your plants will need proper drainage. Being swamped is as bad as being parched when trying to achieve good flower growth. Line your box with a bit of gravel over the holes, then soil, and divide the flowers up symmetrically and evenly. Never plant your flowers in a straight line: not only does this look too regimented, but you will fit far more in if you plant in a zigzag pattern. Think about your design: larger plants should go near the center or back, bulbs should be protected, while trailers should tumble off at the sides or front to give that lush and overflowing effect that you will be aiming for.

Planting your bulbs

Ideally, bulbs should be planted for spring blooming before Halloween as, nothing spooky, after this date the ground and soil will get too hard for them to get settled before the big chill.

Dig your hole, be it in a garden, pot, or a window box – the same process applies for all. Make sure that it is deep enough, and also that there is enough fresh soil all around, at the sides and below. Make the earth really moist and turn it over with a trowel, as if making a mud pie. Place the roots about two to three inches down in the soil. Make sure the bulbous end is pointing up, and the roots and rounded side look down, or else you will be growing an upside-down flower bed and getting covered in mud will all have been for nothing. Once the bulbs are planted and positioned, cover them with earth and lightly pat the fresh soil down. Do not pack it so tight that the bulb can't breathe – imagine how you would feel.

Ensure your bulbs are at least two-thirds of the way down in the box, and also try to protect the bulbs with trailers or greenery that are already growing and can shelter the early stages of the bulb. Once you have chosen and planted your daffodils, tulips, and busy Lizzies, all you have to do is wait for them to bloom.

When planting, if you fear that squirrels or other pests will be attacking and eating your bulbs, you can sprinkle broken eggshells on the surface of the soil. But another way to prevent the critters from having supper on you is to make sure the bulbs are planted nice and deep so they do not get exposed through overenthusiastic watering. (For more pest control, see page 361.)

One final requirement is to make sure your box is secure on the windowsill, on the ledge, or screwed in place. Be safe or else the neighbors will complain. This is particularly important to remember the higher you are placing the box. A piece of Brie thrown from the top of the Eiffel Tower can slice a man's head in half, so imagine the damage a mini Kew Gardens could do to someone.

Aesthetically speaking, while making one window box it might be better to try to do at least two window boxes, if architecture allows; then they can frame your home.

If window boxes are not an option, and yet you want to have some creativity, foliage, and growth to see out of the window, would hanging baskets be a happy alternative? You can buy them ready potted, but for a real sense of achievement, as with the window boxes, you should plant them yourself, mixing a combination of ready-grown plants and bulbs. But always, in your enthusiasm, be careful not to overcram – this will lead to a short-term affair because all too soon the roots will have nowhere to go. Lobelia, fuchsias, trailing geraniums, dwarf nasturtiums, begonias, french marigolds, and morning glory are all great for hanging baskets.

Be as generous as you must be sensible with your watering; this is why you have to ensure your boxes have the correct drainage. If your window/sill is sheltered from rainfall, make sure you don't leave them parched. Likewise, if there have been weeks of torrential rain, they might be drowning and gasping for shelter. Keep an eye on the buds and protect them and this will help them blossom and grow.

How to create a garden

Contrary to stereotyping, gardening is not the preserve of retired people and perky television presenters. Gardens are well worth cultivating as not only do they add color to the entrance they can also add to the value of the property. Once you get started, and the fruits of your labor start to come into bloom, it is as addictive as it is rewarding, honest.

Decide on what you want, a theme, a purpose, or a goal. Do you want all-year greenery, perennial flowers, or fresh herbs and vegetables? Are you going for color? For privacy? For greenery? Plan your garden, and shop accordingly for what you need. Start in the garden centers at DIY stores like Home Depot and then, as your ability improves, work up to more specialized shops.

Your green fingers and creativity can really explode if you have a garden. First select your plot and where, what, and how many you want to plant. You can draw it out à la landscape gardening, roughly plotting lawn, plants, and who goes where; it doesn't matter what size your garden, it's the attention to detail that counts.

If you are laying a lawn you can by all means use seed, but, just like growing a carpet, it is far easier, and instant, to measure up and lay turf. This is easy to roll out and push into place. Then you can go on to select your flowers to frame the garden.

The best spring bulbs are daffodils, tulips, and crocuses, but snowdrops are very good at surviving the winter freeze. For flowers that continue to flower, from spring through to summer, you want to plant geraniums, daisies, and fuchsias. It is also wise to plant some permanent greenery, so your garden is not dependent on what is in flower. The best way to spot evergreens is to look for plants with a slight rubbery feel to the leaves, such as ivy; most garden centers have the sections divided and signposted to help you. Climbing ivy, myrtle, and other trailing plants are good for window boxes, balconies, and breaking up large expanses of brick wall, and they grow relatively fast.

Herbs such as sage, rosemary, and bay look good, or you could add another dimension to the garden with fragrant plants such as mint, jasmine, and lavender. Lavender will not only attract butterflies but you can dry the heads for pot-pourri, or put sprigs in clothes drawers to freshen linens – a real home sweet home plant. If really ambitious and your local grocer isn't up to much, you can even try to plant your own vegetable patch.

Rocket is supereasy to grow. Cut a large square hole in a grow bag, sprinkle seeds on the surface, and with your fingers gently rub some earth over them. Water every day and four weeks later you'll be tossing your own leaves. And once you've cut it, it keeps growing back. Magic.

When flowers die, and if they are perennials, rather than dig up all your handiwork you can cut them right back, wait for next year, and see if they bloom again. If they are a one-flower wonder you will have to replace with something else.

Annuals and perennials

Annuals are plants that last a year, from seed to bloom to seed. Removing dead flower heads can prolong a plant's life, but once they reach the final fade, they have to go.

Perennials are faithful friends that return each year, and grow in size and status as they reach their full maturity. They can grow from seeds or cuttings and can last three to four years before needing to be replaced.

When it is time to replace plants or flowers, you must ensure that you use fresh compost, as old and used compost will have gathered germs from previous occupants. You cannot expect plants to flower without all the necessary minerals and nutrients to help them. In addition you must care for your plants, pruning as well as protecting them.

Gardens to inspire

To help your ideas grow, consult gardening catalogs such as White Flower Farm and magazines such as *Fine Gardening.* Or find the nearest botanical garden and aspire.

Garden decor

Giant terracotta pots and elegant watering cans are great props to have around the garden. As well as giving a garden a dramatic look, they can also serve a purpose: you can either fill with ready-grown flowers, or use them to shelter delicate new clippings, it all depends how addicted to the outdoors you get. Remember that trees and plants that need deep roots and grow big are best saved for gardens and parks; just as it was silly for the

Ugly Sisters to try to squeeze their toes into Cinderella's slipper, so should you, too, know what will fit and what will grow too large.

Facts and flowers

Amaryllis denotes passion and adventure and its name means "splendid beauty" or "pride." When you buy cut stems you can place straight into water; you do not need to recut as the stem is hollow.

Daffodils bring bad luck if a single flower is given, but a bunch will ensure happiness.

Daisies picked between noon and 1:00 P.M. have magical qualities, and are a symbol of good luck.

Honeysuckle is bad luck in Wales, but foretells a wedding in Somerset, England; careful where you pick it.

Hydrangeas are magic plants as they turn blue or pink, depending on the type of soil they grow in.

Lavender is considered an aphrodisiac.

Pansies must not be picked in fine weather or rain will occur.

Roses are the rulers of the English garden. White roses illustrate purity and innocence, the yellow rose perfect achievement and sometimes jealousy, while the red rose denotes passion and sensual desire.

Snowdrops are said, in the West of England, to be bad news. It is said that if they are brought into a house before the first chickens have hatched, all the eggs will be addled.

How to work with the weather

No one can control or really predict the weather, but you can make an educated guess as to what is suitable for your environment. You need to fill your garden with plants that can thrive with the rainfall, wind, temperature, and sunshine that affect your garden.

High summer may ripen your tomatoes, but it will also dry the earth out more quickly. Feel the soil to gauge how moist it is, and water in the early morning or sunset; don't water them while they are gasping in the midday sun as they will not be able to absorb it efficiently.

Gale-force winds can cause havoc, but so, too, can the persistent breeze. Windbreakers or hedges could be necessary; alternatively tie delicate plants into shape so they don't get battered and bent in half.

It isn't just humans that don't like frostbite, plants hate it, too. Frost can be one of the most damaging things of all for plants, as ultimately it cuts off the water supply. Check your garden to see if you have any "frost pockets" (areas that defrost slower than others). Also be warned if your garden is located at the bottom of a ditch – you might need to bed the plants in safer areas. You can minimize the damage if you keep soil heavy and moist and have branches and other plants around to protect plants while they grow.

How to prune

Pruning is an important skill in gardening. Not only does it improve the appearance of your bush, it can stimulate growth, as well as raise the quality and quantity of the flowers. The most popular plant to get pruning practice on is the rose bush.

Tall thin canes produce smaller blooms while thicker canes result in fewer but superior beauties. You can only improve and rarely kill with pruning, just don't get carried away. You will need to get your pruning shears out in mid-March and mid-November each year.

First, take off all the dead wood, dead heads, and any twigs that are choking the plant's growth.

Cut all canes down to where there is a white or pale green pith; any brown coloration on the twig means it is dead or dying.

Use a sharp saw or shears to cut the rose, and always wear gloves as you don't want to get scratched by its thorns.

Cut between a quarter and a half inch above the bud, on a downward-sloping cut.

If you cut an outside bud to make the plants grow wider, and the inside bud for a more upright growth, you can shape your rose bush. You want to encourage the plant to open up outward for better air circulation and exposure to sunlight.

How to deal with pests

Keep an eye on how things are growing. There are all kinds of creepy crawlies to dread.

When you plant your garden, sow the seeds, lay the turf, and turn in fresh compost, also invest in a pest and disease guide. Know how to spot the enemy in its early stages. Do the leaves have spots or teeth marks on them? Carefully learn to tell good from bad.

Only use chemical fertilizers sparingly, if you use them at all; weed killers and strong products can strip plants of their good minerals as well as the harmful ones. Add organic composts and good soils so that the plants have good grounding to sink into. Watering with a hose or sprinkler can dislodge new settlers, and it is also a great idea to have lots of varieties of plants so no invader can sit and munch through a whole flower bed.

Slugs need to be eradicated. Water the garden in the morning rather than in the evening, as this will leave the slugs dehydrated and unable to attack, or put down copper strips to slow them in their path. When digging up gardens, or planting fences, put on your gloves and be sure to throw all the slugs out while you can, rather than trap them in.

Rabbits are not a gardener's friend as they like to nibble at leaves and can dig up painstakingly planted bulbs; so rather than being on sentry duty you will need repellent to rid yourself of these. Deer, moles, and other non-pets can also invade, so be on your guard.

Soil disease can be the kiss of death, and you will need to solarize it to get it out, and dig out any plants in the affected area. Then you have to turn over the fresh soil and mix in fresh compost to restore its health.

Above all, learn to outsmart and outwit your enemy.

How to keep plants alive and well indoors

It goes without saying that plants need to be watered regularly. If plants are particularly leafy you can use a spraymister to freshen and moisturize with even more precision. Think about their well-being and try not to place them in direct sunlight, or in the shade. Read their labels, or know what type of plant goes well where. As with Christmas trees, you should not place your plants next to a radiator; you would pass out, too, if you sat in a sauna all day. Think of where you would want to stand if you were that flower, and no doubt they will agree.

How to choose the best cut flowers

No home is complete without a regular supply of flowers. Whether they are grown in your garden, delivered to your door with love, or you've sent yourself a delivery to the office, they are an essential addition to spruce up the home.

Buy an odd number of stems – even numbers look contrived and are harder to position in the vase – and do not be stingy with the content. If you are on a budget, get the florist to cut you some foliage and extra leaves to fill out the display, or choose a vase with a small hole. Be careful of what you mix, as larger flowers, such as lilies, will demand all the attention.

When filling the vase, twist and view from every angle to check it is totally aesthetically pleasing. Do not neglect to do an overhead view, as this is in reality the flowers' best angle and they want to turn to the sun.

Have a selection of vases on hand as different flowers suit different shapes and lengths. Tulips need tall glasses while freesias get lost in anything too elongated. Impressive displays need pride of place on a coffee table; anything wilting should go straight in the trash.

What flowers to choose and when?

It is often best to see what looks the liveliest when you are in the florist, but you can also have an idea of what is in bloom when. Peonies and tulips are always popular, but there are other alternatives.

January	Snowdrop and daffodil
February	Violet and primrose
March	Jonquil and tulip
April	Sweet pea and daisy
May	Lily of the valley and hawthorn
June	Rose and honeysuckle
July	Larkspur and water lily
August	Poppy and gladiolus
September	Aster and morning glory
October	Calendula and cosmos
November	Chrysanthemum and freesia
December	Holly, ivy, mistletoe

Bridal bouquets

The Roman bride and groom would wear floral garlands as a symbol of their fertility and long life together, and some even had garlic in the mix to ward off evil. Today they are more to symbolize a maiden, and the scents hopefully will forever hold memories of that day. The throwing of the bouquet came from America, clearly originating from a woman once on a volleyball team. Unwed women have to get in training to catch it, as it is said that she who does will be the next to wed.

But what to have in your big day bloom? Flowers have so many meanings it is important to send your beloved the right message.

Flower	Meaning
Apple blossom	Better things to come
Anthurium	No secrets from you
Birch	Longevity
Camellia	Gratitude
Cornflower	Admiration and hope
Daisy	Innocence
Fern	Fascination and sincerity
Forget-me-not	Remembrance and true love
Hollyhock	Devotion
Honeysuckle	Generosity
Hyacinth	Loveliness
Iris	Faith and wisdom
Ivy	Eternal fidelity
Jasmine	Amiability
Lavender	Sweetness and joy
Lilac	Youthful innocence
Lily of the valley	Happiness renewed
Mimosa	Sensitivity
Moss	Affection always
Peony	Captivation
Rose (red)	Fascination
Rose (coral)	Passion and desire
Rose (yellow)	Friendship
Rose (dark pink)	Thankfulness
Rose (pale pink)	Grace
Rose (lavender)	Enchantment
Rose (white)	Innocence
Snowdrop	Hope
Tuberose	Dangerous pleasure
Tulip	My perfect lover
Violet	Faithfulness

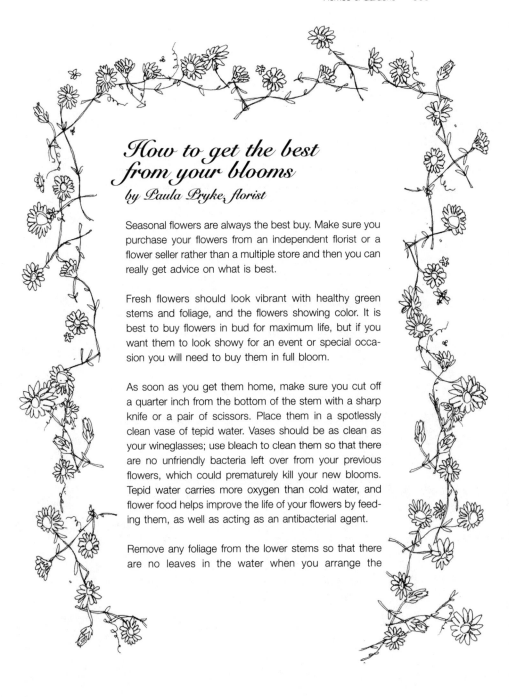

How to get the best from your blooms
by Paula Pryke, florist

Seasonal flowers are always the best buy. Make sure you purchase your flowers from an independent florist or a flower seller rather than a multiple store and then you can really get advice on what is best.

Fresh flowers should look vibrant with healthy green stems and foliage, and the flowers showing color. It is best to buy flowers in bud for maximum life, but if you want them to look showy for an event or special occasion you will need to buy them in full bloom.

As soon as you get them home, make sure you cut off a quarter inch from the bottom of the stem with a sharp knife or a pair of scissors. Place them in a spotlessly clean vase of tepid water. Vases should be as clean as your wineglasses; use bleach to clean them so that there are no unfriendly bacteria left over from your previous flowers, which could prematurely kill your new blooms. Tepid water carries more oxygen than cold water, and flower food helps improve the life of your flowers by feeding them, as well as acting as an antibacterial agent.

Remove any foliage from the lower stems so that there are no leaves in the water when you arrange the

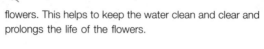

flowers. This helps to keep the water clean and clear and prolongs the life of the flowers.

The best way to maintain the life of your flowers is to change the water daily and recut the stems every three days. This is a little tedious, but worth it for longer-lasting beauty. Keep them at a constant temperature and out of any drafts.

Fruit gives off an aging hormone that can prematurely kill flowers, so do not buy flowers that have been kept with fruit, and do not place near any of your own fruit. Sometimes we use fruit decoratively with flowers, but only for special occasions and when the life of the arrangement is not paramount.

Always have one vase of scented flowers in your home. I usually place my scented vase in my bathroom or in the hallways, never in the kitchen or dining room because they can overpower the food. All scented flowers, with the exception of lilies, have a shorter life than nonscented varieties because they expend most of their energy being fragrant. Sweet peas, lily of the valley, tuberose, mimosa, freesia, and stocks are all examples.

Lilies will last longer if you remove the stamens of pollen. Just pinch these out when you first arrange the flowers and before they go brown and dusty. Pollen will stain, so be careful of your furnishings and clothing. If you get pollen on your clothes, remove it immediately with masking tape.

Most people like to keep their flowers until they drop. It is best to throw them out when they start to fade as they end up smelling vile and often make a mess on furniture.

To make an impact on a budget, use vases of seasonal branches such as blossom, berries, or leaves. I adore cherry blossom in spring, the new silver-green leaves of whiteleaf in early summer, crab apples in autumn, and ilex berries in winter.

The current fashion is to have a collection of vases that look good together and have one stem of an exotic flower in each. This "deconstruction" style works well with anthuriums, orchids, and calla lilies.

I also like to use this style for my dining table, using lots of small glass votives filled with one type of flower or flower head. This allows you room for big serving plates and lots of wineglasses (and bottles!) but still looks impressive. A personal favorite at the moment is the blue vanda orchid which, although expensive, lasts at least three weeks.

Expensive flowers are often the ones that last the longest and are nearly always a better value than cheaper ones; like everything in life, flowers are graded and sold according to quality, and the most expensive are always the best. Tropical flowers (helliconia, anthuriums, gingers) and orchids are very good value, as are lilies and amaryllis.

How to care for tulips

Everyone has their preferred spray, but tulips are a very popular choice because when they are youthful they are the loveliest thing to lift a room, and when they droop they don't drop their pollen. When you get tulips you have to go through a rigorous care ritual to encourage them to live and come into a long bloom. First, take cut flowers and plunge immediately in a basin of cold water. Also fill the chosen vase with water. While under the water, cut a small diagonal tip off the stem so you make a fresh cut that has not been exposed to the air. Repeat this process for the whole bunch, then transfer into a vase one by one, quickly, to avoid the tulip getting air in the raw cut. Take a pin and prick a hole an inch below the head, all the way through the stem. This air hole will ensure the tulips stand upright for longer.

How to purchase flowers for gifts and groveling

If the "bouquet" you receive comes from a garage, or contains garish shades of carnations, slam the door back in their face. This was a cheap, ill-considered gift. Similarly, warning bells should ring if you get a huge unexpected floral delivery; yes, suitors and admirers may be earnestly trying to woo you, but if it comes from the person you are dating you might want to check what they did last night. Know your favorite flowers, and have a favorite florist on hand to recommend in each of the major cities. Question what someone really thinks of you if they send you a Venus fly trap or a cactus plant.

Joining the Jet Set

The Owl and the Pussy-Cat went to sea,
In a beautiful pea-green boat.
They took some honey, and plenty of money,
Wrapped up in a five-pound note.
—*Edward Lear*

How to Get the Travel Bug

Only mad dogs and Englishmen go out in the midday sun.
—*Noël Coward*

How to get started

You might have fifty-seven channels on cable, or be able to google any piece of information you like on the Internet, but the only real way to find inspiration is to get out there, see it, and experience it. Travel should start at an early age; children under two travel free so there is no excuse. Ideally you should aim to discover one new city or country a year. Go to as many places as you have pages in your passport.

The tourist can be a horrible stereotype; the trick is to blend in with the locals, respect their culture, and the doors will open for you to explore.

Picking a destination is like deciding which chocolate to pluck from a box: you can see what it looks like in the picture, but you don't know what it is like on the inside until you have taken a bite. Take a risk and find a new favorite.

Films and books are a brilliant source of inspiration. *The Sound of Music* will send you to Salzburg, *Moulin Rouge* to Paris, *Picnic at Hanging Rock* to Australia, and *Amadeus* to Prague. If you are feeling literary, a dip into *Tess of the D'Urbervilles* will have you heading to Dorset, E. M. Forster's *A Room with a View* to Florence, while Bram Stoker's *Dracula* will pack you off to Transylvania, and Vikram Seth's *A Suitable Boy* to India. Alternatively the truly cultured could seek inspiration through paintings; let Gauguin send you to Tahiti, Monet to his garden in Giverny, France, or go to a country for its galleries.

Everyone should visit the *Mona Lisa* in the Louvre in Paris at least once. The view from the top of the Empire State Building in New York and sunsets on an exotic island are also essential. Borders and equators are there to be crossed. If you love Thai food, why not visit Thailand? If you have a shoe collection to rival *Sex and the City*'s Carrie Bradshaw, perhaps go to New York to compare styles. Holidays are great opportunities for role-play. But there is also much to be said for lying on a white sandy beach, where your only worry is what factor sun cream to wear.

You will, of course, need the appropriate wardrobe whatever the destination, so you need to investigate the culture of the country you are visiting. In some countries, such as Saudi Arabia, shoulders should be covered. In Japan it is considered the height of bad manners to blow your nose in the street. Likewise, two blonde girls in a traditional Arabic state may raise eyebrows; it might be best to cover your head. It is worth checking things out before signing off on the deposit.

If you still don't feel you've found the place you're after, you could *cautiously* ask to see a *selection* of your friends' holiday snaps, or could go to *www.expedia.com* or *www.lastminute.com* and see what destinations they have on offer.

How to decide when you are going

You need to know, roughly, what the weather will be like and what to expect at your chosen destination. If it is for work that is not too important, as they will be responsible for transporting you from office to airport to office to hotel. Air-conditioned environments are not weather-sensitive. If you are going to exotic climates, check when the rainy season is; likewise, do not go to Australia expecting a white Christmas. Do your homework.

Cities are great for Christmas shopping and short weekend breaks, while it would be rude to do the wilds of the Tuscan countryside in anything less than a week.

Once you have chosen the location, you have to decide on where to stay. This is budget, as well as holiday, dependent. It will also help you decide who your travel companion is and how long you will be away. Decide if you want self-catering or catered, to be able to do it yourself, or simply be able to dial up room service. Be honest, sometimes the whole "rustic" thing is really exhausting.

How to be inspired – gorgeous places to go to
by Christopher Bailey, creative director, Burberry

You can be inspired by many different things, but travel is the most obvious. Time and time again, I find myself inspired by England, and where I grew up, which fits perfectly with my work at Burberry, but you should also open your eyes to adventures and see as much of the world as you can.

Salts Mill Gallery, West Yorkshire

At school I learned that in 1853, Mr. Titus Salt's mills employed three thousand people, and a whole village grew around them. But when the textile industry started to flourish elsewhere, it became a sorry sight on the landscape. When it was transformed into studios and then became the home for the largest collection of David Hockney's works, as his hometown of Bradford is nearby, I thought it was perfect. I love the combination of the old mill and the vibrancy of Hockney's art.

The V&A and the Metropolitan Museums

Grand museums are the most inspiring places to wander around. I love walking through all the different cultures of the world, and forgetting all my problems and soaking in the reverential hush, even if it is only for a short while. I love the peacefulness and tranquillity, and how things have been preserved. You must also go to the National Portrait Gallery. I really love museums for their artefacts and the Portrait Gallery for all the unspoken stories. I love the Tudor room, and the way that only recently did they break with the tradition that said you had to be dead to hang in there – only in England!

The Meiji Jingu Shrine, Tokyo

This shrine was built in 1920 by Emperor Meiji to inspire advancement, for people to build trains, universities, banks, and governments. He was the emperor who really opened Japan up to the rest of the world. The cedar-wood temple is set in 175 acres of woodland, and it has one of every tree that grows in Japan in it. It is the most soulful and restful place in the heart of the city. It's at its most magical in April when the cherry blossom is in full bloom. Its shrine means *shinto* (heaven) and when you go in, you have to wash your hands, rinse your mouth, clap your hands, and bow, and in return for observing their rituals you become Japanese and are able to revel in its calm. If you are lucky you might be able to witness a ceremony.

Antwerp

Last but by no means least, I love this city because of the architecture, the people, and the blend of cultures and life in Belgium. They have the best bars and the best restaurants and everyone should go there at least once in their life, if not once a year. The best hotel to stay in is the White Lily, which is owned by two sisters who let you wander 'round every room and choose the one you want to stay in.

How to book your holiday

When you have agreed on budget, dates, and details of your trip, you are finally ready to book. Hooray. This can be done direct with the hotels, on the Internet, or through an agency. Even if you don't book at a travel agency, it is still worth going in and getting a selection of brochures to browse, and seeing if they have any alternative suggestions.

If you are going overseas for a wedding, or any other specific event, it is worth asking if the bride and groom have any suggested venues, as big events tend to get group discounts or special rates for the occasion. If you have any friends or relatives in the hospitality trade, now would be the time to drop them an e-mail, and see if they like you enough to hook you up with a good deal.

Just before you book, check that you can get adequate time off from work and that it's a sensible time to go. Confirm and reconfirm your flight and hotel reservations as these, particularly the travel bookings, tend to be set in stone once made. Make sure you have booked what you want, or else you may not make check-in on time.

It is also sensible when booking to check that your passport is up to date and in order. This will avoid any last-minute panics, and hours in a queue to renew it. Passports tend to take at least three weeks to renew in the post. Emergency ones can be issued, but they are often only a short-term solution and are a hassle your blood pressure would be much happier to pass on. Passport panics will also cause you to miss out on lots of last-minute shopping. Check with the agent when you are booking if you need any visas or vaccinations to get to, or be safe at, your chosen resort. Vaccines are usually only for the more exotic locations; cities tend to be full of man-made hurdles.

While thinking of your health, check that you have travel insurance and coverage for any unforeseen emergency. You do not want to discover problems when you arrive. Deal with it before departure. Pick up travel insurance from an agent or at the airport. Get annual coverage so you are protected for all your little flurries overseas. Or indeed, check to see if you already have it, as many credit cards offer it inclusive in their joining packages.

Photocopy your passport and leave a copy, along with your travel itinerary, with your parents/emergency contact. This may sound over-cautious, but should you and your passport be parted by, say, a light-fingered local, back home can furnish you with all the details you need to speed your departure.

Most countries will have an American consulate, and if where you are going doesn't, check the country is safe to travel to. Do not visit war zones, leave these to Mother Teresa and Kate Adie types. Remember: life is not like the Bond films. Consulates cannot get you out of jail, act as your personal guide, or give you a work permit. They are able to vouch for you, stick up for you (limitedly), and hook you up with help in *emergencies only*.

How to pack the essentials

Make a list of what you want to take and what you think you should take. Try to think about where you are going, what you will be doing, and who you will be seeing. See if you can make the two lists tally.

Leave some room for shopping abroad. If you don't manage this – well, let's face it, a suitcase is there to be filled – try to squeeze an extra holdall flat into your case for the amazing bargains and essential mementos of your trip.

Toiletries, toothbrush, makeup/sun protection, first aid, and hair products are all essential. Yes, quite possibly you can buy shampoo in New York, sun cream in Sydney, and a toothbrush in Tokyo, but who really has time to look for these sorts of things? Far nicer to bring your own, and do not be fooled into thinking the hotel will have nearly enough shampoo to keep your locks luscious; those bottles are never quite big enough. Phone chargers and contact numbers and addresses you might need on location should be accounted for here.

Pack in stages. Ideally, lay stuff out in piles the week before so you can live with your choices. Things should be subject to a brutal edit, before passing the final selection and getting consigned to the case.

Write a list of what you are packing as you fill your case. Not only will this show you what you are taking in black and white, so you can assess whether seventeen white vest tops for a two-day trip is excessive, but it is also a godsend if the suitcase doesn't manage to rejoin you at the other end.

How to shut a suitcase? Ah, now that's another thing. Try everything, push and pull, squeeze and plead, and if all else fails sit on it and hope that you don't have to open it till the other end. If only Mary Poppins's bag was a reality. Just remember that the more you squash the more creases you have to deal with at the other end.

You do not have to pack a suitcase that you can lift, but one that some-one else can lift, or at very least help you drag across to a trolley. You only need to be able to stagger from house to cab, cab to trolley, arrivals to trolley and cab driver to cab, and then hotel staff take over. If a frequent traveler, get one with wheels and aim not to greet your public after a long-haul flight.

Yes, flights do have a weight restriction – see what this is on your ticket. In an emergency you could always pay excess baggage or have it sent sepa-rately to your destination. As long as you do not exceed restrictions, or requirements that vary with every journey, there is no law about what fash-ion you put in your case, just try to contain it all inside. There is nothing worse than seeing underwear flying all over Terminal 2. Try to travel with a gentleman who aims to prove the age of chivalry is not dead. Travel husbands are great for carrying cases, finding trolleys, and dealing with check-in, leaving you to focus on Duty Free.

Just before you leave, put the padlock on the suitcase (if you are allowed), check your reservation and that tickets are all in order. You can e-mail the night before you fly to re-reconfirm, as this will help them avoid any double bookings that are really too much to deal with, especially after a long-haul flight. But don't come over as too needy and neurotic before you arrive.

As you shut the front door, leave a note canceling the milk delivery, check that you have passport, ticket, Visa.

How to pack
by Anya Hindmarch,
accessories designer

This is an ideal time to spring clean your bags, and ditch any receipts and rubbish that are languishing at the bottom of them.

I use what I call the "Russian Doll" formula to make sure you can change your handbag at a moment's notice. Have little loose leather pockets inside, one for makeup/medical, one for money, one for receipts, one for camera, one for passport, etc. That way you can lift all pockets into a new handbag and not have to dig out a million little bits, which takes hours. This also means that you can minimize easily by only taking the relevant pockets when you need them, so leave the makeup pocket in the bathroom, but take the correct-currency money pocket to lunch, rather than dragging the whole bag everywhere. I love to color code them, that way it is easy to know what is what. I go for gold kid for money, silver for receipts, pink for passports.

The case
Packing your suitcase requires a similar methodology. I have categories of things that I pack regularly and that I leave presorted, so I can grab them without having to think. Each category has a container to prompt me and keep it all organized. I have a wash bag for toiletries, one

for hair/makeup, an amenity case for jewelry. I use my shoe bags for underwear and hosiery and laundry. Ziploc bags are great, too, but you should not store anything in these that can get snagged. There is nothing worse than arriving in Tokyo and realizing you have forgotten something; this way you can count the containers and know if all the pieces are present and correct.

Line the base of the case with jeans and woolens, heavy bulkier items. The next layer should be any dresses or coats or long, trailing items; work your way lighter and lighter till you reach the top. Fold shirts inwards, mirroring the way they are packaged when you get them in the store, roll light cardigans and tops to fill the gaps, and ensure all explodable items – such as shampoo, perfume, and toothpaste – are wrapped in carrier bags as the air pressure may cause them to pop, and you don't want that stain all over your silks. Shoes should also always be packed in their own bags as you don't want to get mud on your best stuff.

I often pack things on hangers, with tissue in between so I can lift them out of the case and straight into the wardrobe. Hotel hangers are notorious for not having hooks, or just being too few in number.

Above all, never let your case embarrass you; pack as if you were being spot-checked at customs. Better to have your "smalls" cozied away in a drawstring bag than on show to the sniffer dog. Finally, adorn the outside of your case with a unique marking, a bow or a belt or a way that you can quickly recognize it as yours when it falls off the conveyor belt at arrival.

Model Angela Lindvall on what to pack:

Packing has become an art form. Whether going on a short trip or long journey, you don't want to find yourself with "nothing to wear." Avoid packing too much and try and bring things that are interchangeable. For example, with each pair of trousers you should have at least three tops that work.

It's good to choose layered outfits so you can add or take away, as no one can ever really predict the weather.

Never pack too little.

Always bring a jacket, even if you're going to a warm place; you don't want to get stuck in the cold when the sun goes in.

Avoid bringing too many shoes – easier said than done – but they are bulky to pack. Try to plan outfits around two pairs, plus the ones you're traveling in, which should be the ones that are least easy to pack, say, your biker boots. Be versatile. Also stuff the toes of heels with tissue paper, scarves, or rolled-up tights so that they keep their shape in the case.

Accessories are key for the traveler. They are small, and a great way to change and modify your looks (belts, jewelry, and scarves all pack well). Dresses are also great travel items as you can roll them into your case, and they are a whole look in one. It is always good to have one dressy look, just in case you end up somewhere fancy. Lastly, a great pashmina or shawl is a must have. It is as stylish as it is adaptable, from wrapping 'round you on a plane, to draping over your shoulders in the evening.

How to travel

Daisy, Daisy, give me your answer do . . . 'Cause you'll look sweet upon the seat of a bicycle made for two.

—*Lyrics by Harry Dacre*

This is up to you, as obviously when you travel you will be doing it in style. However, that is not dependent on being in first class, or having a complete set of Vuitton luggage, although both of these certainly help.

Do consider all your options: the most uncomfortable – the tandem (a bicycle made for two); then there is most expensive – a private jet; the most romantic – the gondala; the most environmentally friendly – a glider or sail boat. The decision is yours. There is always a car, coach, and train, but why not jazz things up and look at a trip on the Orient Express? Sailing encompasses everything from canoes to cruises. Then of course there is flying. Sadly there is no longer a supersonic trip on the Concorde on offer, but private helicopters and hot-air balloons are very nice. Horse-drawn carriages, elephants, and camels are also options, but they are rather slow and have limited onboard entertainment.

A brief history

I love flying. I've been to almost as many places as my luggage.
—*Bob Hope*

Although man always looked to the sky, until the 1400s it remained exclusively for birds. In 1492 Leonardo da Vinci started to draw and theorize about flying machines, but things didn't take off until the Montgolfier brothers invented the hot-air balloon in 1783. The bicycle was invented in 1790, the railway locomotive in 1814, but nothing else successfully left the ground until 1899, when Ferdinand von Zeppelin invented the first airborne dirigible. In 1903 the Wright brothers invented the first engined airplane, five years before Henry Ford and his automobile. Man landed on the moon in 1969, and in 1970 the first jumbo jet took off. With commercial flights and the Concorde, the world became a much more accessible place. Next thing you know the holiday in space will finally become reality. Lift off.

Airport amusements

It is essential to arrive early at the airport. Not only does it give you time to do all the necessary check-in and security rituals, but the early bird baggeth the best seats.

Upgrading is not an everyday occurrence, but it is more frequent than winning the lottery. It is at the discretion of those behind the counter who gets the bulkhead and who gets seated next to the toilets. Smile. Remember that happiness is mainly dependent on the mood of the person at the check-in desk, rather than the number of seats sold on the flight. Be nice. Ooze charm. Dress smartly, but not so smartly that you will feel uncomfortable; ballgowns are bulky, corsets and excessive underwiring will set off all the metal detector alarms, and wide-brimmed hats will prevent you from viewing the in-flight movie.

In economy good seats to ask for are the ones next to emergency exits, as they often have more leg room, although they can be colder. On long-haul flights opt for the middle section at the front of the plane, as this is where the fold-down area for travel cots and tots is and so there's a bit of extra room. The downside is that a screaming infant may be brought on to use the area. But if you have to be ousted to make room for the travel cot, there's a chance that you could be upgraded.

Also try to have compact hand luggage, ideally all contained in a fabulous designer label; but if you are on your way to Taiwan to get a knockoff, maybe save this for your next trip. Take a heavy moisturizer, face spray, a digital camera, a book to scribble in and a book to curl up with, a large bottle of water, and an extra pair of socks.

Don't underestimate what can be found at Duty Free. This obviously applies only at main International Airports; at some outbacks you are lucky to get last week's English-language newspaper. It is worth holding out and getting a supply of Touche Éclat and a fresh bottle of perfume, or whatever your poison is, here. The shopping is akin to a few hours in a department store at rock-bottom prices. The only thing to be wary of is that they do not always carry the most up-to-the-minute colors, but when is red lipstick or Chanel No. 5 out of fashion?

How to avoid jet lag, travel sickness, and home sickness

The average airplane is sixteen years old. And so is the average airplane meal.
—*Joan Rivers*

If you are being totally jet set and crossing time zones, it will catch up with you sooner or later. Avoid caffeine and alcohol, food you can't identify, and small talk, and try to adapt to the time zone you are heading to as fast as possible.

If you are traveling west, it is best to arrive in the late afternoon, then it is not too long until bedtime and you will be fresh when you rise. If you are traveling east, try to arrive in the morning. Take the night flight, watch one movie, then lights out. Wake up when you land and arrive in sunlight. Don't give in to the desire for a nap as it will send your body clock into chaos. If you can't sleep on the plane, put the radio on with soft calming music and shut your eyes; it should drown out the sound of the engine and any screaming children.

It is a fact that due to the air pressure in the cabins your emotions will be at fever pitch, and to avoid really joining the mile-high club with a total stranger or, indeed, falling head over heels for someone over your plastic food, it's best to focus on all the lame films you have been harboring a burning desire to see, but been too cool to admit to.

Do not risk watching anything too taxing in the in-flight movie department, such as films involving airplane crashes or death, horror, and mutilation; the latter particularly applies if you are daring to do a night flight alone. Also, do not start to watch a movie half an hour before you land, you will never know what happens, never track down the film to rent, and it will always bug you. Curl up and settle down for the ride.

If you view a flight from London to New York as the equivalent time of watching two films and flicking through your favorite glossy, your fear of flying will seem unfounded and evaporate. If not, tightly clutch the hand of the person next to you, as nervous flying is contagious and they can shake for the journey with you. Calming someone else will calm you down.

It is never great to be sick when away from home, but sometimes even the motion of the journey is enough to set some people off. Do not let this put you off adventuring. For travel sickness, be prepared. In car journeys, do not read while the vehicle is in motion, especially if you are the driver. This includes maps.

On planes and trains the faint-hearted should get an aisle seat. You may think you want to be sandwiched safely into your seat, but it is preferable to be able to get up and move rather than leap over someone when your stomach tells you it's time to go. On planes and trains, close your eyes and try to sleep it off, while on long car journeys make frequent stops or open your window to let some fresh air in. You can buy wristbands that put a slight pressure on your wrist's pressure points, which really helps prevent nausea. That or sit next to a good-looking stranger and persuade yourself that this trip you will not feel sick, as it would not be cool to turn a shade of green and vomit on them.

There is another type of sickness when traveling that has no drugs to cure it: homesickness. Call or e-mail a loved one, bring photos with you, and drink tea.

How to look stylish after a long-haul flight

Basically impossible if it's been a really long flight, and if there was any turbulence – forget it. But for shorter flights, and for style devotees, slip your sunglasses on, carry only one handbag, and whip on the heels.

How to sleep

If you have too much on your mind, it is very hard to roll over and sleep. Try to leave all your worries in the office, the sitting room, or for another day. You do not want bags under your eyes. If you are away from home, jet-lagged, and don't know what the time is, close the curtains and your eyes and try to relax.

Listen to tranquil music. Have a soothing bath, a calming cup of camomile tea. Is there anyone who can make you a cup of cocoa? Make the room dark and cozy, and choose a bed that is soft and comfy. Put lavender essence on the pillows. If all else fails, read till your eyes are too droopy and tired to stay open. But only read fairy tales or nice dream-enhancing stories.

Counting sheep, counting receipts, counting calories, counting bills are so so boring, you're bound to nod off.

Counting mistakes you have made, shoes, or things you want to do will wake your brain up and keep you ticking.

However gorgeous you are, everyone needs to make sure they get the correct quota of beauty sleep. Ideally this is eight hours a night, so that you are ready to fight another day with style.

How to get a room with a view

Mrs. Richards: When I pay for a view, I expect something more interesting than that.

Basil Fawlty: That is Torquay, madam.

Mrs. Richards: Well, it's not good enough.

Basil: Well . . . may I ask what you were hoping to see out of a Torquay hotel bedroom window? Sydney Opera House, perhaps? The Hanging Gardens of Babylon? Herd of wildebeest sweeping majestically . . .
—*Fawlty Towers*

Sadly we are not all like Helena Bonham Carter, but if new in town, or it's your first visit, it is nice to get a Room with a View. Ask if this is possible when you book, but also enquire how much extra, if at all, this privilege will be. Weigh up whether you want to pay for it, and whatever you get, try to appreciate the scenery. A parking lot may not be as conventionally beautiful as the sea, but perhaps there is an opportunity to see the local architecture, some great cars, or if there is any other talent out there.

When you arrive at your hotel, confirm your reservation, rate, and length of stay, and check that the room is what you were expecting before you start to unpack. It is harder to change a rate or room after you have moved into it. Curmudgeonly staff and cockroaches can all be part of the charm of the holiday. You can always do the five-star luxury hotel next year. But do be careful when you are staying with friends, or enjoying someone's hospitality, that you don't outstay your welcome. Take heed of F. Scott Fitzgerald, who wrote, "I entertained on a cruising trip that was so much fun that I had to sink the yacht to make my guests go home."

How to make your hotel room feel like home

Even if you have to travel a lot, there is no place like home, however luxurious your surroundings. Unpack as soon as possible and spread your personal belongings, and character, artistically around the room. Bringing a few "special" items can help to make you feel more at home, but if packing space was limited, drape shoes and dresses so you wake up and see something familiar.

Candles, books, incense, pictures from home are all great to help re-create your space, but this all depends on how long you will be staying. Always purchase fresh flowers as this will bring life to even the drabbest of hotel rooms. Collect items like rocks, shells, leaves, branches to freshen up the space and bring a sense of nature and comfort, but just make sure that the hotel staff don't think it is junk and trash all your efforts. Music is also key; iPods are great as you can store a wide selection of your favorites, which can transport you to any city in the world, or even back home, if you shut your eyes.

Don't forget to bring all your favorite bath and beauty products, so if it all gets too much you can just soak your troubles away.

Manners

Whatever you do, don't be tempted to become a petty crook. Extraordinary as this sounds, hotels can bring out a bizarre side to some people's usually impeccable character as delight is found in pilfering from the hotels. But do check your hotel bills. Housekeeping are wise to all the tricks and will snitch on you. Soaps, shampoos, and the basic toiletries should be free, so it's fair enough to stock up on these. Ashtrays, towels, blankets, and dressing gown are extra. Before slipping them in your bag, ask yourself, Why? Why would you want something you already have at home and which will be quadruple the price and triple the inconvenience to pack? Leave it. Buy decent souvenirs.

How to use a compass

"Second to the right, and straight on till morning." That, Peter told Wendy, in *Peter Pan*, was the way to Neverland.

Some can get their bearings from the tides, some from the stars, while others use a compass. A compass is basically a very primitive ball with a little needle or arrow that is pulled by the magnetic field attached to the North Pole. Thus, once you locate North, which you do by wiggling and twisting the ball till the arrow stops twitching and it points in one direction, you will be able to find South, its opposite, and from this you will, in theory, be able to work out where East and West are. (Think "Never Eat Shredded Wheat" for the order.)

This is only helpful if you know what direction you need to be going in, or indeed, where you are coming from. Compasses may be fine to navigate oceans and skies, but far more successful methods are reading a map, asking for directions, or hailing a cab.

How to read a map

If you are lost, or are searching for a specific location, you need a map. Don't think treasure maps, think A–Z.

A map is a visual guide to help you find your location. If a man is attempting to wrestle a map from you, let him; you may like to borrow Roseanne Barr's line: "Men can read maps better than women – because only the male mind could conceive of one inch equaling a hundred miles."

Ye Olde Mappe was drawn up by cartographers so voyagers like Columbus could show what they had discovered. In the 1930s Phyllis Pearsall woke every morning at 5:00 A.M. and walked eighteen miles a day, mapping out by hand the streets of London. Its first buyer, W. H. Smith, could barely keep up with demand as finally the A–Z map was born, a map of London in a book, with easy-to-follow grids. This system was adopted to map cities across the globe. To find your location, you look up the road and then turn to page reference and grid reference, usually a letter and a number.

On fold-out maps and long-distance journeys, the detail is less and less and the miles become inches or millimeters, but as long as you start with the map the right way up you can't go far wrong.

The Internet has revolutionized journeys with *www.yahoo.com/dd* and the AAA offering sites that will plan your route and give you detailed instructions on how to get from A to B, so log onto these, or try *www.randm-cnally.com* and print details before you set off. The only thing to be cautious of with maps and preplanning is that one-way systems, road works, and diversions are rarely shown. What may look good on paper may be an impossibility in reality, so always have an A–Z, or idea of alternative routes, just in case – traveling "as the crow flies" only works if you have black wings.

How to hail a cab across the world

TAXI! A word that needs no translation and is understood in every tongue. The trick is not how to hail one, but rather how to find one and get it to stop. Of course, in most U.S. cities, taxis are something you call for in advance, rather than hail. So for those unused to the art of hailing a taxi, a few pointers:

There are nineteen thousand taxis in London, four times the number in Paris; and around twelve thousand in New York City (and of course none are around when you need one).

In London, cabbies have to pass "the knowledge," which involves learning all the routes 'round town, and can take anything between one year and four to complete. The word "taxi" is an abbreviation of "taximeter," which was the meter invented by Wilhelm Bruhn in 1891 to measure the distance traveled and the fare to charge. Drivers have been licensed since 1838, although coachmen have been operating since the sixteenth century, starting with the mail coach. How very Jane Eyre.

In London you can simply flag them down, that is if you see one with an orange light illuminated. Finders keepers. In New York it's a white light that shines when it's free, but this is very similar to the not-so-welcome sign saying "off duty." And in the rest of Europe it's in the luck of the draw. In Paris, like most of Europe, taxis are only required to stop at official taxi ranks, and are loath to do anything to go out of their way and bend the rules to rescue a stranded and confused traveler. There are 487 well-hidden ranks in Paris, but if you don't see one of these, yank your skirt above the knee. A flash of some leg, on heels, and a whistle, will hopefully awaken the passionate side of a Parisian, but could cause a pileup in Italy.

When hailing a cab the aim is to get one pointing in the direction you are going – easy enough in Manhattan, less so if you are lost. If this is the case just leap in and appeal to the driver's sense of direction.

As for minicabs and gypsy taxis, it's a bit like eating a doner kebab. You don't, unless you first check they have a license and look legit. Only play Russian roulette and get one of these if you preagree a fare with the driver and are in a group. Aim not to be the last one left in the cab alone, but, if you are, keep your mobile on and in prominent view if you feel at all nervous. If you feel at all anxious, get out with your group of friends. Far better to get a black cab in London, a yellow one in New York, and whatever pulls up sporting a TAXI overhead light in Paris.

Try not to be a backseat driver, unless, as the meter is ticking, you feel that after going past a landmark for the third time, you should say something. But always be polite, you don't want them dumping you out in no-man's land; taxis are hard enough to find in the city.

How to tip when abroad

Tipping varies the world over. It makes sense to check the local customs in advance of departing for wherever you're going. In some places not tipping is certain to give offense, and in others tipping is certain to offend. Damned if you do, damned if you don't – so you need to know.

In Japan and China, tipping is out. Do not try slipping anything extra on top of the bill or into their pockets as service is included. However, in many foreign and domestic hotels, service might be included, but there's no guarantee the nice man who brings you your breakfast will ever see any of that. So slipping in a few bills is always appreciated (and will get you nicer service the following morning). Again, check ahead what the rules are where you're going.

The tip-o-meter rises to 10 percent in Germany and India; 10 to 15 percent in the UK, Ireland, and Italy (though here it's only optional, not obligatory). In Europe, tipping is almost always restricted to restaurants – and it should say on the bill whether the gratuity is included. Of course, a restaurant tip of up to 20 percent is expected in the U.S., with 15 percent being standard.

How to be jet set

A real jet-set traveler goes to countries off the beaten tracks. The seven wonders of the ancient world might have included the Hanging Gardens of Babylon and the Great Pyramid of Giza, but you should compile your own list of wonders.

These might include:

Paying homage to Elvis at Graceland.
Drinking cocktails in the Hemingway Bar in the Ritz Hotel, Paris.

Passing under the Bridge of Sighs on a Venetian gondola.

Successfully hiring a *vaporetto* at the Venice Film Festival.

Being served a Caesar salad at the Carlton,
    during the Cannes Film Festival.

Rolling your own cigar in Cuba.

Going up the Empire State Building on Valentine's Day.

Having tea at Claridges at the far secluded table.

Gambling in Las Vegas.

Throwing a coin in the fountains in Rome.

Paddling in the sea at Brighton.

Going to Red Square in Moscow.

Climbing to the top of St. Paul's Cathedral.

Dancing at Rio's Carneval.

Seeing in the New Year under Big Ben.

Buying tulips in Amsterdam.

Building a sandcastle in the Bahamas.

Watching a cabaret in Berlin.

Walking along the Great Wall of China.

Swimming along the Great Barrier Reef.

Surviving Delhi belly.

Being the first to discover something wonderful.

How to Prevent Motoring Horrors

Somebody actually complimented
me on my driving today. It said,
"Parking Fine."
—*Tommy Cooper*

How to learn to drive

There are two things no man will admit he cannot do well: drive and make love.

—*Stirling Moss*

When behind the wheel think more Daisy Duke than *Driving Miss Daisy*. What car you drive says a lot about you, how successful you or your partner are, and what stage of life you are at. But really, boys worry about this far more than is necessary; your prime concern is that it runs, all the tires look healthy and full, there is enough gas to get you from A to B, and there is a nice, easy parking space waiting for you when you get there. If you have reached the dizzying heights of going to a gas station to refuel, it must be assumed that:

    a) You have passed your driving test.

    b) You have a car.

    If you have answered NO to question a) you need to go and get lessons immediately.

Driving is a vital skill that everyone should have in their repertoire, and the later you learn it, the harder and worse it is. A bit like the measles. Book driving lessons without delay. Note: however cute your boyfriend is, **NEVER** get lessons from someone you want to remain friends with. When you're deciding what kind of car to learn on, think small and friendly. The vast majority of cars in the U.S. are automatic, so unless you're planning on investing in a European sports car, don't bother learning to drive stick at this point. Of course, if you can't drive stick, you won't likely be able to drive in Europe. But ask yourself: Are you planning to drive in Europe anytime soon? If so, then by all means learn to drive the stick. If not, don't torture yourself unnecessarily.

    Beyond those initial decisions, the two most important things when driving are that you wear a seat belt and that you wear soft, thin-soled flat shoes, "driving" shoes. As with many things, practice makes perfect – but it is a known fact that women are better drivers. Not only are they more rational, they are more safety conscious and they get lower insurance rates that reflect this.

Knowing which side of the road to drive on

The British do get a bad rap for driving on the left-hand side, and for making all their colonies do so – but they had history, heritage, and tradition behind the decision. In Medieval times, jousting knights kept their lances under their right arm, and traditionally gentlemen walked on the left-hand side of the road with their sword arm, the right arm, between the lady and danger. Japanese Samurai warriors walked on the left-hand side for the same reason, and the Japanese have maintained a left-hand-side drive in honor of this.

Even if you're not driving it's useful to know which side of the road a country favors, as it makes road crossing much less dangerous.

Popular left sides: Australia, Bahamas, Cyprus, Falkland Islands, Guernsey, India, Indonesia, Ireland, Japan, Jersey, Maldives, Malta, Nepal, United Kingdom.

And right sides: Afghanistan, Argentina, Belgium, Bosnia, Canada, Cuba, Denmark, Egypt, Ethiopia, Finland, France, Greece, Iraq, Italy, Kuwait, Morocco, United States, Vietnam.

The last left-hand-side country to go to the right was Sweden, on September 3, 1967.

There is one exception to the left-hand-drive rule in the UK, and this is Savoy Court in London. On the driveway leading to the hotel, the cars need to drive on the right so that ladies in fancy gowns can get out of cars without being rained on.

Sensible as it would be for us all to be united on one side (of the road), the cost would be in the billions and is therefore far too pricey to entertain.

How to mirror, signal, makeup, maneuver

Clearly a car was designed for a woman: there are mirrors everywhere! You will have a wing mirror on either side of the car, a mirror in the fold-down sun shield, and a large rectangular rearview mirror, which is so important it is the focal point of the car. This is stuck onto the front windshield, above the dash-board, and as well as showing you what is happening on the road behind you, it is a mirror made for lipstick application and eyeliner top-ups.

Get in the driving seat, buckle up, key in ignition, and adjust the mirror. The RVM should be angled so a side-glance gives you a complete view of any overtakers and talent in the car behind, without you constantly having to look over your shoulder. This really does give you eyes in the back of your head. So carefully tilt the mirror to make sure that you get it to the optimum angle, check your bangs, eyebrows, and eye makeup, and you are ready.

Red lights are deliberately timed to give you enough of a pause to freshen up your lipstick. Do not be put off or rushed by honking beeps; if they rush you they will only have to wait longer while you repair, and they are only doing it to attract your attention. You already have theirs.

Never apply makeup while moving; not only is this extremely dangerous, but it is very tricky, especially with deep colors.

The RVM is also great to do a last-minute check to see if any lipstick has strayed to your teeth, and the overhead visor mirror is great to tell you the honest truth on whether or not it is time to get those roots seen to.

Glove compartments should always have a stash of tissues, a map, a bottle of perfume, clear lip gloss, a comb, and packet of mints.

How to use a mobile when driving

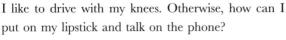

I like to drive with my knees. Otherwise, how can I put on my lipstick and talk on the phone?
—*Sharon Stone*

It is worth noting straight away that this is not only silly, but it is illegal. Naughty Sharon. Illegal unless you have a hands-free kit for your mobile. It is true that long car journeys are boring, and a nice little chat could make the time pass more pleasurably, but you can only do this hands free. As stupid as you may look talking on a hands free (talking to yourself is the first official sign of madness), it is a safety must and will ultimately look much better than having an accident. Mobiles are essential for car journeys when breakdowns, emotional as well as mechanical, require backup, but by far the best option is to switch them off until the engine is off.

How to fill the tank

If you have made it to a gas station you are now an official part of the motoring community. Gas stations are beauty salons for cars. They have gas and car washes for them, magazines, coffee, and cash machines for you.

First rule: You must not use your mobile here; it's a bit like being on an airplane. Some terrible spark could cause everything to blow. Now is not a good time for a cigarette break.

Second: What side is the flap that you need to lift to get the gas in the car? Might be worth checking this out as you get in the car, as it can be very tricky if your pump is on the other side of your flap and you have to stretch the thing over the rear of the car.

Once you have ascertained this information, you need to decide if you are going to fill it up with regular, premium, diesel, and so on. Select the appropriate pump and proceed. Be sure to choose the right gas for your car – you should have been told this when you bought or rented it, so make a note; if you fill your car with the wrong petrol it will have the equivalent of an allergic reaction and you will have to get it pumped out. Best avoided.

Many gas stations, depending on the state or country you're in, are self-service or have a less-expensive self-service option. This means you have to do it yourself. Park alongside the pump, turn off the ignition, and get out of the car. Pop open the gas cap. Great if you can slip on a pair of heeled slingbacks to do the job in, but if not, ad-lib with generous wiggle, and then go over to the pump. Pull the pump, insert the nozzle into said hole, and squeeze until either full, or it has gotten to the required price. It is a skill like icing your name on a cake to squeeze and ease the gas to the exact dollar.

Replace pump, twist lid back on car, and waltz in to pay. (Unless you've already paid using your credit card right at the pump.)

And then that is it: another job well done. If you are enjoying yourself here you can also check your oil and that your tires are pumped up, but don't bring anything else over to be blown up here, the pressure is too great and it will explode.

How to occupy yourself while at the car wash

While you are at the gas station you may as well get your car washed. And no, there is no point in doing it yourself, it simply gets you all wet and soapy. Select the wax, the dry, and go the full Monty. Once you are captive there is no escaping.

It's the ideal time to do a quick outfit change from work to evening.

With the brushes spinning past, people will only get flashes of what is going on inside the car, so you may as well make it exciting. Do not have an argument with anyone in your car while in the car wash as you will not be able to escape; doors as well as windows have to remain tightly shut throughout the procedure.

How to outsmart fellow motorists

There is a definite difference between a "safe, superior" driver and the "arrogant, aggressive" driver. Safety and wit are the two crucial skills a driver needs to possess.

There is something strange that happens to people once they get behind the wheel; do not let this evil streak take you over nor terrify you. You need to outmaneuver rather than outsmart other drivers, so have a few quick reactions up your sleeve. The trick here is to know the rules better than everyone else and play him or her to your advantage. Drive with the law and the Highway Code behind you and you can rule the road.

Don't let another driver intimidate you.

All cars, and all drivers, have equal rights on the road and all took the same test to get there – no one is "better," or has an unwritten priority, however much buses and bicycles blatantly ignore this and treat the roads as if they had exclusive ownership. They don't. This rule, of course, does not apply to emergency vehicles; if you see the flashing lights and hear the siren, it is the law to get out of the way and let them pass. Do not be bullied into doing 50 mph in a 30-mph zone even if they insist on snuffling up your behind and driving so close that you can see the whites of their eyes. Continue driving; you can accelerate slightly, if you feel like it, but do not believe for one moment that they have more of a claim than you.

Do not get road rage; if you are being goaded by some jerk, put a calming CD on, loudly, and ignore the troublemaker's taunts. You'll waste more time if you do stop, and my goodness, they might even pick a fight, so ignore it, don't argue, and if it is getting dangerous, let them pass. Animal.

Red light etiquette

Red means stop. This is a universal rule. There is also no advantage in "revving" your car; what do you really achieve? You waste gas. But if you have to beat the cocky git who has pulled up alongside, are you ready?

Get ready to burn the rubber off the beep alongside. Do not, *do not* take your eyes off the light – do not blink for a second, and the moment it changes GO! Speed through and beat them, but almost immediately, a few yards after victory, slow and they will most likely pass you.

This way you get rid of them, and also beat them, but so can't be bothered to chip a nail over their childish games. The alternative way is to look over, bat your eyes, then turn disdainfully away and apply a flash of lip gloss, as if to say, "So not even going to bother with you." Chic.

 # *How to know the rules of the road*

If you have passed your test and you have gotten your license, chances are you already have some grasp of the Highway Code, but a rule book should always be close to hand, as should the user manual of the car.

Always wear a seat belt and never drive with more people than you have seat belts in your car.

NEVER drink and drive; the same applies for drugs, excessive tiredness, or emotional distress.

Always have enough gas to get to your destination, or the nearest gas station, and keep your car in good service and full working order, just as you do yourself. "Don't drive like you own the road – drive like you own the car," advises *www.teendriving.com,* and this and other nuggets of information make this site a must for anyone, regardless of their age, to log onto while learning the rules of the road.

A standard motorist's vehicle checklist is:

1. **Lights:** Front and rear headlights, are they all working?

2. **Steering and suspension-control, shock absorbers and rear suspension:** Get them checked.

3. **Tires and wheels:** All there and got the correct internal pressure and in good condition?

4. **Brakes:** ABS (antiskid) as well as all the regulars – they all have to work, well – and any worries, get them checked.

5. **Seat belts:** Essential, and should include shoulder straps front and back.

6. **General:** Horn, mirrors, fuel system, registration plates, fluffy dice, and so on. Get a professional to check, they know what to look for.

How to deal with car mechanics

You can learn how to pop a hood open, fill a car up with gas, but anything more adventurous you should leave to the experts. You do not want to meddle with mechanics, just as you shouldn't cut your own bangs. Rumor has it you should be able to change the oil. But why would you want to be lying under a car, unscrewing the large bolt, letting the oil drain into a shallow pan and then screwing the bolt back on – tightly – sometimes even using a bolt grip, and then locating the oil filter which is somewhere near the engine under the hood? You have to know how to use a wrench to free the lid and add the fresh oil that could ruin your clothes, if it gets in contact with them. Far, far easier to ask a mechanic.

Take your car to a garage, explain very simply what you want, i.e., "I want to change the oil," and leave it to them.

The best way to deal with mechanics is to keep it straightforward and simple; do not waffle or engage in engine chit-chat you're not likely to understand or you could lose your vehicle to the garage for days. Know (more or less) what you are asking for. Remember while sparkling about your spark plugs that these mechanics probably have grouped you as having the same motor savvy as the topless calendar girl pinned up in the workroom. Neither confirm nor deny. But take pains to avoid any double-entendre associations with any of the tasks you have in mind for them or else you only have yourself to blame.

Try to use a family-run firm, or one that your family goes to, or a large reputable chain, to avoid the lecherous comments and the cowboys.

When going to the garage it is a jeans, T-shirt, and sneakers moment, no point tottering in on heels as they will have already mentally undressed you; and try to turn a deaf ear to any lewd or patronizing comments. If you cannot, throw out a few fashion references or something from your specialized field. No doubt this will completely baffle them.

It is preferable to keep them on your side, as that way they will also take pity on you and do the jobs that you probably could do, should you have the inclination, which you don't. One such job is refilling the fluid that cleans the windshield. You can follow the instructions in the owner's manual if you want, but it's far easier when getting your car serviced, which you should do every ten to twelve thousand miles, to bat your eyes and ask the nice man if he can do it to save you getting muddled under the hood.

Any real problems and nowadays it is the car itself that will tell you what is wrong: most have internal computers that bleep when something is out of gas, out of battery, or malfunctioning. It will also tell you off if you don't put your seat belt on or forget to take the handbrake off.

How to change a flat tire – part one

When a tire blows you have to deal with it there and then. A blow is an immediate pop/bang that you will hear, whereas a slow puncture is a little hole that will gradually lose air and the tire will get softer, and softer, then go flat. Either way, you can't drive far like that.

Keep an eye on your tires and give them the odd kick to check how perky they are. If they feel soft try to drive them to a tire shop before it's at the crucial stage when you have to perform the op. Tires can be changed by a professional while you wait; they can check the treads while you have a cup of tea in the waiting room.

If you are halfway up a mountain you will have to improvise. Call the AAA or whatever emergency breakdown service you are with. How quickly can they come to a girl stranded, vulnerable, in a car by herself? You should be a top-of-the-list priority; lay the whole Damsel in Distress thing on thick. Ask for an ETA and see if there is a nice coffee shop within eye range; if not, it is an in-car karaoke sing-along.

If you are halfway up a mountain in a country where you don't speak the language you will need a mobile phone signal, a phrase book, or lots of gesticulations. Call the company that lent you this dud and ask them to translate or get over to you pronto as you try and negotiate language barriers, as well as car language barriers.

If help doesn't appear to be forthcoming, and there really is no knight in shining armor galloping toward you over the horizon, roll your sleeves up, take off your designer jacket, and deal with it yourself. All the tools to change a tire should be in the car, and with any luck the user manual will let you know what and where you are looking.

How to change a flat tire – part two

Okay, we were trying to avoid this, but time to make the best of a bad situation. Hazard lights on, emergency brake on, and place a heavy object wedged up against the good rear tire.

Look in the trunk and check there is a tire that is worth swapping with.

Ease off the hubcap, and see if you can unscrew or at least loosen one of the nuts with your gadgets. Can you? No point even grappling with a jack if you cannot shift these.

At times like these you really need to hope that you have good upper body strength.

Take off any clothing you don't want grease on. Put on gloves if available.

Take out the lug wrench, jack, and spare tire. Careful, you can get very mucky doing this.

Loosen nuts, turning them clockwise if the lug has an L on it, and left (counterclockwise) if it has an R on it. Do not remove – just loosen.

Now comes the jack – the car needs to be raised before you take off the nuts (screws). Put jack on ground next to flat tire, under car frame, under something structural – so that you don't damage a weak bit of the frame. You then pump up the jack. Never, ever go under a car when supported only by a jack.

Once it is jacked up, take the screws off and swap tires. Position new one, and hold in place with lug bolts, then rescrew. Retighten and rescrew, lower jack, replace hubcap, and pat yourself on the back.

Then, when you have composed yourself, drive the car straight to the nearest garage to get a fresh tire and things really tightly screwed on by an electric tool.

How to tow or be towed

Ideally this will not ever happen to you. But perhaps you were on an idyllic holiday and the car got stuck in the mud – you need to pull it out. You should leave the fast lane and certainly not travel any great distance. Are you sure your subcompact can cope with towing a U-Haul or RV? Be sensible.

If you tow a small trailer without brakes, the weight has to be less than 50 percent of the weight of your car. Before you start, check the tread and state of the tires, as they will take all the extra strain. Reverse up to a trailer, or if towing, attach strong guy rope and do your best Girl Scout knots. Allow for the extra weight and length when maneuvering, and let traffic overtake you.

If towing a breakdown, get them to put hazards on and write a sign saying ON TOW to have in their back window so as not to scare motorists. And finally, before you set off, see if it wouldn't be better to wait for the AAA.

How to parallel park with style

The idea is to park with the curb in sight. If getting out of the car curbside, you should be able to step from the car straight to the pavement. Ignore all taunts from unhelpful backseat drivers; everyone has their own technique and everyone parks in their own sweet time. When you see the space that is for you, pull alongside it. Brake and indicate, so you have claimed it as yours. Then put the car into reverse. If there is a car behind you this will show them what is about to happen and they need to back off and let you do this. Do not let them rush you or else you might scrape the paintwork of the car parallel to yours. With your rear bumper at the same level as the car in front of the space you are about to park in, turn the steering wheel hard to the right (this is assuming you are driving on the right and parking on the right – flip reverse for other side).

Slowly and easily nudge backward till your back door is in the space, then brake and turn hard in the other direction, and ease back again. Then you should be mostly in the damn space so you can shuffle backward and forward. There are no prizes for speed. Sometimes you can get a hole in one, others it requires precision and patience. Just do it your way and it will line up fine. A similar thing applies to parking in a multistory parking garage; every single floor has lifts to the ground floor, as well as stairs, so there is no harm going 'round and 'round till you pass a space that is acceptable for you just to slide into. If a space seems too tight, leave it to Mr. Thin or Mr. Boy Racer. Multistory car garages are convenient, and they cost a fortune, so at least shop around till you get a good fit, and roll in nose first – only showoffs reverse in – and you need to have easy access to the trunk for your shopping anyway.

How to get out of a car in a short skirt

When a man opens the car door for his wife, it's either a new car or a new wife.
—*Prince Philip, Duke of Edinburgh*

Proper (raised) limousines are the most microminiskirt-friendly vehicles to travel in, should this influence your dress code. As you slide off the seat, smooth skirt down, swivel, and step out, dignity intact. Land Rovers and vehicles that involve climbing to enter and exit are ideal for showing off legs, but also risk showing off a lot more, too.

Fortunately there is a way of getting out of a car, no matter how low the car or short the skirt, and leaving something to the imagination.

Take seat belt off, check shoes are on, lipstick and hair in place, skirt not 'round waist, and then open the door.

Knees together, swivel legs to side-facing exit, with your back to the handbrake.

Stretch leg nearest the door out of vehicle, lightly resting the hand of your opposite arm over your dignity. Try to keep knees together.

Using your other arm (the one on the same side as stretched leg), pull your body out of vehicle with slide and glide.

Curl head and shoulders forward, so you're concealed from hidden paparazzi, as you come up to stand.

Stretch other leg out and over so you are standing.

Smooth skirt, what little of it there is.

Shut door and walk away.

Other means of transport worth mastering include:

Motorcycle and side car, moped, tandem, bicycle, sedan chair, horse and carriage, piggy-back, Rollerblades, skateboard, skis, tram, train, elephant, hot-air balloon, rowing boat, camel, gondola, glider, bus, coach, tightrope.

How to Stay in the Black

'Cause we are living in a material world
And I am a material girl . . .
  —*Madonna*, "Material Girl"

There is no point denying it, money is an essential commodity to make the world go 'round. You not only need to know how to make it, but how to keep hold of it, how to spend it, and what to do if you lose it. Money brings responsibility as well as the highs and lows. Don't bank on winning the lottery; this is as likely as arriving at Manolo and finding a "one-day-only 100 percent discount sale" in your size only. Far better to plan ahead, save for a rainy day, and look a million dollars on a dime.

Consider this. Have you:

a) Bought the winning lottery ticket recently or know anyone who has?

b) Got a fabulously generous, wealthy relative or a doting other half whose only pleasure is to lavish gifts on you? (Note: the latter are quite hard to find.)

c) Inherited a fortune or robbed a bank?

d) None of the above, and, to quote Dolly Parton, are "working nine to five, what a way to make a living," and have very little to show for it?

Being a gold digger or a criminal are both OUT and gambling is unreliable. You need to know how to manage your money.

How to look responsible with money

Looking is one thing, being is altogether another game. When asking for a loan, visiting your bank manager, or going to a money-borrowing meeting, you need to look responsible with money.

Always aim to have your own funds. However attractive a joint bank account may seem, you need to maintain an air of independence for those rainy days when only a splurge can revive your spirits.

As appealing as it may seem, marrying a millionaire is not the modern girl's answer to life-long happiness.

How to be an independent woman

Destiny's Child's anthem "Independent Women" is a great mantra to live by, and it will make you all the more attractive and feel all the more invincible. Other songs worth learning the words to and belting out as theme tunes include Abba's "Money Money Money," Madonna's "Material Girl," Marilyn Monroe's "Diamonds Are a Girl's Best Friend." Dance moves are an added bonus.

But remember the words of Arnold Schwarzenegger: "Money doesn't make you happy. I now have fifty million dollars, but I was just as happy when I had forty-eight million." There are more important things, and there are a whole host of other songs to sing for this.

How to justify a pair of heels each month

Whatever the internal turmoil and financial crisis you are weathering, you must never let standards slip, they need to be kept high, and preferably in heels. When hitting hard times it is customary to throw on a "victim" look. This is not an option. Appearances are everything and you only get one chance to make a first impression, so make sure you always make the right one.

Never leave home shabby and unkempt, because if you don't care, why should anyone else? The worse the situation, the higher the heels should be.

a) Walking in heels will enhance your concentration, making your thinking clearer and speeding a solution to your woes. Tick money saved on therapy and an increased sense of emotional well-being (worth a fortune).

b) Heels, in the greater scheme of things, are an economic investment, as cheap shoes last such a short time that their healing effect is limited and you only have to go and buy more.

c) Heels lift spirits as well as bottoms, and tone thighs. Plastic surgery and therapy in a footstep. A decent enough pair of heels can be equal to a weekly gym workout, a pay raise with a bigger office, and can also lead to lavishing of gifts, dinners, drinks, theater trips, and so on. A real entertainment and health investment.

Look at it like this and you can justify *more* than one pair a month.

How to explain why taxis are economical

Sometimes you simply cannot take another step.

When this happens, and the balls of your feet feel like you are walking on knives, there is only one word that will ease the pain: TAXI.

Taxis minimize the amount of walking time, tricky street maneuvers, and the need to carry a larger bag with driving shoes. How can you possibly be expected to think on your feet if you are wearing something as comfortable as a cheese cutter?

How to spend wisely on Christmas gifts

Christmas shopping can begin as early as you choose. The key things to know are what they like, where to get it, and your budget. The longer you give yourself, the lower your blood pressure will be in December. You should be carol singing on Christmas Eve, not doing battle in a department store. Forward planning is also the key to finding the perfect present, and helps in spreading the cost so you have a kitty for the January sales. After all, "money is like muck, not good except it be spread," said Francis Bacon.

Relatives' and token gifts, as well as cards, can often be picked up months in advance. By the time Christmas comes around *no one* will remember they are from seasons past. Just store them away somewhere safe for eleven months. Gauge the success of your last gift to know if you can do a repeat on a theme, or if it is back to the old drawing board.

You should constantly be on the lookout for great gifts; if traveling, see if there is anything unique that you can pick up, or indeed in Duty Free.

How to get the most from the January sales

Forget Christmas, January is when the *real* credit card action happens. Limber up to the New Year event. A seasoned pro will start staking out the stores early in November. Try styles on pre-Christmas and sales rush. Learn what styles suit you and which scare you. Get acquainted with the store layout, although this often changes at sale time, just to slow the regulars down a notch. Try to "befriend" the staff, find out when the sale is due to start, and if you can get invited to a preview date.

On sale day there is no time for friends. Go alone, and stay focused – this is no time for indecision. Have you got a particular piece in mind, or are you searching for "the perfect jacket"? If it is a particular piece, get there early; no prizes for second place. Find the target as fast as possible, check the size and reduction, purchase.

Do not try stuff on at sales, it wastes valuable bargain-hunting time. Likewise, do not suffer false economy and get spontaneous or crazy creative. Despite the price you only need one pair of hot pants, if any, and there is no point purchasing something today that will be in your donation pile tomorrow.

Department stores at sales are worth watching, and sometimes it's worth risking holding out for the last week, for super-duper reductions. Bloomingdale's will test to see if you have nerves of steel as you wait for first, then second, and third reductions, and gamble on the Proenza Schouler jacket disappearing from the rails completely, despite the homing signal you had locked on it. For more specialized places, such as Manolo Blahnik, it is only worth going on the first day, and, in reality, being in the first ten. Swallow your pride, get competitive; bargains need commitment and earlier queuers get bigger prizes.

Another chic idea is to find out when the sales are on in the other fashion capitals of the world (Paris, London, and Milan). Plan a trip there, or get a business trip to coincide with the dates, and get bargains that only the locals would know the value of.

Remember that the trick of sales is to know what you want, your size, and what suits you. Chances are that if there is a whole rail of red velvet Santa suits that have been unpurchased, it's for a reason – there is a lot of crap that looks good on no one.

How to be economic

Love conquers all things except poverty and toothache.
—*Mae West*

There are ways to reduce your costs, but not your standard of living.

Learning to hand wash, steam, and rotate red carpet looks can reduce dry-cleaning bills.

Answering your phone when it rings avoids you having to call everyone back, so get caller ID and minimize your bill.

Is there any way you can get public transport? Even half the way? If not, is there anyone who could enjoy your company in return for a lift in their car?

Encourage suitors to send weekly bouquets of flowers, and more if they feel they must, as fresh flowers lift every home. Alternatively try growing your own blooms if admirers seem thin on the ground.

Have evenings when you dine at home in front of the television. Being elusive and unavailable is not only economical, it is a way of making you seem far more glamorous. Weigh up the cost of an evening with how much you want to go. Never accept every invitation.

Can you work in an office? If so, you can use their phone and office facilities for free, and stock up on stationery, social life, and so forth.

Visit a department store on your way out and freshen up with the latest sample of perfume; or if you have some time, get the makeup counter to apply their latest shade, under strict supervision.

Get an expense account, share cabs, or indeed find a knight in shining armor.

How to cope with poverty

Like dear St. Francis of Assisi, I am wedded to poverty, but in my case the marriage is not a success.
—*Oscar Wilde*

Oh, woe is you. There will be times when, through no fault of your own, you are poor. Flat broke. Have overspent.

Best ways to cope with this are to tighten the belt and get your financial organization into play.

If you are aware that you are about to reach danger levels, perhaps take steps before you hit a crisis point. But if it sneaks up on you by surprise, here are the easiest ways to deal with it.

List all your outgoing expenses (bills, meals out, in, shopping, travel, and so forth).

Write down all your monthly incoming funds. Do they tally? Are you in profit? Do you break even? Good grief, is it time to start doing extra baby-sitting again? Are there any outstanding payments owed to you? And can you cover all your outgoings and account for them all?

Direct debits are a great, and easy, way to pay, but keep an eye on them. At times like this do you still want to be giving colorblind cats in Cambodia $50 every month?

Is there anyone who could lend you some money? I know Shakespeare said, "Neither a borrower nor a lender be," but desperate times call for desperate measures. Try not to find a Shylock. Are there any favors you could call in or anyone who owes you? Think family? Friend? Or, if desperate, you could always loan something to a pawnbroker. Be very, *very* wary of going to loan sharks – they have this name for a reason – and the interest rates they charge tend to be extortionate. Could you have a spring clean? Are there any trinkets or any past fashion triumphs that you could bear to part with and sell on eBay?

Stay in, and cut down on meals out, taxis, and two-hour calls on your mobile.

Get friends to take pity on you and take you out – this will also shed light on who your real friends are. The poverty week would also be a good week to accept any work lunches, dinner parties (providing transport is included), and blind dates (dinner only, obviously; things are not *that* desperate).

Call the bank. Reassuring them everything will be okay will help you deal with the crisis head-on. A problem shared is a problem halved.

Go to the library to browse and borrow, rather than buy. You don't want to get cabin fever so go window-shopping – there is no fee to try stuff on – and put the perfect little black dress on hold.

If you have to make purchases, make the shopping trips budget sensitive. Therapy is always helpful in times of depression, and retail is one of the most effective drugs. Set yourself a challenge to get the perfect thing for under $20 and if you fail, spring clean and delve deeper into your wardrobe. After all, Sarah Jessica Parker and Jennifer Aniston have made the Gap look like couture. If they can do it, why can't you? Get creative and do some revamping.

The same could apply to the kitchen; baked potatoes à la that jar of something that was lurking in the cupboard could be exciting, a dash of mustard will bring spice to your baked beans, as well as numb the taste buds. The possibilities are endless.

Turn off your mobile for a day while you think about this dilemma.

Limit visits to danger zones, e.g., Manolo Blahnik, Barneys, Fred Segal, etc.

In extreme poverty-stricken moments, remove credit cards from wallets and replace with donor and library cards.

How to stay rich

There is actually no fool-proof way to do this, other than with caution. So perhaps this should also be called *how to invest*. Property is the obvious investment, after art, shoes, and rare pieces of vintage. Racehorses have less reliable returns.

Read the financial sections of the newspapers. It will educate you, and it will also impress fellow commuters on the train.

Or go for the grown-up option, and become a shareholder. Or you could take advantage of the no-tax perk of an IRA. They are tax-exempt special savings accounts where you can store money away in a separate "hard to reach" account that will quietly accumulate interest; brilliant. Alternatively you should either learn how to place bets (see page 115) or, slightly less sexy, invest in a pension. Fewer and fewer of us are saving for when we are older and wiser, but company pension plans are worth considering as an option for your dotage. Both have different elements of risk: there have been major pension scandals in recent years, but the gambling option plays with higher stakes. Play safe; when elderly, you are more susceptible to heart attacks.

Banking

Do you have a bank account? You should. Is it the right one for you? If you are to be a big spender, and a serious investor, you really need to upgrade from shaking the coins out of a porcelain piggy bank and tucking the notes under your mattress. There are not only much easier and safer methods, but looking after your money can make you richer.

It is much harder to rob a bank than pick a pocket; banks also have insurance and security against this. A bank is a bit like a garden – that doesn't mean that money grows on trees, but your cash, like plants, will grow with regular watering (interest rates) and you can do your own pruning (i.e., draw cash out of an ATM machine).

The most vital things you must look for when joining or assessing a bank (apart from any joining perk or promotion) are:

Does your bank freak out or have flexible overdraft facilities?

How about online banking? Can you understand how to view your account or do you need a math degree?

Have you seen a branch of your preferred bank locally and is their card compatible with ATMs near you? The more branches there are of the bank, the fewer fees you will have to pay when using an ATM that doesn't belong to your bank network.

And interest rates?

Banking may diminish the pleasure and interest rate of a person, but, before you glaze over, it does matter. The protocol might be slightly exasperating, but getting the right interest rate is not only interesting, it is vital. An interest rate is the amount, or percent, that you are charged as a fee when you either borrow or lend your money. When you borrow you ultimately want to find the lowest-costing interest rate as this is the figure that you will have to pay back. But when the shoe is on the other foot and you have lent someone some money, or indeed your savings are in a bank, you want to find a nice high interest rate so it can earn some extra for you. Banks get their customers by offering various competitive rates, so you need to shop around.

How to invest and dabble in the city

If you decide to become a real city slicker, fast track your way to becoming a millionaire and get a few bonds, stocks, shares, and shoulder pads. Joining the city gang usually takes a sizeable investment, say the equivalent of a five-star weekend break, and the result is some stocks with more mood swings than the most complex of women. Your choice.

Before you invest, talk to a trained professional, or broker, or someone in the biz. High flyers are usually young yuppie boys who can't speak in full sentences, work silly hours, and generally have to shout all day at work. If that sounds too exhausting you can look online, as well as read the papers to see what the fate of other stocks are. Stocks are, as far as we're concerned, the same as shares.

If you buy shares you become a shareholder; but before you think of turning up at a board meeting and giving the company a redesign, remember that you probably own 0.00005 percent and are a mere blip on the radar. Pharmaceutical companies usually have steady growth, as people will always need curing and medicine, but *all* shares are très volatile, and you will need nerves of steel as well as shares in the stuff, so just go with what your broker and your brain tell you.

Remember: the higher the risk, the higher the gains – as well as the greater the carnage if it crashes.

When buying shares you have to appoint either your bank manager or a broker to haggle and keep an eye on things for you. You do *not* deal with it yourself, you simply sign the check and buckle up for the roller-coaster ride.

Note: if the ride's too much for you, ask your broker, nicely, to let you get off – as near to the top as possible.

How to spend nothing

I don't care too much for money, money can't buy me love.
—*The Beatles*

There is another way to save money – other than shopping on a shoestring – and that is to spend nothing at all.

It sounds very, very clichéd, but it's true, there are many things that you can do without spending a single penny.

Climb to the top of a hill and take in the view.
Paddle in the sea and build sandcastles.
Play games.
Watch the clouds change and make shapes.
Sit in a park, and play designer label I Spy.
Watch a spider weave a web.
Feel the wind blow in your hair.
Kick the autumn leaves and collect chestnuts, or build a snowman.
Visit galleries or museums on free night.
Enjoy a live music concert, courtesy of the buskers.
Laugh till your face and stomach hurt.

Acknowledgments

Once upon a time, I was in Paris, my computer had crashed, I couldn't check my e-mails, and my hotel room had been burgled. . . .

I agree that when people make their thank-you's, it's nauseating, an Oscar moment, but many things can't happen without an awful lot of help, advice, and luck. This book is due entirely to a chain of events that started with Bella Freud, who called Ed Victor and miraculously got the great Wizard of Oz of literary agents to take me on and St. Grainne Fox was assigned to look after me and hold my hand throughout. Jocasta Brownlee was my fabulous editor at Hodder and Stoughton and brought the book to life, along with Natasha Law's fantastic illustrations. The book then went stateside, as only the really stylish do, and I owe a huge debt to Hyperion Books; my editor and interpreter, Peternelle van Arsdale; and Ellen Archer for transforming this book. Kiera Hepford, Allison McGeehon, Rachelle Nashner, and Miriam Wenger are also amongst the army who helped perform the U.S. makeover.

John Galliano inspired this idea, and just about everything I do, and makes my world Technicolor, and it is to him I will be forever devoted. For being a true gentleman and making everyone tall, slim, elegant, and beautiful even on bad hair days, I must thank my favorite Manolo Blahnik, who inspired the title. Stephen Jones for being so encouraging; Steven and Bill for being Steven and Bill; Val Garland who ignored my flu, told me I looked gorgeous – liar – and subtly gave me a touché éclat; and Sam McKnight, who bought me cough medicine. Kate Betts, for being the greatest editor in chief of them all; she told me to be a writer and booked me in at the Costes Hotel. And to Gisele, Stella, and Jacquetta, who give me hope that I do not have the largest phone bill in the land, and dispel the myth that fashion people are *itches; they are not. To Duncan, Anne, Leslie, Jelka, Carrie, Elizabeth, and all the PRs I tortured and stalked in pursuit of my quotes, thank you.

Now, I know it is a cliché, but I really do have to thank my mother, because she's perfect, and my father who knows how to do EVERYTHING – and is actually Super Daddy. One mission included driving over to Paris to change a lightbulb (it was very tricky). My brothers, Oliver and Jeremy, who grew up knowing that Manolo Blahnik was a GOD, were able to help with all things technical, and Coco, my cat, who really thought this whole idea was nonsense and ate half the proofs at a crucial moment and told me to stop working so hard and play with her.

Then the friends who still called even though I was always proofreading: Sarah, Romilly, Posh Natalie, Charlotte, Samira, Lainey, Alexis, Katie Knickers, Robin, Michael and Thakoon, and my fairy godmother, Mrs Burstein, who looked after me with tea and sympathy in Claridges. There are so many wonderful people who helped either anonymously, or on the way, such as my New York Angel, Sarah, and my knights in shining armor: Douglas the Dapper and Kithe the Kind. Did I know how to play poker? Know Heidi Klum? How to turn on my computer? Hell no, but lucky they did, and I am so grateful they took the time to explain it slowly and simply to me, several times.

Finally I have to say a thank-you to all the magazines that have let me write for them; to Abi and Dolly and all the amazing shows I have seen, invited or not, with Robert and Sean; and above all, for those who have let me do it my way. I am now satisfied I have mentioned most people who I might ever have come in contact with. I hope I have thanked all those who have made this possible, who buy the book, and who hold their head high, and walk tall into the unknown in their Blahniks . . . and live happily ever after.

Index

About the Author

Camilla Morton is a London-based fashion writer. She is the runway reporter for Vogue.com, covering all international and couture collections. She writes for several magazines and newspapers, including contributing to *Time* magazine's Style and Design supplement, and *Harper's Bazaar* both in the U.S. and UK.

About the Illustrator

Natasha Law was born and raised in London. Her work appears frequently in the UK Sunday *Times* Style Section.